Byzantine Jewry
from Justinian
to the Fourth Crusade

THE LITTMAN LIBRARY OF
JEWISH CIVILIZATION

EDITORS:
David Goldstein
Louis Jacobs

Byzantine Jewry
from Justinian
to the Fourth Crusade

ANDREW SHARF

SCHOCKEN BOOKS · NEW YORK

First published in U.S.A. in 1971
by Schocken Books Inc.
67 Park Avenue
New York, N.Y., 10016

© *Andrew Sharf 1971*

Library of Congress Catalog Card Number 74–135519

Printed in Great Britain

TO
MY WIFE

Contents

Acknowledgements

This book would probably never have been written, far less published, had it not been for the interest shown by Mr Colin Franklin when we met at Bar-Ilan University. I am grateful to him for thus stimulating me, and for not being too disappointed with the result. At the same time I should like to express my deep appreciation of the patience and acumen devoted by Rabbi Dr David Goldstein to the editing of the typescript. Needless to say, any blemishes that remain are my own responsibility. I am also indebted to the Littman Foundation for supporting this work. Finally, I should like to thank the University for enabling me to spend some months at the British Museum and to visit Istanbul and Greece, for work which could not well have been done in Israel.

Abbreviations

Editions

CMH — *Cambridge Medieval History* vol. 4, ed. J. M. Hussey, (1967)

CSHB — *Corpus Scriptorum Historiae Byzantinae*, 48 vols., ed. L. Dindorf and others (Bonn 1826–97)

Doelger — *Regesten der Kaiserurkunden des ostroemischen Reiches*
Regesten — (Corpus der griechischen Urkunden des Mittelalters und der neueren Zeit, Reihe A Abt. I), ed. F. Doelger, (Munich-Berlin 1924–60)

DTC — *Dictionnaire de théologie catholique*, 15 vols., ed. A. Vacant and others (Paris 1905–50)

Mansi — J. D. Mansi, *Sanctorum conciliorum nova et amplissima collectio*, 31 vols. (Florence and Venice 1759–98)

MGH — *Monumenta Germaniae Historica* (SS = Scriptores) ed. Th. Mommsen and others (Hanover and Berlin 1826—in progress)

MPG — J. P. Migne, *Patrologiae cursus completus*, series graeca, 165 vols. (Paris 1857–86)

MPL — J. P. Migne, *Patrologiae cursus completus*, series latina, 221 vols. (Paris 1844–64)

PO — *Patrologia Orientalis*, ed. A. Graffin and F. Nau (Paris 1907—in progress)

Periodicals

BNJ	*Byzantinisch-neugriechische Jahrbuecher*
BYZ	*Byzantion*
BZ	*Byzantinische Zeitschrift*
DOP	*Dumbarton Oaks Papers*
JJS	*Journal of Jewish Studies*
JQR	*Jewish Quarterly Review*
JAOS	*Journal of the American Oriental Society*
JPOS	*Journal of the Palestine Oriental Society*
MGWJ	*Monatsschrift fuer Geschichte und Wissenschaft des Judentums*
PAAJR	*Proceedings of the American Academy for Jewish Research*
REJ	*Revue des Études Juives*
ROC	*Revue de l'Orient Chrétien*

CHAPTER I

The Community and
its Background

The Jews who are the subject of our story, like any other Jews of
the Dispersion, lived a life in great part determined by the behaviour of the non-Jewish society around them, as expressed in
its laws, its customs, its economic possibilities, and in its administrative and political institutions. The term 'Byzantine', the historical and geographical label of the society which concerns us
here, has been variously used. In its broadest meaning, it has been
applied to the eastern provinces of the Roman Empire, from the
foundation of their capital, Constantinople, on the site of Greek
Byzantium in the year A.D. 330, to its capture by the Ottoman
Turks in 1453—that is, for the whole of the thousand years or
more that, according to Gibbon, it took the Roman Empire
to fall. For our purpose, at least, the usage has to be narrowed
down considerably. The Roman East only began to acquire a
genuine political and social identity during the period of the final
disappearance of one united authority, that is during the reign of
Justinian (527–565), the last emperor who seriously tried to assert
it. In 1204, another sort of unity with the West was achieved:
the Norman and Venetian leaders of an expedition whose ostensible aim was to free Jerusalem from the Muslims, the expedition
which became known as the 'Fourth Crusade', contented themselves with capturing Constantinople instead. Although their rule
lasted for barely fifty years, the old identity was never regained. It

is only for this shorter period, from Justinian to this first capture of Constantinople, that a distinguishing label is really appropriate. During the first hundred years of this period, Byzantine territory included all the old Roman Mediterranean provinces with the exception of Spain: that is, North Africa, Egypt, Palestine, Syria, Asia Minor and Greece. After the Arab expansion of the seventh century, only the last two remained. In the West, there were Byzantine colonies of varying extent in southern Italy and Sicily, the last of which was lost in 1071.

Most of the Jewish communities in these territories were far older than Byzantium, far older, for that matter, than Rome. Many of them lasted after Byzantium was no more than a dim memory. Byzantine rule was a brief episode in the long history of Mediterranean Jewry. However, it is a neglected episode. It is a historical link often omitted between the frequently discussed Jews of the Roman Empire after the destruction of the Second Temple, and the Greek or Turkish Jewish communities of the fifteenth and sixteenth centuries. Similarly, it can be thought of as a geographical link to which insufficient attention has been paid. For most of our period Byzantium was either a bridge or a barrier between Islam and Europe. Its Jewish communities merit discussion in order to complete any survey of early medieval Jewry, for its life under Muslim rule, just as its expansion in the post-Roman West, has attracted a large and ever growing literature. However, the Byzantine communities have an interest of their own. For most of our period, the important ones were at Oria and Bari in Italy, at Thessalonica, Thebes and Castoria in Greece, at Constantinople itself, at Amorium, Attaleia, Seleucia and smaller centres of central and southern Asia Minor. For the sixth century, and for the early years of the seventh, there must be added Syrian Antioch, Tiberias and Caesarea in Palestine, Alexandria and the communities of North Africa. In Palestine and Syria, the Jews were involved, in one way or another, in the events leading up to the Arab invasions. Towards the end of our period, scholars of note arose, some of whom participated in the long and bitter disputes that began to trouble all Mediterranean Jewry between the traditional interpreters of the scriptures and their opponents, the Karaites. On the other hand, it is equally valuable to attempt a reconstruction of ordinary life in the cities of Italy, Greece and Asia Minor. It had many specifically Byzantine characteristics particularly in the sphere of legislation. Special sections of the Byzantine codes of law and, occasionally, special enactments were devoted to the Jewish question. And this was not simply because of the usual, not especially benevolent, concern of any Christian medieval régime for its Jewish subjects. It was also because the Jews constituted an active element amongst the many communities of the multiracial society which Byzantium ruled.

How big was that element? No clear statistical reply can be given. From the first to the twelfth century there exist only two explicit pieces of information about the numbers of the Jews, Roman or Byzantine. The first asserts that, according to the census held by the Emperor Claudius in A.D. 42, they numbered 6,944,000.[1] Some modern scholars treat this figure seriously and accept that the Jews would thus have formed about ten per cent of the general population.[2] The second is derived from an apparently meticulous survey made by one of the best-known of Jewish travellers, Benjamin of Tudela, on his visit to Byzantium in 1168.[3] His total figure is 8,603, but it is highly probable that this is composed of the names given to him by the local synagogues, which would only have been the names of the heads of families. It should therefore be multiplied by at least five. To this should be added an estimate of the numbers in the places which it is known Benjamin did not visit. The final figure may be close to 100,000 of whom, according to this method of reckoning, that is, by heads of families, not less than ten thousand—a tenth of the total— lived in Constantinople.[4] What was the general population? In Constantinople by the twelfth century, it could have been half a million[5]—of which the Jews there thus constituted two per cent. But the proportion for all Byzantium could easily have been higher. Byzantine territorial losses to Seljuks and Normans, together with a persistent drift from the provinces to the capital which for the past hundred years the emperors had been unable to check, showed that the general population of Constantinople certainly constituted far more than a tenth of the total population of Byzantium.[6] An estimate, therefore, of how much the proportion of Jews to the general population exceeded two per cent could be reached if it were known how much more than a tenth of the total the general population of Constantinople actually constituted. In the absence of this information, we can only return to the census of Claudius and, while its ten per cent may seem impossibly large, it is unreasonable to denude it of all reality. For subsequent territorial changes, although they meant population losses, did not necessarily mean changes in the proportion between Jews and non-Jews. It may thus be accepted that the Jews formed a solid and noticeable percentage of the population. It was not an evenly spread percentage. It was concentrated in the cities, though, as we shall see, by no means necessarily in Constantinople. Now, it was Byzantine city life which was important in the Jewish context—and not merely because this was the life which most Byzantine Jews lived. It was because it was this life which so strikingly differentiated Byzantium from western régimes. For this reason Byzantine Jewry, in addition to its interest as a geographical or historical link between Jewries better known to history, has also the interest of a development within a non-Jewish environment exceptional in that age: the Byzantine environment. Before attempting an account of Byzantine Jewry, an analysis has to be attempted of what this exceptional quality consisted.[7]

Roman civilization, like the civilization of the Greeks before it, had depended on cities and could not long survive their decay. The decline of imperial authority was closely connected with the gradual disintegration, caused by external attacks and internal conflicts, of the urban community. This disintegration brought with it restricted trade, uncertain communications, a shrinking population and a neglected agriculture. The impoverishment of the economy eventually destroyed the institutions of an effective central administration, that is, those institutions able to guarantee the day-to-day security of the ordinary citizen. The western inheritors of Rome could not preserve or reconstitute this essential of Roman government because the material prerequisites for it did not exist. When the citizen could no longer hope for

4

the state to give him protection, he was compelled to look for help closer at hand. The provision of this help and, thus, real political power passed to the local landed proprietor who in his turn naturally sought the protection of someone greater than he, and the feudal framework of medieval Europe slowly came into being. The process itself cannot be described here, nor can its causes, immediate or distant, be systematically analysed. It is sufficient to recall that the Emperor Diocletian (284–305), despite drastic financial and administrative reforms, failed to halt it in its very early stages. Some time between the fourth and the eighth century a moment must have come when men could no longer suppose themselves to be living in a Roman world.

The disintegration of the city was a western phenomenon. The eastern provinces showed themselves far better able to meet the challenge of barbarian invasion and civil disorder. It was partly for this reason that Constantine I (324–337) founded the city that bore his name in the heart of those provinces—the new Rome which survived the disasters overwhelming the old. Her economy, perhaps because the old Greek city-state had deeper roots in the East, remained comparatively stable. Traditional industries—the manufacture of silverware, of glassware, the weaving of silk cloth—continued to flourish, while the absence of a serious decline in population ensured a steady demand for foodstuffs and for raw materials. Constantinople, from her strategic position at the meeting point of Europe and Asia, developed and maintained a network of trade routes throughout Greece, Asia Minor and in what remained of imperial territory in South Italy. Egyptian and Syrian trade, integral to Roman prosperity for hundreds of years, as well as the old Roman contacts with Persia, India and the Far East, were attracted to the new centre. The conquest of Syria and Egypt by the Arabs, and their political domination, by the end of the seventh century, over the whole eastern and southern Mediterranean coast-line was no more than a temporary inter-ruption. The volume of trade did not diminish. After an initial setback, Byzantium continued to benefit substantially from it. As a result, the Byzantine gold coin, the 'bezant' or *solidus*, despite many devaluations in its gold content, remained the only reliable medium of exchange throughout the Mediterranean world—and far beyond it. The strength of the currency was the best indication that Byzantium had succeeded in preserving a genuine money economy—that is, the availability of cash for goods and services. One aspect is particularly to be noted. The operations of such an economy could be properly financed only by interest-bearing loans or investments—as, of course, they had been in Roman times. Thus, the taking of interest could not, in itself, be considered sinful in Byzantium as for centuries it was in the West. Nor, as formally at least in the West, was it ever forbidden. Indeed, the church itself financed trading voyages. On the other hand, the rate of interest was low and there were other strictly enforced conditions indicating that some moral reservations did exist.

Byzantine economic resources were fundamental to the whole social and political structure. First of all, they enabled the government, at the time of the Arab invasions, to begin a far-reaching agrarian and military reform. The provinces of Greece and Asia Minor were reorganized into military districts, called 'themes', each with its own militia drawn from communities of small farmers, whose holdings were dependent on this service. They and their commanders, the governors of the themes, were paid from the capital. The themes saved Asia Minor from the Arabs, that is, they saved the main source of food supply after the fall of Egypt. But they did far more. They saved all Byzantine agriculture from disaster. Barbarian onslaughts were just as dangerous for the East as for the West. But the Byzantine countryside did not become deserted. The theme system not only stabilized the size of the existing population but also helped Byzantium to absorb her hordes of Slav invaders with considerably greater success than Rome had absorbed her Germans. For, in a remarkably short time, the Slavs not only became useful soldiers (which Germans had often enough been for Rome) but also productive cultivators. The themes gave Byzantium security, for they gave the central administration the nucleus of a professional standing army and effective control over distant areas. They halted the division of power between feudal landowners—that process of disintegration which in the West developed unchecked. Secondly, Byzantine finances were able to afford a professional civil service. This meant that the state could pay experienced officials to collect taxes efficiently, to operate the machinery of the law with some prospect of fairness and consistency and to ensure good communications between capital and provinces by supervising road conditions and maintaining a state post. It meant, in other words, the preservation of the basic administrative achievements of the first Rome. But, in Byzantium, the civil service had wider responsibilities. It had to regulate much of economic life. Important trades and industries had appropriate associations organized by the state, membership of which was compulsory. In some spheres, for example in the manufacture and sale of silk cloth, the state itself owned enterprises and from time to time enforced a monopoly. At all times it concerned itself with conditions of work and with the fixing of prices in every sphere. Both the theme and the trade association had superficial parallels in western society. It was usual for land to be granted on condition of military service, while guilds of craftsmen became common enough in the cities. Both institutions, however, were derogatory to the exercise of any central authority. The first produced the local noble's independent army and, in effect, his private system of law and justice. The second fought for its private privileges against a king or an emperor. It was precisely the opposite in Byzantium where these institutions were set up by a strong central authority and themselves helped to perpetuate that strength.

Thirdly, Byzantine resources helped to maintain a remarkable level of education. It is true that the schools of philosophy at Athens were closed by Justinian and never recovered their ancient glory, while the universities of Alexandria and of Antioch were lost to Byzantium at the beginning of our period. In the year 425, however, a university was founded at Constantinople by Theodosius II with professors paid by the state and freed from all taxes. Despite many vicissitudes of fortune its studies were only occasionally interrupted. It performed the practical task of training candidates for senior administrative posts while, in the eleventh century, its Greek classical tradition made it the focus of a great

7

cultural efflorescence. Some of the emperors were themselves more than patrons of higher education. Leo III (717–741), Basil I (867–886) and Leo VI (886–912) all had a hand in the codification of the laws associated with their reigns. The last gained the sobriquet of 'the Philosopher' and we know that he also composed poems and a treatise on military strategy. Theophilus (829–42) excelled in many branches of knowledge including astronomy and natural history. Constantine VII (913–959) described and classified the machinery of government, court ceremonial, and the relations of Byzantium with her neighbours in extremely detailed works which today constitute a historical source of first class value. However, Byzantine education had a wider context than university graduates and emperors. Both elementary and secondary schools existed in many cities and in not a few villages, open to anyone who could afford the comparatively small fee. Not only basic literacy, but a knowledge of arithmetic, grammar, and Greek literature was the rule in any relatively well-to-do family. The most important characteristic of this structure was that it was wholly secular both in respect of subject-matter and of purpose. Theology and training for the priesthood were the business of quite separate institutions. Byzantine education produced an educated lay public. Thus the whole picture differed profoundly from the situation in Western Europe where education was provided by the Church for churchmen and where the literate layman, however rich or noble, was a great rarity.

The character of the economic, administrative and educational structure was reflected in the character of the ruling institution—in the position of the emperor and in the scope of his activities. It is true that, in one vital respect, nothing had changed since Roman days. The death of an emperor was likely to bring confusion. The virtual acceptance, for hundreds of years, of some sort of hereditary principle could never ensure a peaceful transfer of power. Six emperors rose and fell before Leo III succeeded in establishing his dynasty. Basil I established his by murdering his predecessor. Constantine VII was kept from the throne for over twenty years by his father-in-law. However, such palace revolutions, together with the wider conflicts they frequently engendered, never

8

damaged Byzantium any more than they had Rome before her decay. The reason was that professional civil servants ensured administrative continuity, which helped the state to survive both serious internal disorder and the attacks of external enemies for which such disorder was the natural opportunity. During most of our period, a professional civil service meant that the ruling institution was not hampered in the way that Western medieval rulers were in their efforts to achieve stability. The Byzantine emperor did not have to curtail his sovereignty by the need to distribute land and privileges in return for the performance of some administrative task, nor for the sake of assembling an army. A professional civil service left no place for the Western sort of feudal aristocracy. The high officers of state had their carefully graded honours, their perquisites, their family wealth and their influence at court. Their ambitions and intrigues were often an emperor's biggest problem and the natural cause of many palace upheavals. But however insecure the position of a particular emperor, the imperial office itself had no rivals. Its powers could not be encroached upon by persons or institutions exclusively entitled to the exercise of some special authority. It ruled through a hierarchy of rank, not of status. This was true throughout Byzantine society. There were no specific functions assigned by hereditary right, nor did any disabilities result from hereditary limitations. In other words, there was nothing in Byzantium corresponding to the rigid divisions between the magnates, the knights and the villeins of the feudal West each with their privileges and limitations strictly defined. On the contrary, there was considerable social flexibility. The smallholders of the themes, despite their strategic and economic importance, were not bound to the soil. The absence of great landlords throughout much of this period and a measure of co-operative responsibility in the payment of taxes meant that there existed in the countryside a rough equality. There was a parallel situation in the towns. Those who, during the later years of the Roman Empire, had become bound to their trade or calling and had sunk to the level of bondsmen, had, by the end of the seventh century, regained their professional mobility. Distinctions of status were only significant in court

9

ceremonial (which was eventually abolished), for example that between guildsmen and senators. When Constantine V, the successor of Leo III, wished to assure himself of the loyalty of the capital he caused exactly the same oath to be administered to the senate, to senior army officers, to shopkeepers and to craftsmen—an inconceivable procedure according to Western ideas.

This same rough equality, under the ruling institution, was strikingly illustrated by the active political life of the urban population as a whole. At the beginning of our period, its principal expression was through the 'circus parties'—the supporters of the hippodrome chariot races organized under two rival colours: the Greens and the Blues. The struggle between them, although probably sporting in origin, had come to reflect a genuine clash of interests: the Blues were the party of the rich, the Greens of the poor. The Blues were likely to support the authorities, the Greens to oppose them. This was not always so. Twice in the sixth century the two parties joined forces and the emperor had nearly to abdicate as a result, while during the reign of Phocas (602–610) their allegiances were very confused and Phocas benefited from considerable Green suppport. The circus parties were closely associated with the 'demes'. These were district organizations, of popular composition, with remarkably wide powers. At one time or another, they were responsible for public order, for the collection of local taxes, for the raising of a militia, perhaps for the exercise of certain judicial powers. They were closely connected with the guilds, since each district tended to be the centre for a particular trade; indeed it is not always easy to draw an absolute distinction between the two. In 583, the militia of the demes defeated four Slav attacks on Constantinople. In 1040, the guilds defended Thessalonica against the Bulgarians, and in 1185 against the Normans. But the demes, directly or through the guilds, also continued to lead the towns politically, long after the circus parties had ceased to matter. On the whole, they were more conservative than either of the two colours had been, and would declare against anyone, whether an emperor or a rebel, whose policies were likely to upset the established order. And their support or opposition was usually as decisive as had been that of the parties. Thus, in one form or another the population of the towns preserved its independent importance within the framework of a recognized tradition. This democratic element was as typically Byzantine as the autocracy of the ruling institution—from whose prerogatives it took nothing, any more than did the court nobility. It was an element also somewhat reminiscent of the Greek city. And this is not surprising. Byzantium preserved elements of the Greek tradition in politics, just as it preserved elements of the Roman achievement in administration.

From both Greece and Rome it inherited another institution—slavery. Its jurists excused it just as had the jurists of Rome and not a few philosophers of Greece. There was a distinction between 'natural' or 'universal' law on the one hand, in which slavery cannot exist, and various contingent laws on the other which permit it—such as the laws of war which prescribe it for the captured. Byzantine slaves were legally either prisoners of war or their descendants, and they might easily be as Christian as their masters. They were not infrequently freed, sometimes on condition that they continued to be orthodox in their faith. But there was nothing to say that a non-Christian slave who converted to Christianity would automatically be granted freedom. The slaves performed many functions. They were not only unskilled labourers and craftsmen but also doctors and notaries. Their sale and purchase was meticulously regulated. In the ninth and tenth centuries there was a lively demand for them on the part of a prosperous urban middle class. Even monks bought them despite repeated prohibitions, and an organized slave market grew up in Constantinople. It is impossible to assert that they were as necessary to the Byzantine economy as they had been to the Roman, but there is no doubt that they were a valuable possession.

However, it was in the relations between the emperor and the church that this double heritage from Greece and Rome had its most striking results. On the one hand, an unimpaired sovereignty and an efficient administration allowed him to exercise the same authority as had the strongest of his Roman predecessors. Just as in 325 the First Ecumenical Council at Nicea had been summoned and presided over by Constantine I, so the Sixth Ecumenical

Council was initiated and organized in 680 by Constantine IV. Just as the codes of Theodosius II in the fifth century had indifferently included secular and ecclesiastical legislation, so did the codes of Justinian in the sixth century and the rescripts of Leo VI in the tenth. And the emperors, whether during the Roman or during the Byzantine periods, unhesitatingly decided on matters of doctrine or of usage. The Nicean Creed, the basis of Christian theology to this day, was partly the work of Constantine himself —although at the time almost certainly not a Christian. Heraclius (610–641) enforced his own definition in an attempt to end a centuries-old dispute between the Monophysites—those who believed that Jesus possessed only one, divine, nature—and the formula of the Council of Chalcedon according to which he had two, divine and human; accepted by the orthodox, but itself largely an imperial decision. Leo III forbade holy pictures, icons, which by his day had become the tradition in churches. Iconoclasm was finally abolished by imperial decree in 843. Leo VI laid down the correct age for baptism and the exact rank which married clergy could attain. Now, while there was often fierce opposition to the substance of such decisions, it was rarely claimed that the emperor had no right to make them. And the opposition was never specifically ecclesiastical. No conflict developed between the spiritual and the secular authorities as it did between the popes and the German emperors. In this sense, the Byzantine church was as much an integral part of the ruling institution as was the civil service or the army command. Indeed, it had the same function: to guard the empire by guarding its internal unity, in this instance through religious conformity. Of course, it should not be forgotten that for the emperor this function had as much religious as political meaning. His decisions were intended to strengthen the church whose head and defender he was. Religious conformity was important for political unity, but the extirpation of theological error was the first responsibility of a ruler whose titles, at least from the end of the seventh century, proclaimed that he was 'both king and priest'.

On the other hand, the Greek heritage was as alive in the Byzantine church as it was in the Byzantine city. The Greek philosophic and cultural tradition, the language itself, provided particularly suitable tools for elaborate doctrinal interpretations, while the high level of literacy ensured widespread and enthusiastic participation in theological disputes. The Greens were monophysites, the Blues disciples of Chalcedon. The destruction of the icons and their rehabilitation had both popular support and opposition. Within the church, there was an interesting parallel. The leading part in a dispute was usually taken by the monks, and it was the monks who within the church constituted the popular element. They were closest to the mass of the ordinary people. There were strong links between the monastery and its immediate surroundings—not merely because of the medical and social services it provided, common enough, of course, in the West (though at a later period and not nearly so efficiently carried out). Often the monks were originally local people, while the monastery might be built with the help of volunteer local labour. It was for these reasons that the locality would look to the monastery for its secular as well as for its spiritual needs. The monks were both moral examples and a source of practical advice. The biographies of those famous for their holiness or their miracles were as well known as the scriptures. And the monks constituted the popular element in another equally important sense: their great numbers made them a substantial proportion of the general population. Thus, the monks who opposed iconoclasm were an obvious danger, and became a special target of imperial anger. Constantine V paraded them with every circumstance of ignominy in the Hippodrome, and had many executed. But there were iconoclast monks too. This kind of division continued. From the end of the eighth century, there were two tendencies within the church on a number of issues, two more or less explicitly organized parties in both of which the monks played their part. One was more likely to be stricter in its interpretation of dogma or custom than the other, and less likely to accept an imperial decision. It was the stricter party, for example, that aroused popular opinion against the probably uncanonical appointment of the patriarch Photius in 858, as well as against Leo VI's insistence on a fourth marriage in 906. But the fundamental significance of both parties was the simple fact of their existence and influence, whatever side they took—just as the fundamental significance of the demes and the guilds was their particular political power in the city, and not their attitude to any issue. The church parties, like the city parties, were the democratic elements, the Greek tradition, in Byzantine society; elements which never directly challenged the sovereignty of the ruling institution, the embodiment of the Roman tradition, but which could never be left out of account.

These, then, were the ways, important for our understanding of Byzantine Jewry, in which the Byzantium of our period differed from the West: a strong central authority, a flourishing economy, a measure of social mobility, a genuinely democratic (and, in comparison to the West, an educated) element actively involved in religious or political quarrels. Of course, this situation was not static. Byzantine institutions, like any others, were subject to change and decay. In particular, our period saw not only the establishment but also the destruction of the most influential of any single one of them—the theme system. By the middle of the eleventh century there had appeared in Asia Minor precisely what the themes had been intended to prevent: great private estates, whose tenants had been the soldiers of the theme but whom the great landowners could now use for their private armies in their quarrels with the emperor or with each other. The rich soil of Asia Minor may have been especially attractive when a low rate of interest and controls of various kinds on trade and manufacture made profitable investments difficult to find. In any case, at least from the end of the ninth century, there was a growing pressure to buy out the smallholder. Romanus I (920–944)[7a] understood the danger, but neither his decrees nor those of his immediate successors, forbidding the alienation of theme property, could halt the process. The tenth and eleventh centuries saw a bitter struggle for power between the emperors and these new provincial magnates. And the magnates won. The emperors were forced to recognize in practice, if not in theory, the claims of a semi-feudal nobility, whose irresponsible squabbling ruined Asia Minor and damaged the whole structure of the state. It says much for Byzantium's inner resources that under Alexius I

(1081–1118) it recovered much of its military and administrative efficiency. Modern Byzantine studies have corrected exaggerated ideas of general decay during the fifty years before Alexius. But the crisis had been severe, and the recovery was incomplete.

The menace of external enemies was, at times, no less serious. The first of these enemies was Persia. The crisis came during the reign of Phocas and the early years of Heraclius. Syria, Palestine and Egypt were overrun, Constantinople besieged. The next crisis was the Arab onslaught. The same provinces, regained by Heraclius, were lost—this time permanently. Every summer, from 673 to 678, the Arabs raided as far as Constantinople. In 717–18 came the great siege whose failure was a turning point, not only in Byzantine, but probably also in world history. One way or another, the struggle with Islam continued during the whole of our period. A Byzantine counter-attack began under Michael III (842–867) and reached its climax a hundred years later when a narrow coastal strip from Antioch to Jaffa was temporarily re-conquered. After that, however, it was not long before new Muslim invaders, the Seljuk Turks, appeared, who, with the weakening of the Byzantine military system, were able to make permanent conquests in Asia Minor. The Muslim danger was not the only one that Byzantium had to face. By the end of the seventh century, the Slavs on the northern frontier had been absorbed into an aggressive non-Slav state—the so-called first Bulgarian empire—which destroyed army after army, both before and after its acceptance of Byzantine Christianity and customs, until it was finally crushed by Basil II in 1018. In Byzantine eyes, the First Crusade was no more than another threat to imperial security—this time from the west. Its Norman leaders had driven the Byzantines out of Italy and Sicily by 1071. Shortly afterwards, they were raiding Greece. Their appearance at Constantinople in the last years of the century, in the guise of Crusaders, was thought of as part of a general plan of conquest—the plan that was carried out in 1204. Indeed, during the whole of our period it would be hard to find a year of peace. Yet it would be a mistake to think of the Byzantines as living in a perpetual state of emergency. Wars, and rumours of wars, did not in themselves seriously

15

disturb the régime. The really critical periods did, especially the losses in Asia Minor whether to rebellious generals or Seljuk amirs. These losses damaged the whole economy. Concessions had to be made to foreign merchants. The Venetians demanded payment for help they had given Alexius to establish himself over his rivals and solve his financial problems. By the beginning of the twelfth century, Venetians, Pisans and Genoans each had their own quarter in Constantinople with various preferential conditions. At the same time, the successes of the First Crusade and the rise of the Crusader Kingdoms in Syria and Palestine, forced the empire into some remarkably useless Western alliances in an effort to balance these new elements. The final result was the disaster of 1204.

One consequence of all these changes was that Byzantium lost her pre-eminence and became just one of several Christian or Muslim states struggling for supremacy in the eastern Mediterranean. Yet, until 1204, a basic aspect remained unaffected. Changes in the balance of power, however revolutionary, hardly injured trade, whoever might be profiting most from it. The lands of the eastern Mediterranean remained a thriving economic unit of which Byzantium was a part. It continued to benefit, in however reduced a measure, from the general prosperity. So long as Constantinople with its surrounding territories remained intact, Byzantium continued to command resources enabling it until the end, despite western pressures and the infiltration of western ideas, to preserve something of the typical institutions which gave it a different character from the West.

Byzantine institutions influenced Byzantine Jewry in two fundamental respects. Firstly, the absence of rigid social hierarchies under the ruling institution meant that there was no special category into which, as in the West, the Jews had to be fitted. They were never an isolated element. From the middle of the fourth century to the middle of eleventh, they lived in the heart of Constantinople, in the Chalkoprateia, among the bronze and copper workers.[8] Subsequently they began to settle in Pera, on the other side of the Golden Horn, a move officially confirmed by Alexius I in his general allocation of quarters for different communities. The Jews were not denied access to the old city, where they had their own landing stage, just like the Venetians.[9] This freedom of movement was true of Alexandria, of Antioch and of Thessalonica; contact between Jew and non-Jew was everywhere very close. Similarly, the character of the economy discouraged distinctions of the Western sort. The Jews could own houses and land; they could be farmers. The need for interest-bearing loans and their legality prevented moneylending, as in the West, from being a particularly Jewish occupation. Such concepts were meaningless in Byzantium. The Jews followed many different occupations, some of which will be discussed in the context of various events in their history. They were an integral part of the economy, though their actual contribution is difficult to assess for the same reason that it is difficult accurately to estimate their numbers: the extant information is for widely separated periods. Sometimes that contribution was important: at the beginning of our period they were sharing in the responsibility of shipping corn and other food commodities to Constantinople; by the twelfth century they had become exceptionally skilled workers in the silk industry.[10] Secondly, as against this positive aspect, Byzantium was a powerful Christian state with an extraordinary interest in its religion. If the Jews were not isolated, they were not loved. Legally enacted or extra-legal discriminations arising from some theological principle were not lacking. The absence of confinement to specific occupations did not mean unrestricted entry to all. Thus, two opposing forces acted upon Byzantine Jewry: the opportunities of a comparatively open society and the inherent threat of a theologically oriented ruling institution. The situation was not static. The vicissitudes through which the empire passed often determined which force was in the ascendant.

Notes

1 Bar-Hebraeus, ed. and trans. E. Pococke, *Historia compendiara dynastiarum* (London, 1663), text, p. 73, translation, p. 116

2 For a summary of the arguments, see S. W. Baron, *A Social and Religious History of the Jews*, 2nd ed. (New York, 1957), vol. 1, pp. 370–2 (note 7)

3 ספר מסעות, ed. and trans. M. Adler, *The Itinerary of Benjamin of Tudela* (London, 1907), text pp. 11–17, translation, pp. 10–14. On the date of Benjamin's visit, see Adler, *op. cit.*, pp. 1–2 (note 2)

4 For this total, see Baron, *op. cit.*, vol. 3, pp. 322–3 (note 29); p. 284 (note 48); Z. Ankori, *Karaites in Byzantium* (New York and Jerusalem, 1959), p. 159; for Benjamin's figures see Adler, text, p. 17, trans., p. 14; see below, pp. 134–7

5 See S. Vryonis, 'Byzantine $Δημοκράτια$ and the Guilds in the Eleventh Century', DOP 17 (1963), p. 293; A. Andréadès, 'La population de l'empire byzantin' *Bulletin de l'institut archéologique bulgare* 9 (1935), p. 121

6 See J. L. Teall, 'The Grain Supply of the Byzantine Empire 330–1025', DOP 13 (1959) pp. 105–8

7 On Byzantium generally, the best in English is G. Ostrogorsky, trans. J. Hussey, *History of the Byzantine State* (Oxford, 1956)—and subsequent editions; see also the new fourth volume of the *Cambridge Medieval History* (1967). Its bibliographies are the best guide to the specialist literature on the various aspects briefly mentioned here

7a In this period Romanus thrust aside the legal emperor Constantine (see p. 8), but both appear together in all Byzantine regnal lists; see e.g. Ostrogorsky, p. 516 and below, pp. 95–6, p. 98, p. 100.

8 See A. Galanté, *Les Juifs de Constantinople sous Byzance* (Istanbul, 1940), pp. 23–5; cf. C. Emereau, 'Constantinople sous Théodore le Jeune', BYZ 2 (1925), p. 112

9 *Annae Comnenae Alexiadis* V. 10; ed. and trans. B. Leib, *Anne Comnene, Alexiade*, vol. 2 (Paris, 1943, 1967), p. 54

10 Galanté, *op. cit.* p. 51; cf. R. S. Lopez, 'The Role of Trade in the Economic Readjustment of Byzantium in the Seventh Century', DOP 13 (1959), p. 83. On Jews in the silk industry, see *Benjamin of Tudela*, ed. Adler, text, p. 12, p. 13, p. 17, trans. p. 10, p. 11, p. 14

CHAPTER II

The Jews under Justinian

Byzantium, then, was a society of law and order, a centralized state whose decisions were likely to be carried out by a loyal cadre of trained administrators. In such a society, legislative action was more likely to have results than the decrees of contemporary Western rulers, which often remained mere expressions of personal intention. Byzantine legislation was closer to modern situations: a reflection of commonly held attitudes and an application, usually effective, of commands or prohibitions inspired by religious or moral axioms. Thus, an account of the Jews under Justinian, a formative period for them as for all his subjects, must begin with an account of his legislation. Just as his famous codification of Roman law fixed much of the administrative and juridical framework within which his successors continued to rule, so did his legislation on Jewish matters impose a pattern of life for the Jews which his successors did not disturb for very long.

Justinian's Code was based on a similar one completed by Theodosius II in 438, itself compiled from the legislation of the previous hundred years, from the time of Constantine I, the emperor who accorded Christianity its status of the ruling and exclusive religion. Yet Theodosius was careful to preserve as far as possible older traditions and to perpetuate the juridical concepts of pre-Christian imperial Rome. The body of legislation, then, which was completed by Justinian and which assigned to the Jews their place in society, was Roman as well as Christian. The dis-inclination to alter the old laws applied equally to Jewish matters.[1] In 212, Roman citizenship had been universally granted to all the inhabitants of the empire. The civil status of the Jews, that is their right to the protection of the law, became identical with that of every other race and nation ruled by Rome. They did not lose this right.[2] The various disabilities laid upon them from Theodosius to Justinian never derogated from it, any more than a law disabling everyone below a certain age from performing specific acts would turn all that class of persons into outlaws. Thus Judaism remained an explicitly permitted religion.[3]

However, this situation was not only the result of incorporating pre-Christian enactments into a Christian code. It was also deliberate Christian policy. Judaism had to be preserved as a living testimony to the Christian interpretation of the scriptures, to the victory of Christianity.[4] Jews were thus sharply distinguished from both pagans and heretics—who had no rights and no civil status. Their situation contradicted the common view that 'the dogmatic exclusiveness of the Christian religion also meant that all other religions were proscribed and completely denied any legal protection.'[5] Of course, the doctrine that gave the Jews this paradoxical privilege in a medieval Christian state was not confined to Rome or Byzantium. But it was carried out there more consistently and effectively than anywhere else in the Christian world.

This doctrine, once accepted, had not only to permit Judaism but, in a society of law and order, could not but protect its institutions. First of all, circumcision continued to be permitted. This had been an exceptional Jewish privilege in Roman law, which normally associated circumcision with castration, an illegal mutilation attracting the death penalty and confiscation of property.[6] Next, both Codes declared synagogues to be legally recognized places of worship, and protected from violence or desecration.[7] If a synagogue had been seized, it was to be returned. If it had been consecrated for use as a church, the community was to be compensated by a sum of money and, if judged necessary, by a building plot suitable for erecting another.[8] Just as the synagogue was recognized, so were Jewish courts of law. Their decisions in civil cases between Jews had full legal force and were to be executed by the imperial magistrates as though they were their own.[9] The Jew was protected in his daily life. He could not be forced to desecrate his sabbath or his festivals.[10] A non-Jew could not fix the price of the goods a Jew offered for sale.[11] A non-Jew could not be directly in charge of Jews at work.[12] Finally, the Jew, if he himself was causing no offence, was not to be molested: 'not to be trampled upon for being Jewish and not to suffer contumely for his religion . . . the law forbids private revenge'.[13]

But this doctrine of preservation had another side. The same theological reasoning which protected the status of the Jews and their religion assigned to them a position of permanent inferiority. The Codes gave legal form to this principle in three ways. First of all, they progressively disabled the Jews from performing public functions. In 404, they were excluded from certain government posts,[14] in 418 from a great many more.[15] In 425, all posts, whether civil or military, were closed to them.[16] It was this last regulation which was repeated by Justinian.[17] Yet there was one public function which the Jews were not only allowed, but compelled to perform. Together with all other financially qualified citizens, they had to accept membership of city councils, to serve as 'decurions'; for this service could mean serious financial loss. The decurions had to collect the local taxes and make up the deficit from their own pockets, a system intended to compensate the treasury for the growing poverty of the cities in the Western provinces. The large number of edicts, beginning in 330, re-affirming Jewish responsibilities shows how often Jews, no less than others, tried to evade this honour.[18] But here, too, there was progressive discrimination. According to the Theodosian Code, the Jew, in common with the Christian on whom the lot fell, was allowed to pay for a substitute, particularly if the Jew held an official position in his own community.[19] Some such rights remained in the Code of Justinian, but they were all abolished by a 'novel' or separate promulgation in 537, which stressed the principle involved: the Jews must never enjoy the fruits of office but only suffer its pains and penalties.[20]

Secondly, the Jews were not allowed to own Christian slaves. This disability was also punitive. Slavery, as we have seen, was important to the economy and there was no disapproval of Christian slavery as such. The later sections of the Theodosian Code tended to prohibit purchase, as distinct from ownership, which was permitted on certain conditions, particularly if acquired by inheritance. Penalties were confined to the loss of the slaves, usually by means of a forced sale for the price paid.[21] Justinian abolished this distinction and increased the penalties. Any non-Christian lost his Christian slaves without compensation and had to pay a fine of 30 lbs. in gold.[22] A Jew might suffer death.[23]

Thirdly, the same theological principle that enjoined the preservation of Judaism emphasized that it must not be allowed to flourish. No new synagogues could be built.[24] The repair of old ones could be a risky step since, if building operations were judged outside that category, the structure was confiscated and a fine of 50 lbs. in gold had to be paid.[25] In 545, Justinian published a novel making the whole issue legally problematic: possession of a synagogue which could be shown to occupy a site belonging to an ecclesiastical institution was automatically null and void.[26] While existing Judaism was thus restricted, its spread was of course strictly forbidden. One motive for the prohibition of the possession by Jews of Christian slaves was that their conversion to Judaism by their masters was thought to be the most likely way in which the spread of Judaism might be attempted.[27] In both Codes, the penalty for circumcizing a Christian slave was the old Roman penalty for castration—death and confiscation of property.[28] Justinian, when he repeated the permission for Jews to circumcize their own children, declared this penalty for circumcizing any non-Jewish child.[29] The penalty for circumcizing a free adult was normally confiscation of property and exile for life.[30] Here again Justinian introduced the possibility of a death penalty —even for attempted conversion.[31] A Christian who had become a Jew was also subject to penalties—though they were lighter. He might be restricted in his testamentary powers, or his property might be entirely confiscated.[32] These laws imply that the Codes

22

recognized, while they condemned, the Jew by conversion as they did the Jew by birth.

Finally, it is to be noted that most Jewish legislation, whether conferring a right or declaring a disability, was prefaced by unambiguous expressions of hatred and contempt for Judaism. If recognition was necessary, it was a detestable necessity. Reiterations of the degraded and superstitious character of Jewish religious practices derived from the same theology that was the basis of the legislation. They proclaimed the irredeemable inferiority of the 'living testimony', and were a greater threat than much of the legislation itself. They were a general encouragement to interference on allegedly moral grounds without reference to any particular laws, and in virtual contradiction to those intended to safeguard the inviolability of the synagogue. Thus, for example, it was not accidental that Justinian omitted from his Code an earlier injunction that heads of communities especially must not be insulted.[33] It was in this same spirit that, unusually preoccupied with morals and theology even for a Byzantine emperor, he set out to reform two grave abuses.

It was disgraceful that the Jewish Passover should in any way have precedence over the Christian Easter. And so he commanded that 'if ever the season brought the Passover before the Easter of the Christians, the Jews were forbidden to hold it at the time laid down, to pay honour to God, or to perform their legitimate rites'.

It is necessary to add that, although this information is given by the major contemporary historian, Procopius of Caesarea, its authenticity is not beyond doubt. It appears in a work largely consisting of stories derogatory to Justinian, many of them known to be invented, written when Procopius was in disfavour at court. It closes a chapter of miscellaneous allegations of Justinian's disregard for 'all the laws of the Romans', and is followed by a chapter with the opening, 'I will now relate how false and cunning he was'.[34] Nor is there any reference to such a restriction in Justinian's own legislation, in subsequent legislation, or in any other source. But it is undeniably consonant with Justinian's views and fits in well with his second piece of interference about which there can be no possible doubt.

It was disgraceful that the Jews should be prevented from understanding the teachings of their own sacred writings. In 553, he published a novel with two instructions for the service of the synagogue.[35] It was forbidden to insist that the readings from the Pentateuch be in Hebrew from the sacred Scroll of the Law, the readings that then as always were an integral element in certain services. The Pentateuch could be read in Greek, in Latin or in any other tongue, according to the wishes of the congregation. In practice, this tongue was likely to be Greek. The vast majority of Justinian's Jewish subjects were Greek-speaking, whatever the state of their Hebrew knowledge. For the past four hundred years, there had existed an acceptable Greek translation of the scriptures though, of course, it was in no sense a substitute for the readings from the Scrolls. It was by Aquila, a convert to Judaism, who had worked under rabbinic supervision, and who had been praised in the poetic language of the Psalms as 'the most comely of men, who had made the beauties of Japhet (i.e. Greece) dwell in the tents of Shem'. And if the Hebrew of the scriptures was to be translated, Greek, said the Rabbis after careful examination, was the only language which met all requirements.[36] Justinian, aware of the regard in which Aquila was held, permitted it as an alternative to the Septuagint in order to give his reform a maximum chance of success. Secondly, no passages from the 'Deuterosis', that is the Mishnā, the traditional rabbinic interpretation which followed the readings, whether part of the actual service or not, could be given at all. The second instruction was in consonance with the common suspicions of all Jewish post-biblical literature, which was supposed to contain defamations of Christianity. But the novel said nothing of this. The reason it gave was that the Mishnā did not belong to the scriptures and was not divinely inspired. It was but the work of men and thus could only mislead. Similarly, the first instruction was meant to prevent misleading explanations of the Pentateuch if read out in a language which the majority of the congregation could not easily follow. Justinian himself claimed that he was settling a Jewish dispute on this very point, though the only evidence are his own words in the preamble to the novel. However that may be, the prime purpose of the first instruction as of the second was to improve Jewish morals and eradicate false beliefs by ensuring that the Pentateuch was understood without intermediaries, that is without rabbinic interpretation, whether by the rabbis of the Mishnā or by the rabbi of a community. Here was a contradiction: the Aquila translation itself had rabbinic sanction. But the novel did not only declare that the degraded condition of Judaism, affirmed by the Codes, was the fault of the rabbis—a conclusion reached by many other Christian rulers. It also decided precisely which rabbinic sanction was acceptable—just as the emperors were accustomed to do with the interpretations of Christian theologians. When Justinian asserted that he was settling a Jewish dispute, whether he had really been invited to do so or no, he was applying a fundamental principle of the Byzantine ruling institution to the Jewish sphere. Just as every emperor was the final arbiter of Christian beliefs and practices, so Justinian was now the final arbiter of the beliefs and practices of the only other legal religion in his dominions. And his purpose was not only to eradicate the false beliefs and practices of that religion. A correct knowledge of the scriptures could not but convince of the truth of the Christian interpretation. The novel had conversionist undertones and has to be considered in the context of what the authorities had to say on this subject.

The principle of the 'living testimony' had a corollary. The existence of the Jews as an inferior sect proved one truth of the Christian interpretation. Another would be fulfilled by the conversion of all of them to Christianity—a sign of the second coming of the Christian Messiah. No human obstacle must stand in the way. In this sense, there was no 'racialism'. The converted Jew was as heartily and unreservedly welcome as the Christian convert to Judaism was condemned. The Codes reserved their fiercest punishment for the Jew found guilty of molesting a convert to Christianity—death by fire.[37] On the other hand, the last days could not be brought nearer by force. Jews could not be pushed into conversion. It had to proceed from a genuine change of heart. The baptismal formula that the Jew had to recite included, in all its many versions, his declaration that he had not been induced by fear or by hope of gain.[38] Innumerable popular tales repeated the lesson that the desired result was only obtainable by convincing the Jew—either by argument or by a miracle—of the truth of Christianity.[39] This prerequisite of sincerity was official church policy in the time of Justinian and was embodied in canon law at the Second Council of Nicea (787).[40] The avoidance of inducement did not preclude encouragement, however slight this distinction might be. In the eyes of the church, the best result the disabilities of the Codes could achieve would be to encourage the Jews to change their beliefs. Later in the sixth century, Pope Gregory I encouraged Jewish tenants on his estates in Byzantine Italy by offering to excuse converts some of their rent.[41] And Justinian's novel intended that the reading of the scriptures without incorrect interpretations should encourage conclusions inevitably leading to conversion.

However, just as the repeated denunciation of Jewish customs incited interference, so did the great theological weight attached to the conversion of the Jews provide a strong temptation to direct action, whatever the Codes or the church itself might say. Here, too, Justinian was the first example. In 535, he announced that he would no longer permit the existence of synagogues in North Africa, while both the Jews and the heretics there were forbidden henceforth the practice of their religious rites. In so doing, he expressly contradicted the two fundamentals of Byzantine Jewish legislation: the protection of the synagogue and the distinction of Jews from heretics. The decree was never seriously applied. It was omitted from many collections of his laws, including their first modern edition.[42] Nevertheless, it set a precedent. The threat of repetition was a constant possibility. And it was a possibility symptomatic of the whole legal situation of the Jews under Justinian. A comparison of the two Codes, together with their relevant decrees and novels, shows how it had deteriorated. Restrictions and disabilities had increased. Punishments were more severe. Interference had received the sanction of law. In the formal sense at least, the Jews were noticeably worse off.[43]

For the period between the two Codes, no legislation on Jewish matters is extant, but the circumstances make it probable that some was enacted.[44] The relations of the Jews with the state from

Theodosius II to Justinian were frequently turbulent. The Jews were often involved with general upheaval. Thus, in 415, the Jews of Alexandria were victims in a quarrel of the fanatically strict patriarch Cyril with the liberally inclined imperial governor. The people of Alexandria, famous at that time for their exceptional love of violence, enthusiastically joined in the quarrel. The patriarch's faction murdered Hypatia, an expounder of Greek philosophy and the governor's friend. The governor's faction rioted at a theatrical performance. The manager was known to be the patriarch's agent, and Jewish voices were raised accusing him of provocation. Cyril blamed the Jews for the riot. When they armed themselves in fear of reprisals and several Christians were killed, the synagogues were destroyed and the Jews expelled from the city.[45] A Jewish issue had certainly been at stake. Cyril wanted to rid Alexandria of all non-Christian elements, whether Jewish or Hellenistic. On the other hand, the Jews had participated in the conflict because it was as normal for them to do so as for other communities. The sources do not suggest that their support of a particular faction was unusual. Of course, it is not surprising that as on other occasions they should be the first to suffer.

Their complete exclusion did not last long. There were already Jews in Alexandria at the time of the Council of Chalcedon in a secure enough position to risk petitioning for the re-building of their synagogues, on the grounds that the Council's decision for the double nature of Jesus had automatically exculpated them from the age old charge of crucifying a god.[46] The details in an account of an alleged miraculous conversion to Christianity, during the reign of the monophysite patriarch Timothy (518–535), suggest a settled Jewish family life.[47] There is some evidence of Jews in Alexandria during the reign of his successor Theodosius I (535–567). Monophysites 'take counsel together to build a church, so as not to be like the Jews'—presumably meaning the local community still without its synagogue.[48] An Alexandrian Jewish 'sophist' is mentioned in a theological polemic of the first half of the sixth century[49]—conceivably evidence of some Jewish learning. On the other hand, the comparatively unimportant examples of papyri with a Jewish context assignable to the sixth

27

century show that Jewish impact on Egyptian events then was slight.[50] The Jews did not return to Alexandria in any numbers until shortly before the Arab conquest. Until then, it was at Antioch and in Palestine that they were most prominently involved in imperial politics.

At Antioch, they participated in the politics of the hippodrome, that is, in the factions of the circus. As early as the year 40, a clash between the Greens and the Blues led, for unexplained reasons, to the burning of synagogues.[51] In the period of the Codes, the connection between the Jews and the circus factions was clearer. They had become a prosperous community, they were shop-keepers, artisans and merchants.[52] The Emperor Valens (364–378) is said to have presented them with gardens for their private use.[53] There were Jewish farmers outside the city and Jewish tenants on the great estates.[54] Their social position made them naturally loyal to the Blues. In 484, the Blues supported a revolt against the Emperor Zeno which the Greens helped to crush. In their reprisals, the Greens destroyed synagogues and burned bones they had exhumed from the Jewish cemetery, thus fulfilling a curse often shouted in circus quarrels: 'may the bones of your ancestors be exhumed!'. Zeno's comment was that they would have employed their time better by burning the Jews themselves.[55] In 507, it was the Emperor Anastasius who had reasons to encourage the Greens of Antioch, and again the results included the destruction of synagogues, this time in the suburb of Daphne. The riots spread and order was restored with difficulty.[56] There is little comparable evidence regarding the hippodrome at Constantinople. Jews may have joined in the so-called *Nikē* (victory) riots when the two factions combined and nearly forced Justinian to abdicate. But the reference is ambiguous; 'Jews' may be here simply a term of abuse.[57] There is, however, some reason to suppose that the Jews were as active in the factions at Constantinople as at Antioch.

One of the *midrashim*—allegorical or anecdotal commentaries on the scriptural text—illustrates Solomon's glory by giving him a circus or hippodrome.[58] Its description suggests a Byzantine rather than a scriptural context. The dimensions of its track are close to that of the hippodrome at Constantinople.[59] The

spectators wear garments coloured according to their rank: blue
for the king, the priests and the rabbis; white for the Jews of
Jerusalem; red for spectators from neighbouring towns; green for
the heathens. These colours are explained as symbolizing the
seasons of the year, and this was precisely the explanation of a
sixth-century scholar for the colours of the circus parties—
originally those four.[60] The blue of the highest rank and the green
of the lowest recall the social status of the Blues and the Greens.[61]
This ascription of a Byzantine hippodrome to Solomon strongly
contrasts with Jewish distaste for the old circus of the Romans—
the place of death or of unworthy frivolous spectacles.[62] It was
when gladiators and clowns were replaced by chariot races that
Jewish participation became acceptable, and it was then natural to
endow the greatest of Jewish rulers with an institution which had
become for Jews no less than for other citizens the centre of public
activity in an imperial city.

In Palestine, the protagonists of political involvement were the
Samaritans, a distinct community from the eighth century before
the Christian era. Their centre was Shkhem (Nablus), their holy
sanctuary was on Mount Gerizim, overlooking the town. From
the time of Constantine I, they were fervently nationalist, and by
the end of the fifth century they were a serious threat to imperial
rule. During the disorders of 484, which had affected Palestine as
well as Syria, they captured Shkhem, killed its bishop, proclaimed
their independence and chose a king. They were suppressed with
difficulty. A strong garrison was put into Shkhem, and the sanctuary was turned into a church.[63] The troubles in the reign of
Anastasius gave them a fresh opportunity. The garrison was
massacred and, for a brief moment, Shkhem again was theirs.[64]
The next revolt was in 529. This time they became masters of all
ancient Samaria from Caesarea on the coast almost to Tiberias
on the Sea of Kinneret. After their suppression they were altogether denied access to Gerizim on which five churches were
built, with a high wall around them.[65] They rose again in 555,
murdering the commander of troops at Caesarea.[66] This Samaritan struggle for independence was an integral element of the
situation of the Jews under Justinian. It is true that the Samaritans

were often as hostile to Palestinian Jews as they were to the imperial authorities. They were known to burn straw over their footprints in order to obliterate their presence. In 529, they killed both Jews and Greeks. Justinian, on his part, clearly distinguished between Jews and Samaritans, if only because in his day the latter were much more militant. After 529, he almost abolished their civil status. He virtually prohibited Samaritans from inheriting property, and ordered their wives and children to be brought up in Christian beliefs.[67] Nevertheless, the connection between the two communities was as obvious in official eyes as the difference between them. The novel dealing with Samaritans was automatically repeated by Basil I next to his Jewish legislation, although he had no Samaritans to rule.[68] A great deal of imperial legislation applied to both communities, for example exclusions from the public service in their progressive severity from Theodosius to Justinian.[69] Even the novel that interfered with Jewish synagogue ritual may have had a Samaritan reference. The specific false belief arising from an unwitting or malicious misinterpretation of the scriptures was said to be the denial of angels and of the Last Judgment. These were two heresies often listed by the church as having been acquired by the Samaritans from the Sadducees.[70] It is unlikely that Justinian could have been worried about the latter who had long since disappeared from the Jewish scene. Finally, Jews had joined in the revolt of 555. It was the most dangerous of them all; to crush it, troops had to be brought from as far afield as North Africa.[71] There was another sense in which the Jews and the Samaritans were comparably dangerous. Both had links outside their communities. The Jews participated in the factions. The Samaritans had friends at court. Samaritan pressure on the Empress Theodora nearly stopped Justinian from promulgating his penal legislation.[72] In 551, he was somehow persuaded slightly to ameliorate its effects.[73]

All these political involvements arose in circumstances affecting the general population, which themselves were threats to the peace and security of the empire. The conflicts of the factions, with their Jewish participation, like the first two Samaritan revolts, were connected with some general challenge to imperial authority whether aimed at Theodosius through his governor in Alexandria or at Zeno and Anastasius in Syria. These upheavals were followed by an economic crisis in Palestine. A flow of gold from the middle of the fourth to the middle of the fifth century had lavishly embellished its holy places with expensively adorned churches and shrines. It had enriched individual ecclesiastics who hoarded it in defiance of the law.[74] Little had been used for productive enterprises; instead it had added to the population the liability of numerous pilgrims and beggars. By 529, the situation was so bad that the government was forced to cancel two years of taxes owing to the treasury.[75] Eventually, the decline of the economy produced a most striking instance of contact between the communities. Towards the end of the century, Jews and Christians, deprived of their livelihood, worked with guerrilla bands openly operating in central Palestine.[76]

The political involvements of the Jewish question had an international aspect. The strategic and commercial value of the Gulf of Suez, then joined to the Nile by a canal, and of Aila (Eilat), from which there were routes to Palestine via Gaza, depended on conditions at the southern entrance to the Red Sea, the Perim Strait (Bāb-al-Mandāb). In the middle of the fourth century, both sides were controlled by Ethiopia. On the eastern side this control was exercised through the kingdom of the Himyarites, a group of tribes which included star-worshippers, then also the religion of their Ethiopian overlords, and Jews who had settled there after the destruction of the second Temple. The Himyarites ruled over a territory roughly corresponding to the present Republic of the Yemen and the South Arabian Federation. The empire protected its interests at Bāb-al-Mandāb by endeavouring to spread Christianity both in Ethiopia itself and in its Himyarite domain. In 350, permission was given to build a church at Najrān, in the central Yemen, officially for the use of Roman merchants. But it was a precarious success. The gradual spread of Christianity among the Himyarites was balanced by a growth in Jewish influence, which, after Ethiopia lost her hold in 378, steadily increased.[77] From 385 to 420, the Himyarites may already have had a Jewish ruler.[78] The situation became so serious that, at the beginning of the sixth century, an archbishop was sent from Alexandria to encourage the Christian Himyarites. A debate lasting four days resulted in the traditionally miraculous conversion of the archbishop's Jewish opponent, a victory with no lasting result.[79] About 518, another Jewish ruler, Dhū Nuwās, was in power. His first act was to lay an embargo on imperial trade and imprison a number of merchants in declared reprisal for the ill-treatment of Jews by the imperial government.[80]

This setback to imperial interests administered by a Jewish state had other consequences involving the Jews of the empire. Dhū Nuwās not only represented the Jewish tribes, he had the support of many Christians and pagans who rightly feared Ethiopian attempts to reconquer their Himyarite domain. He unsuccessfully tried to make an alliance with Persia, a permanent threat to the empire in the east and often supposed to have contact with Palestinian and Syrian Jews. Meanwhile Christianity and, accordingly, support for imperial policy, had grown stronger in Ethiopia. In 522, with imperial encouragement and assistance, part of the Yemen was retaken, and an imperial fleet of seventy ships was got ready for a fresh campaign. The king of Ethiopia demonstratively declared himself a Christian, and the Christian Himyarites began to turn to him. The unity of the defenders of Himyarite independence was broken, and Dhū Nuwās had to look for other sources outside his country. This time he was more successful than he had been with Persia. For some years Himyarite Judaism had been reinforced by periodical visits of rabbis from Tiberias.[81] With their help he temporarily re-established his position and began a vigorous attempt to convert to Judaism, and thus to Himyarite loyalty, the remaining pagans and the newer Christians who were not yet firm in their faith.[82] However, he was unable to make any impression on the oldest Christian centre, Najrān, and had no alternative but to destroy it as a dangerous pro-Ethiopian stronghold. Stories of the atrocities he was alleged to have committed there made a great impression and were repeated many times.[83] In 524, he was dead and his country once more under Ethiopian rule. It had been a war of two Christian States against a Jewish state. The Jews of the empire were held responsible for interference in imperial policy; their leaders had helped the ruler of the Jewish state; they could be held responsible for Najrān. Before the final Ethiopian victory, the suggestion in fact was made: let rabbis in Tiberias be imprisoned as hostages for the good behaviour of the Jewish Himyarites.[84]

The defeat of Dhū Nuwās had a sequel in the time of Justinian. Since 473, there had been a semi-autonomous colony of Jewish and Christian merchants on the island of Yotabē (Tirān) at the entrance to the Gulf of Aila, together in control of the imperial customs which, as was common, had been farmed out to private individuals.[85] Both the profits from trade and the income from duties were worth having; items that passed through the Gulf included spices, scents, linens, silks, precious stones and exotic animals.[86] After 524 the colony was swelled by Jewish refugees from the Yemen, who had drifted up the coast to Makkā, about fifty miles south-east of Aila. The Christians objected violently to this potential threat to their profits; the Jews seized a fort and were only dislodged by an expeditionary force from the mainland after a fierce struggle.[87] In 535, Justinian abolished the autonomy of Yotabē and all its inhabitants, whether Jewish or Christian, became ordinary subjects of the empire.[88]

Jewish involvement in politics and public life had another aspect. Judaism itself was attractive. The official establishment of Christianity had not meant complete victory for its ideas. In Egypt a widespread cult of observing the sabbath on Saturday lasted into the fifth century.[89] At Antioch, there had been continuous Christian interest in Judaism from the time of the apostles. In the fourth century, listening to Jewish preachers became fashionable among the upper classes, particularly among the women.[90] At the beginning of the sixth century, there were Christians observing the Jewish sabbath and festivals; there were those who even practised circumcision. Some brought tefillin (phylacteries) and mezuzot (the sign on the doorposts) into church.[91] There they might have been reminded of the synagogue service by certain elements of the Kontakion, a hymn or sung sermon in which Greek religious poetry reached its height, and which was the creation of the deacon Romanus (died about 555)—himself a Jew by origin.[92]

Such disciples—the apostle Paul had called them 'God-Fearers'—did not have to become converts to Judaism. Jewish tradition explicitly welcomed them in the category of 'strangers within the gate'.[93] In the cities of North Africa, with their old-established Jewish communities, judaizing tendencies, as at Antioch, were contemporary with the spread of Christianity. Christians often had close relations with Jews; many regulations were promulgated at Carthage to deal with these canons.[94] In the fifth century, a Judaeo-Christian sect arose which combined circumcision with baptism and denied the trinity. The church called its members 'Caelicolists' or sky-worshippers, after the usage in the Jewish liturgy of sometimes substituting 'the heavens' for 'God'.[95] On the other hand, in the countryside there were actual converts to Judaism among the native Berbers. Their numbers had been increased by Jewish refugees from the first period of Ethiopian rule over the Himyarites and, by 483, there existed a powerful Jewish Berber tribe. Its influence spread through the Berber villages, and it was the Berbers who continued fighting imperial troops after 534, when Byzantium subjugated the Vandals who had been masters of North Africa for the previous hundred years.[96]

Obviously, these instances of Jewish influence angered the clergy. In Egypt, the persistence of a Jewish custom made the patriarch Cyril particularly glad of a pretext to expel the community. At Antioch, the 'God-Fearers' had especially reverenced the synagogue containing the bones of the Maccabean martyrs. At the end of the fourth century, in defiance of the law, it was turned into a church. In 551, perhaps to avoid future risks, Justinian had the bones transferred to Constantinople.[97] The rescript of Theodosius in 423 re-affirming the inviolability of the synagogue as a place of worship was openly denounced by Simon Stylites, famed for his pillar-squatting, and the leader of monastic extremism at Antioch. He was powerful enough to cause the city governor who proclaimed it to be dismissed and nearly murdered.[98] His pressure even caused it to be momentarily ignored at Constantinople, where a synagogue in the Chalkoprateia was confiscated.[99] In North Africa, the Caelicolists were threatened with charges of high treason and with outlawry as heretics.[100] Nor is it surprising that Justinian increased the penalties for Jews suspected of proselytizing. The political implications of Jewish influence also had their consequences. Justinian's novel of 535 prohibiting Judaism in North Africa was aimed at Jewish ascendancy among the Berbers. The only known instance of its application was at a little place there called Borium, where the Jews had long lived in amity with the local population.[101]

Thus, in the eyes of the authorities, the Jews under Justinian had amply justified their frequent denunciation in the preambles to legislation. For the past hundred years and more they had been associated with disorders inside the empire. They helped the empire's enemies abroad, and could be held responsible for the notorious atrocities in the recent Himyarite wars. And they were particularly to be feared and hated on account of the Christians they had seduced to their degraded customs. There was enough in the official record to explain the harsher regulations introduced by Justinian, his interference in the service of the synagogue and his ominous step towards a policy of forced conversions. But Justinian was very far from conducting a general retaliatory campaign. The picture was not so simple. The reaction of the authorities was limited. There were no reprisals for Najrān either by Justinian's predecessor Justin I, or by Justinian himself when he came to the throne only two or three years later. Nor did the various legal or extra-legal measures which he did take against the Jews bring about any change in their juridical status. Their religion continued to be recognized. Their fundamental privileges remained untouched. One reason, of course, was the unaffected validity of the theological principle of the 'living testimony'. Another was indicated by a proviso to the inheritance restrictions placed on the Samaritans after 529: land in active cultivation must be allowed to pass unhindered from father to son, so as not to risk its profitability or its taxable value.[102] The milder law of 555 for the Samaritans had also this consideration. The depression in Palestine made it inadvisable to damage any of its productive sources. But Palestine was not the only weak spot in the economy. The mounting costs of Justinian's attempt to recreate the old Roman world, the financing of an extensive building programme

4

in Constantinople, an exceptionally bad outbreak of plague in 547, were among the reasons why the whole empire was passing through similar difficulties. It was clearly inadvisable to withdraw the protection of the state from any community which had an economic contribution to make. The continuance of this protection for the Jews meant that their social relations, no less than their juridical status, remained unchanged. They continued to participate in the public life of the Byzantine city and to mingle freely with their fellow citizens.

Notes

1. Expressed in C.Th. XVI.8.15 and 20; trans. C. Pharr, M. B. Pharr and T. S. Davidson, *The Theodosian Code and Novels and the Sirmondian Constitutions* (Princeton 1952), pp. 468–9; cf. A. H. M. Jones, *The Later Roman Empire* (Oxford 1964), vol. 2, p. 949

2. 'Judaei Romano et commune jure viventes'—C. Th.II.1.10 (=Pharr, p. 38); cf. C.I. I.9.8, ed. P. Krueger, *Corpus Iuris Civilis*, vol. 2 (Berlin 1954), p. 61

3. On the distinction between civil status and personal status, of which this is an example, as it affected Roman Jewry, see J. Juster, *Les droits politiques des Juifs dans l'empire romain* (Paris 1912), pp. 23–5.

4. For references to the copious Christian sources, see J. Juster, *Les Juifs dans l'Empire Romain* (Paris, 1914), vol. 1, pp. 226–9 (note 6)

5. Ostrogorsky, *History*, p. 70

6. *Digesta* XLVIII.8.11, ed. Th. Mommsen and P. Krueger, *Corpus Iuris Civilis* vol. 1 p. 853; cf. Juster. *Les Juifs*, vol. 2, pp. 190–5

7. C.Th. XVI.8.9–11 (=Pharr, p. 468); cf. C.I. 1.9.14 (=Krueger, p. 62); C.Th. VII.8.2. (=Pharr, p. 165); cf. C.I. 1.9.4 (=Krueger, p. 61)

8. C.Th. XVI.8.25, 27 (=Pharr, pp. 470–1); cf. C.I. 1.9.15 (=Krueger, p. 62)

9. C.Th. II.1.10 (=Pharr, p. 39); cf. C.I. 1.9.8 (=Krueger, p. 61)

10. C.Th. II.8.26; VIII.8.8; XVI.8.20 (=Pharr, p. 45; p. 210; p. 469); cf. C.I. 1.9.13 (=Krueger, pp. 61–2)

11. C.Th. XVI.8.10 (=Pharr, p. 468); cf. C.I. 1.9.10 (=Krueger, p. 61)

12. C.I. 1.9.10 (=Krueger, p. 61)

13. C.Th. XVI.8.21 (=Pharr, pp. 469–70); cf. C.I. 1.11.6 (=Krueger, p. 63). On all the foregoing references to privileges, cf. G. Ferrari dalle Spade, 'Privilegi degli Ebrei nell'Impero Romano Cristiano', *Muenchner Beitraege zur Papyrusforschung und antiken Rechtsgeschichte*, 35 (ii) (1945), pp. 102–17

14. C.Th. XVI.8.16 (=Pharr, p. 469)

15. C.Th. XVI.8.24 (=Pharr, p. 470)

16. Sirmondian Constitutions, 6 (=Pharr, p. 480); this was a compilation of material not in the Code but antedating its completion; see Pharr, p. 477, note 1

17. C.I. 1.5.12/4 (=Krueger, p. 53)

18 E.g. C.Th. XVI.8.2, 3, 4, 13 (= Pharr, pp. 467–8); C.Th. XVI.8.24 (= Pharr, p. 470)

19 C.Th. XII.1.99 (= Pharr, pp. 356–7); C.Th. XII.1.157 and 165 (= Pharr, pp. 364–6)

20 C.I. X.32.49 (= Krueger, p. 413), Novel 45, ed. R. Schoell and W. Kroll, *Corpus Iuris Civilis*, vol. 3, pp. 277–9

21 C.Th. III.1.5 (= Pharr, p. 64); C.Th. XVI.9.5 (= Pharr, p. 472)

22 C.I. 1.9.18 (= Krueger, p. 62)

23 C.I. 1. 10.1 (= Krueger, p. 62); cf. C.I. 1.3.54(56)/8 (Krueger, p. 38) and C.I. 1.9.10 (= Krueger, p. 61). Justinian may have been repeating a stricter law of Constantine (not extant), see Pharr, p. 469, note 25

24 C.Th. XVI.8.25 and 27(= Pharr, p. 470); cf. C.I. 1.9.15 (= Krueger, p. 62)

25 Th.Nov. III.3 and 5 (= Pharr, p. 489); cf. C.I. 1.9.18 (= Krueger, p. 62)

26 Novel 131 (= Schoell and Kroll, p. 663)

27 See e.g. C.Th. XVI.9.3 and 4 (= Pharr, pp. 471–2)

28 Th.Nov. III.4 (= Pharr, p. 489); cf. C.I. 1.9.16 (= Kreuger, p. 62)

29 *Digesta* XLVIII.8.11 as in note 6, above

30 C.Th. XVI.8.26 (= Pharr, pp. 470–1); cf. C.I. 1.9.16 (= Krueger, p. 62)

31 C.I. 1.9.18 (= Krueger, p. 62)

32 C.Th. XVI.7.3 (= Pharr, p. 466); cf. C.I. 1.7.2 (= Krueger, p. 60) and C.Th. XVI.8.7 (= Pharr, pp. 467–8); cf. C.I. 1.7.1 (= Krueger, p. 60)

33 C.Th. XVI.8.11 (= Pharr, p. 468)

34 *Procopii historia arcana*, c. 28, 29; ed. J. Haury (Leipzig 1963), p. 174

35 Novel 146 (= Schoell and Kroll, p. 714); cf. Juster, *Les Juifs*, vol. 1, pp. 372–3 (note 6); p. 374 (note 1); pp. 375–6. English translation in J. Parkes, *The Conflict of the Church and the Synagogue* (London 1934), pp. 392–3. For references to the literature on this best known Jewish legislation of Justinian, see Baron, vol. 3, p. 233, note 11

36 Jerusalem Talmud, *Tractate Megillā* I.71c, quoting Psalms XLV.3. The superiority of Greek is stated in the same passage:
בדקו ומצאו שאין התורה יכולה להתרגם כל צורכה אלא ביוונית

37 C.Th. XVI.8.1 (= Pharr. p. 467); cf. C.I. 1.9.3 (= Krueger, p. 61)

38 The prototype is in the so-called 'Clementine Recognitions', MPG vol. 1, cols. 1456B–1461B; trans. Parkes, *op. cit.*, pp. 397–400. For others, see F. Cumont, 'Une formule grècque de renonciation au judaïsme', *Wiener Studien* 24 (1902), pp. 230–40; V. Ermoni, 'Abjuration', *Dictionnaire d'archéologie chrétienne et de liturgie* vol. 1 (1924), cols 98–103; V. N. Beneshevitch, 'On the History of the Jews in Byzantium from the Sixth to the Ninth Centuries', *Yevreiskaya Misl*, 2 (1926), pp. 305–18 (Greek texts), pp. 197–224 (commentary in Russian)

39 See e.g. the instances in A. L. Williams, *Adversus Judaeos. A bird's eye view of Christian Apologiae until the Renaissance* (Cambridge 1935)

40 See *Timothei Presbyteri De Receptione Haeriticorum*, MPG vol. 86, col. 72 for the time of Justinian; Mansi, vol. 14, col. 427 for the Second Council of Nicea

41 *S. Gregorii epistolae* II.38, ed. P. Ewald and L. M. Hartmann, MGH Epistolae I (1891), pp. 133–4; cf. S. Katz, 'Pope Gregory the Great and the Jews', JQR (new series) 24 (1933), p. 125

37

42 Novel 37 (= Schoell and Kroll, pp. 244–5).
It only appears in recensions up to 575, see P. Noailles, *Les collections de novelles de l'empereur Justinien*, vol. 1 (Bordeaux 1912), pp. 179, 184, 195, 258. It is omitted in Theodore Balsamon's comprehensive twelfth century collection of Roman laws, ed. W. Voellus and H. Justel (Paris 1661), and by Zachariae von Lingenthal in his fundamental *Jus graeco-romanum*, vol. 3, (Leipzig 1881). See also A. H. M. Jones, *The Later Roman Empire* (Oxford, 1964), vol. 1, pp. 274, 286

43 Cf. P. Browe, 'Die Judengesetzgebung Justinians', *Analecta Gregoriana* 8 (1935), pp. 101–46

44 Juster, *Les Juifs*, vol. 1, pp. 166–7

45 John of Nikiu, a major source for Egypt, trans. C. H. Charles, *The Chronicle of John of Nikiu* (London 1916), LXXIV. 87–9 (= pp. 101–2); *Socratis historia ecclesiastica* MPG vol. 67, cols. 760–5; repeated by the twelfth-century but usually reliable Michael the Syrian, VIII.2, trans. J. B. Chabot, *Le Chronique de Michel le syrien*, vol. 2, pp. 11–12, cf. Parkes, *op. cit.*, pp. 234–5

46 Michael the Syrian VIII.12, repeating a lost portion of the sixth-century chronicle of Zachariae of Mytilene (= Chabot, vol. 2, p. 94); cf. F. Nau, 'L'histoire ecclésiastique de Jean d'Asie', ROC 2 (1897), p. 458

47 John of Nikiu, XCI (= Charles, pp. 144–5)

48 Ibn al-Mukaf'a (Severus), *Kitāb siyari-l-ābāi al-baṭārikati*, ed. and trans. B. Evetts, *History of the Patriarchs of the Coptic Church of Alexandria*, PO vol. 1, p. 467

49 *S. Anastasii Sinaitae Adversus Acephalos*, MPG vol. 89, col. 249D; cf. O. Bardenhewer, *Geschichte der altkirchlichen Literatur*, vol. 4 (Freiburg 1924), p. 86

50 See V. A. Tcherikover, A. Fuks and M. Stern, *Corpus papyrorum judaicorum* (Harvard 1964), vol. 1, p. 93; vol. 3, pp. 88–105

51 *Joannis Malalas chronographia* (late sixth century), ed. L. Dindorf, CSHB (1831), pp. 244–5

52 See C. H. Kraeling, 'The Jewish Community at Antioch,' *Journal of Biblical Literature* 51 (1932), pp. 132–3; 140–5

53 Michael the Syrian, VII.7 (= Chabot, vol. 1, p. 294); cf. Parkes, *op. cit.*, p. 181

54 See the Jerusalem Talmud, *Tractate Horayot*, III.48; cf. *Libani orationes* XLVII.13, ed. R. Foerster (Leipzig 1906), bk.3, p. 410

55 Malalas, Dindorf, pp. 389–90; a fuller account is given by the Slavonic version, trans. M. Spinker and G. Downey, *The Chronicle of John Malalas*, Chicago (1940), pp. 111–12. For the curse, see *Theophanis chronographia* (a principal source for the sixth to the eighth centuries), ed. C. de Boor, vol. 1 (Leipzig 1883) (= Theoph.), p. 182 (line 16); cf. J. B. Bury, *A History of the Later Roman Empire* (London 1923), vol. 2, pp. 71–4

56 Malalas, Dindorf, p. 395

57 Theoph. 230 (lines 5–8), somewhat similar to the abuse exchanged between Blues and Greens in Theoph. 182 (line 16); cf. note (55), above

58 *Kissē ve-ippodromin shel shlomo ha-melekh*, ed. A. Jellinek, *Beth Hamidrasch*, Leipzig (1853), vol. 2, pp. 83–6; cf. J. Perles, 'Thron und Circus des

Koenigs Salamo', MGWJ 21 (1872), pp. 122–39; *Jewish Encyclopaedia*, vol. 11, p. 442

59 Perles, p. 127; cf. Malalas, Dindorf, pp. 173–6; A. Vogt, 'L'Hippodrome de Constantinople', BYZ 10 (1935), p. 472

60 *Cassiodori senatoris variae* LI, ed. Th. Mommsen, MGH *Auctores antiquissimi* XII (Berlin 1894), p. 105; cf. Perles, p. 124

61 The first to notice this parallel was H. Grégoire, 'Le peuple de Constantinople ou les Bleus et les Verts', *Comptes rendus de l'Academie des Inscriptions et Belles Lettres* (Paris 1946), p. 577

62 See e.g. Babylonian Talmud, *Tractate Avoda Zara*, 16b, 18b; *Tractate Baba Kamma*, 39a; *Midrash Eikha Rabba*, 3 and 18

63 Malalas, Dindorf, 382; cf. J. A. Montgomery, *The Samaritans* (Philadelphia 1907), pp. 110–12

64 *Procopii De Aedificiis*, V. 7 (= Haury, pp. 165–6)

65 Malalas, Dindorf, p. 455

66 Malalas, Dindorf, p. 487; Michael the Syrian, IX. 31 (= Chabot, vol. 2, p. 262); Nau, *op. cit.*, p. 489; on the correct date, cf. E. Stein, *Histoire de Bas Empire*, vol. 2 (Paris 1949), p. 374, note 2

67 Novel 144 (= Schoell and Kroll, pp. 709–10); C.I. 1.5.17–21 (= Krueger, pp. 56–60)

68 *Basilicorum libri XX*, ed. H. J. Scheltema and N. Van der Wal, Groningen-Gravenhage (1955), Series A, vol. 1, pp. 11–12 (copy of Novel 144)

69 C.Th. XVI.8.16 and 24 (= Pharr, p. 469, 470); Sirm. Const. 6 (= Pharr, p. 470); C.I. 1.5.12/4 (= Krueger, p. 53)

70 E.g. *Epiphanii Adversus Haereses*, MPG, vol. 41, cols 240A–241B; cf. Montgomery, p. 239; pp. 250–1

71 John of Nikiu XCIII (= Charles, p. 148)

72 *Cyrilli Scythopolitani vita Sabae* LXX, ed. E. Schwartz, *Texte und Untersuchungen zur Geschichte der altchristlichen Literatur* XLIX.2 (1939), pp. 172–4; p. 177

73 Novel 129 (= Schoell and Kroll, pp. 647–50)

74 C.Th. XVI.2.20 (= Pharr, pp. 443–4); Th.Nov.V (= Pharr, pp. 566–7)

75 See M. Avi-Yonah, 'The Economics of Byzantine Palestine', *Israel Exploration Journal* 8 (1958), pp. 39–51

76 *Joannis Moschi Pratum Spirituale* CLXV (= MPG, vol. 87, col. 3032C–D)

77 Philostorgii historia ecclesiastica III.4–6, ed. J. Bidez, *Philostorgius Kirchengeschichte* (Leipzig 1913), pp. 32–6 (= MPG vol. 65 cols 481C–489A); cf. R. Devreesse, *Le Patriarcat d'Antioche depuis la paix de l'église jusqu'à la conquête arabe* (Paris 1945), pp. 256–8)

78 P. K. Hitti, History of the Arabs (London 1956), p. 60

79 *Gregentii episcopi Tephransis disputatio cum Herbano Judaeo*, MPG vol. 86, cols. 621–784; cf. Williams, *op. cit.*, pp. 141–50

80 Malalas, Dindorf, p. 433; John of Nikiu, XC.72 (= Charles, p. 142); Michael the Syrian, IX.17 (= Chabot, vol. 2, pp. 183–4); on the probable date cf. Bury, *op. cit.*, vol. 2, p. 323; Baron, vol. 3, pp. 66–7

81 Simeon of Beit Arshām (contemporary monophysite source), trans. A. Jeffery, 'Three Documents on the History of Christianity in South Arabia', *Anglican Theological Review* 27 (1945), p. 204

82 *The Book of the Himyarites* (perhaps written by a companion of Simeon), ed. and trans. A. Moberg (Lund 1924), p. cv.

83 Jeffery, pp. 195–203; Jacob of Sarug ed. and trans. R. Schroetter, 'Trostschreiben Jacob's von Sarug an die himjaritischen Christen', *Zeitschrift der Deutschen Morgenlaendischen Gesellschaft* 31 (1877), pp. 369–95 and *Martyrium S. Arethae* MPG vol. 115, cols 1249–1289—both from lost portions of *The Book of the Himyarites*; Joannes Psaltes (died 538), *Hymn on the Homerite Martyrs*, ed. and trans. E. W. Brooks, PO vol. 7, pp. 613–14; Zachariae of Mytilene, trans. F. J. Hamilton and E. W. Brooks, London 1899, pp. 192–203; Theoph. 169; Michael the Syrian, IX.18 (=Chabot, vol. 2, pp. 184–9). On the authenticity of the original report (Simeon was not an eyewitness) see J. Halévy, 'Examen critique des sources relatives à la persécution des chrétiens de Nedjran par le roi juif des Himyarites', REJ 18 (1889), pp. 16–42; 161–78; 21 (1890), pp. 73–7; L. Duchesne, 'Note sur le massacre des chrétiens himyarites', REJ 20 (1890), pp. 220–4; Jeffery, p. 188

84 Jeffery, *op. cit.*, p. 204

85 Theoph. 141 (lines 15–17); cf. M. Abel, 'L'Ile de Jotabé', *Revue Biblique* 47 (1938), pp. 522–4

86 *Digesta* XXXIX.4.16/7 (=Mommsen, p. 651)

87 *Choricii Gazei laudatio Aratii ducis et Stephanis*, LXVI–LXXVIII, ed. R. Foerster and E. Richsteig, Leipzig (1929), pp. 65–8; cf. Abel, pp. 529–32

88 *Procopii Bella* I.ix.3–4 (=Haury, p. 101)

89 Tcherikover, *op. cit.*, vol. 1, pp. 43–87, p. 110

90 *S. Joannis Chrysostomi Adversus Judaeos*, MPG vol. 48, cols. 843–942; cf. M. Simon, 'La polémique antijuive de S. Jean Chrysostome et le mouvement judaïsant d'Antioche', *Annuaire de l'Institute de Philologie et d'Histoire Orientales et Slaves* 4 (1936), pp. 404–5; p. 407

91 S. Kazan, 'Isaac of Antioch's Homily against the Jews', *Oriens Christianus* 47 (1963), pp. 94–6

92 P. Maas, 'Die Chronologie des Hymnes des Romanos' BZ 15 (1906), p. 30; cf. Baron, vol. 7, pp. 80–2; p. 127, p. 142; F. H. Marshall and J. Mavrogordato, 'Byzantine Literature', *Byzantium*, Oxford (1948), p. 223; pp. 240–1

93 οἱ φοβούμενοι τὸν θεόν: *Acts of the Apostles*, XIII.16, 26, 43; XVII.4, 17. On 'strangers within the gate', see S. Bialoblocki, *Die Beziehungen des Judentums zu Proselyten und Proselytentum* (Berlin 1930)= 'Jewish Attitudes to Proselytes and to Proselytism' (in Hebrew), *Bar-Ilan Annual* 2 (1964), pp. 44–9

94 *Fulgentii Ferrandi breviatio canonum*, 69, 185, 186, 196= MPL vol. 88, cols. 827–8; cf. P. Monceaux, 'Les Colonies juives dans l'Afrique romaine', REJ 44 (1902), p. 27

95 *Augustini epistolae* XLIV.6.13= MPG vol. 38, col. 180; cf. J. M. Fuller, *Dictionary of Christian Biography* (London 1877), vol. 1, p. 589

96 See N. Slouchz, 'Hébréo-Phéniciens et Judéo-Berbères—introduction à l'histoire des Juifs et du Judaisme en Afrique', *Archives Marocaines* 14 (1908), pp. 192; 378–86

97 M. Rampolla y Tindaro, 'Martyre et Sepulture des Maccabées', *Revue de l'Art Chrétien* 10 (1899), pp. 457–65

98 C.Th. XVI.8.25–6 (= Pharr, p. 470); *Symeonis Stylitae vita* XII.50 = MPG vol. 114 cols. 381D–384A; *Evagrii historia ecclesiastica* I.13, ed. J. Bidez and L. Parmentier (London 1898), p. 22; cf. Rampolla, p. 389

99 Theoph. 102 (10–12); cf. F. Nau, 'Deux épisodes de l'histoire juive sous Theodore II', REJ 83 (1927), pp. 205–6

100 C.Th. XVI.8.19 (= Pharr, p. 469) cf. C.I. 1.9.12 (= Krueger, p. 61)

101 *Procopii De Aedificiis.* VI.12 (= Haury, p. 175)

102 Novel 144 (= Schoell and Kroll, p. 710)

CHAPTER III

The Arab Invasions

The political and social identity which the Roman east began to acquire under Justinian achieved its full form in the seventh century. The defeat of the Persians and the check to the Arabs were signs of the comprehensive political and social consolidation which gave the ruling institution its final range of secular and sacred functions. Arab successes actually helped this consolidation. The loss of North Africa deprived the empire of a province whose re-conquest by Justinian had brought no benefits. The loss of Alexandria removed a permanent challenge to the commercial and political pre-eminence of Constantinople. The loss of the eastern provinces had the advantage of leaving the empire easier to defend. It was no longer necessary to accept the risk of doubtful religious or cultural loyalties: the themes were recruited from the native populations of Greece, of Asia Minor and from the rapidly assimilated Slav immigrants. The new situation also improved internal security. The loss of Antioch put outside the frontiers a reservoir of riot and rebellion which had troubled governments for years. The new army of the themes not only checked the Arabs but also lowered the value of the democratic military organizations—the militia of the demes. Thus, the demes lost that element of their prestige, and the emperors were able to crush the most troublesome activity with which they had been connected: the circus parties were deprived of the power they had enjoyed from

42

the days of Zeno, and, instead, were allotted elaborate functions in the various ceremonies of the imperial court.[1] To the new stability in the capital and in the provinces there was added, at least for the time being, a new stability within the church. The Arab conquests solved the doctrinal dispute which had divided the empire since Justinian. Both the monophysites, whether in Egypt or Syria, and the Chalcedonian extremists of North Africa or Palestine who had rejected the compromise offered by Heraclius, were now safely under Muslim rule. And the new frontiers rid the patriarch of Constantinople of all his rivals—whether at Alexandria and Antioch or at Carthage and Jerusalem. The significance of all these developments was that the freeing of the ruling institution from many restrictions on the exercise of its secular and sacred functions had been the result of a closer social unity achieved by the fortuitous extrusion of foreign, religious, cultural or political elements. In this respect, the new identity of the Roman east was the opposite of the old. The aim of pre-Christian Rome had been to unite all the peoples under its rule by one universal legal system, with little interest in religious or cultural differences. The aim of Byzantium, the final crystallization of Christian Rome, was to seek such unity in religious and cultural homogeneity.

For the Jews, these developments meant the opposite of what they did for the ruling institution. The losses of territory left the rest of the empire enjoying a closer cohesion, but the Jews of South Italy, of Greece and of Asia Minor found it more difficult to make contact with the Jews of Egypt, of Palestine or of Syria when one state no longer ruled them all. Until another change in the politics of the eastern Mediterranean at the end of the tenth century, they remained seriously impoverished by this partial isolation. The improved internal security which benefited the empire threw an unwelcome light on their community as the one remaining foreign element, and affected the balance of the two forces acting upon them: it put into doubt the peculiar advantages of Byzantine society, and increased the inherent dangers of the Byzantine kind of theocracy. In 632, the second force took control: the Emperor Heraclius ordered the conversion to Christianity of all the Jews in his dominions.[2] But this tilt of the balance was not decisive. Although the decree was the first of its kind in Byzantium, its causes and consequences were comparable to those associated with the decrees of Justinian.

The condition of the Jews during the second half of the sixth century was influenced by the same factors that had influenced it for the previous hundred years. Relations with the authorities were often bad. In Palestine, the economic depression continued and with it the active hostility of both Jews and Samaritans. A pilgrim from Piacenza who was there about 570 noticed how at Sebastea, near Shkhem, Samaritans, assuming he was a Byzantine, followed him to wipe out his footprints, and made him throw the money for his purchases into water in order to avoid the pollution of his touch.[3] Jews used Na'arān (near Jericho) and Beit Ramlā (across the Jordan) as bases for raiding the vicinity.[4] The contemporary chronicler, John of Ephesus, recorded that in 578 both Jews and Samaritans broke into a revolt serious enough for the Emperor Justin II to send a special officer who, in addition to the normal executions, could only suppress it by the unfortunate expedient of destroying a great deal of property.[5] But there was another side to this picture. The same pilgrim from Piacenza noted that vast crowds of Jews from all over Palestine prayed unhindered at the tombs of the patriarchs in Hebron, with the co-operation of the authorities who had allotted them a separate entrance.[6] The mixed guerrilla bands mentioned in the last chapter showed that the poverty of the land also produced co-operation between the Jews and the local Christians—not only enmity. In 579, a disturbance at Constantinople had familiar characteristics. Demonstrations by Christian extremists protesting that the judges had been bribed to favour the accused in a trial for 'hellenism' led, in the words of John of Ephesus, to violence by which

> the whole city was troubled. The shops were shut and Jews, Samaritans and heretics of all kinds rushed from every quarter, ready both to set the city on fire and steal whatever came to hand. ... They had joined in for the loot and were meaning to burn churches, supposing that the Christians would be blamed for it. They acknowledged under the scourge other crimes, and were

condemned to various punishments including crucifixion and banishment.

Those responsible for the riot were treated with great leniency, which the Emperor Tiberius II, not a year on the throne, thought it prudent to conceal by having their backs painted with vermilion stripes to convince their opponents that they, too, had had a whipping.[7] As in the time of Justinian, the well-known militancy of the Samaritans automatically associated them in an upheaval involving the Jews. And the language of the chronicler, however tendentious, suggested another parallel. As in the quarrel of the patriarch Cyril with the hellenistically inclined governor of Alexandria, the Jews had participated in a conflict of their non-Jewish neighbours to their own detriment—and for the same reason: the government would not seriously antagonize the real protagonists. Yet, two years previously, there had been a happier illustration of Jews in city politics. When Eutychius, the patriarch of Constantinople was reinstated after a long doctrinal dispute, masses of Jews joined his welcoming supporters with loud cries of 'May the faith of the Christians be strengthened—blessed be he who cometh in the name of the Lord!'.[8]

An incident in 592, at the beginning of the reign of the emperor Maurice, had similar contrasting elements. The Jews were attacked in Antioch on suspicion of having desecrated an icon of the Virgin Mary. The allegation itself was a common pretext for violence, but the detail that the icon had been in a house rented by a Jew from a Christian confirmed the normality of Jews living side by side with Christians and conducting transactions of this kind.[9]

The official reaction of the authorities to all these events was not decisive. In 572, Justin II revoked the ameliorations that Justinian had been persuaded to make in the disabilities suffered by the Samaritans.[10] Maurice, suspected of being influenced by a mystic of doubtful orthodoxy, proclaimed the purity of his own beliefs by getting his nephew Domitian to issue orders for the compulsory baptism of Jews and Samaritans. It was an empty gesture: Domitian was the governor of distant Melitene in Byzantine Armenia.[11] The Jews were told to leave Antioch after the attack upon them in 592. But the expulsion was at most only effective until the reign of Phocas.[12] None of these measures altered the general situation. Contacts between Jews and non-Jews remained as they had been—both close and ambivalent. It is difficult to agree that, during this period, there was 'an irreconcilable hostility between the Jews and their Christian neighbours and rulers'.[13]

At the same time, the extra-legal actions typical of the preceding period continued to occur. In 569, for no known reason, a synagogue at Constantinople was seized and turned into a church, perhaps the same synagogue that had suffered from Simon under Theodosius.[14] John of Ephesus, the biographer of another Symeon Stylites, related with satisfaction how he himself had improved on his hero's burning of a synagogue by successfully turning seven into churches during the course of a preaching journey through western and central Asia Minor.[15] In the second half of the sixth century there was added to the liturgy of the church a special order for the consecration of synagogues to Christian uses.[16] But these actions did not indicate a general change of policy. John's Symeon bitterly complained that ecclesiastical protection had hindered the accomplishment of his holy purpose.[17] A similar complaint had been heard when the rabbis of Tiberias had been left in peace after Najrān.[18] At the end of the sixth century, Pope Gregory I, who acknowledged Maurice as his emperor in Byzantine Italy, scrupulously observed the provision of the Codes. On three occasions he ordered that synagogues which had been illegally seized must be returned together with their appurtenances, their adjacent buildings and their surrounding land. If they had already been consecrated for Christian use, their communities must be financially compensated according to valuations fixed by arbitrators from both parties. For, he reminded the local clergy, just as the law forbade the building of new synagogues, so it allowed the Jews to possess undisturbed those they already had.[19] Thus, the relations of the Jews with the state, with their neighbours and with the church was no different under Maurice from what they had been under Justinian. The fundamental laws had not been changed. The measure of social integration had not lessened. And the community continued to suffer from the occasional outbursts against it, whether legalized or illegal.

The shift in the balance of forces affecting Byzantine Jewry, the crisis of relations with their environment which culminated in the decree of 632, was the result of the general crisis through which the empire passed after the murder of Maurice with all his family and the usurpation of the imperial throne by Phocas in 602. Afraid of the senior administrators and of those army officers who had not directly helped him, he tried to rule through the Greens, usually the opponents of the ruling institution. They made good use of the opportunity. At Constantinople, they burned down the hippodrome. At Antioch in 609, they demonstrated their love for Phocas by inciting the crowds against the monophysite patriarch Anastasius II who had been installed, and had ruled for years expressly in defiance of imperial instructions.[20] Anastasius was killed, disgustingly mutilated, and dragged through the main street. When Phocas saw that party rule was causing his empire to disintegrate around him, he turned against the Greens. His emissary Bonosus slew thousands of their supporters as he marched through Asia Minor and restored order at Antioch, but it was too late. He was lynched by the Greens on his return to Constantinople and Phocas himself was overthrown by Heraclius with the help of elements from both parties. Between 602 and 610, it was the circus parties who were in control. Even in Spain it became known how 'at that time the Greens and the Blues made civil war throughout the East and Egypt and destroyed each other in mutual slaughter'[21] But stories spread, and were copied into later Byzantine sources, that the Jews had taken the lead in these disorders, and that they were directly responsible for the murder of Anastasius.[22]

Jews had certainly been involved, but exactly as they had been in the past: as members of the circus parties, except that this time the confused situation affected their usual party allegiance. This is how a hostile eyewitness, Jacob, a Jew shortly after converted to Christianity, described it:

> Because I was possessed of the Devil and hated Christ . . . when Phocas was reigning in Constantinople, I, as a Green, denounced

the Christians as Blues, calling them Jews and bastards. And when the Greens burned the Hippodrome and committed misdeeds, I, as a Blue, denounced the Christians as Greens, insulting them as incendiaries and Manicheans. And when Bonosus took vengeance on the Greens at Antioch and slew them, I went into Antioch and denounced many Christians as Greens, as one well intentioned to the emperor and a Blue. And when the Greens turned upon Bonosus in Constantinople, I also turned upon him—and that most heartily, seeing that he was a Christian.

There followed a detailed account of the killing of Blues in various places throughout Asia Minor.[23] However, with all these accusations, there was no word about the killing of Anastasius. Equally silent on this point was a seventh-century monophysite source. Not unnaturally, the bloodshed at Antioch was the fault of the Chalcedonites, but there was no allusion to Jewish participation.[24] Finally, a chronicle written about 629, a year when the Jews were very much in disfavour as will be seen, recorded that Anastasius was killed by regular soldiers who were trying to quell the party riot.[25] In 610, the continuance of disorder in the eastern provinces after the fall of Phocas and the seizure of power by Heraclius produced the rumour that the Jews were planning a mass slaughter of Christians in Tyre and near-by cities; in order to forestall them, the Christians killed many of them instead.[26] Once more, the Jews probably suffered for their participation in some general movement against the authorities. There is no reliable information that the Jews were officially punished for all these alleged misdeeds. The statement in one chronicle, still occasionally accepted, that it was not Heraclius but Phocas who published the decree of forced baptism, was the result of a confusion in chronology.[27] But, as on previous occasions, it was the part, real or supposed, played by the Jews in these events that was remembered.

Meanwhile, the disorders had given the Persians an unusual chance. They poured into Syria and Palestine, driving before them the remnants of organized defence. In 614 they took Jerusalem. The following year they were masters of Egypt. For Byzantine Jewry, these disasters to the empire brought a heightening of the crisis in relations that had begun in 602. They served to stress the links that were supposed to exist between the Jews and the Persians. Dhū-Nuwās, kept in power with the help of Jews within the empire, had tried to get the Persians on his side against the Byzantine-Ethiopian alliance. When, during Justinian's endless wars against them, the Persians had captured Antioch in 540, a great fire broke out which left the Jewish quarter untouched.[28] The authorities would remember that Persian Jews served in the Persian army. Commanders gave them the same consideration they gave to other sects, and even avoided fighting on their holy days.[29] And it was when the Persians had conquered Egypt that the Jews returned there in some numbers. Between 620 and 622, according to an eighth-century source, monks from the monastery of St Anthony in the hills of Kulzum above the Gulf of Suez, converted to Christianity the Jews of Tumai, a small town not far off. There is no record of this event in the history of the monastery, while the only other of that name was on the banks of the Nile. The Jews were said to have been converted on the first day of their Feast of Tabernacles, which was supposed to have co-incided with the second day of the Feast of the Exaltation of the Cross in the Coptic Church. This is 15 September—an impossible date for the Jewish feast. These and other difficulties make the story itself as doubtful as most of its kind. But the surrounding details it gives sound vivid and authentic. They show how Tumai had a flourishing community of three hundred and seventy-five Jews including merchants and scholars, the important among them with their households of slaves and servants.[30] In Alexandria the Jews became established enough for the Muslims to insert a special clause regarding them in the treaty they made when they, in their turn, captured the city.[31]

In Palestine, the Jews of Caesarea, the first important place to be besieged, immediately submitted to the Persians.[32] Elsewhere, the occupation encouraged the militant elements among the Jews as against the peaceful pilgrims. In Khozibā, near Jericho, the Christians went in fear of them.[33] Jacob the convert related how Jews suspected of Christian sympathies were attacked at Acre.[34] The climax came with the fall of Jerusalem. The Jews were held responsible for much during the siege and after. According to one contemporary chronicle they had deliberately started fights with the Christians which had weakened the defence.[35] According to Sophronius, the future patriarch who was in Alexandria at the time, their treachery had been more direct.[36] And when the Persians began the sack of the city, the Jews were said to have helped them by searching out Christian victims.[37] This picture of collaboration between Jews and Persians, direct or indirect, has to be modified. It is unlikely that Byzantine Jews admired the Persian government as such. Conditions under it, during the sixth century and the early years of the seventh, were no better than their own. Legal toleration, including the privilege of serving in the army, did not prevent the outbreak of a fierce persecution in 520, when a reforming sect of Magians, the ruling Persian religion, caused the death of the head of the community and the closing of the great academies of Talmudic learning at Surā and Pumbeditā. There was another persecution in 581 and another in 590 when the Jews were accused of supporting an unsuccessful claimant to the throne. And, immediately after the Persians had established themselves in Jerusalem, many of the Jews were executed by crucifixion and the rest expelled.[38] It was only in the reign of Khosroes II (628–640) that the Persian Jews regained some calm and prosperity.

However, the invasions gave Byzantine Jews certain opportunities. In Egypt, there was the chance to re-establish themselves, a process which had proved difficult after their expulsion. In Palestine, it was not the coming of the Persians but the collapse of imperial rule which was welcomed. It was this which encouraged nationalist hopes after more than a century of struggle. However, the extent of actual Jewish retaliation is difficult to assess. The only eyewitness account of the siege and capture of Jerusalem asserted that it was dissension over the readiness of the patriarch himself to negotiate a surrender which led to treasonable contacts with the Persians and to bloody riots. And those immediately responsible were once again the Blues and the Greens who had brought their party quarrels from Antioch.[39] Of course, as elsewhere, there could have been Jews among them. The account told how afterwards the Christians reproached the Jews for burning churches and for ransoming prisoners in order to kill them.[40] But a detailed description of the massacres, giving the exact number that died in every quarter of the city, made no reference to Jewish participation.[41] Yet all these events of the Persian invasion, so far as the authorities at the time were concerned, showed how the Jews of the empire were potential traitors, as well as leaders of disorder. Later historians have sometimes taken the same view, as they have of the events involving the Jews at the end of the reign of Phocas.[42]

Even so, these suspicions did not lead to immediate reprisals after Heraclius had re-organized his armies and had begun to push the Persians out of the territories they had conquered. When, in 628, the Persians after a long struggle abandoned Edessa in eastern Syria, he rejected the advice of his general to massacre the Jews there, who in fear had shut the gates of the city against him, and allowed them to go in a body, so long as they left imperial territory.[43] The following year, in his triumphal progress through Palestine, he accepted the hospitality of Benjamin, the head of the community in Tiberias, and gave him his solemn promise to respect Jewish rights. The reprisals began when he entered Jerusalem. Monks took him to the spots where Christians had died and filled his ears with tales of Jewish atrocities. They assured him that they would take the sin upon their own souls if he broke his promise to Benjamin, and he was persuaded to expel the Jews from the city, perhaps to permit their indiscriminate slaughter.[44]

In 630, the Arabs began their invasion of Palestine. The new threat to the empire revived all the fears of Jewish disloyalty. Just as there were supposed to have been treasonable contacts with the Persians, so was there supposed to be Jewish support for Islām because of a common hatred of the Christians, although it was known that the two religions differed.[45] The latter supposition was as doubtful as the former. The Arabs, once in power, usually permitted both Jews and Christians to live in peace if they paid the *jizyā*, the tax on unbelievers who were counted with 'the people of the book'—those who accepted the scriptures which were common ground to all three faiths. The treaty with Alexandria provided that, after the surrender, the Arabs would not meddle in Christian affairs, and that the Jews would be allowed to remain in the city undisturbed. After the surrender of Jerusalem in 636, the Arabs allowed the Jews to return and, in their general arrangements with the patriarch Sophronius, allotted to them their living quarters. They also carefully defined the site of the Temple and told the Jews to keep it clean by sweeping it every day.[46] But it was known that the Arabs spared no one who had not submitted. Muḥammad himself had destroyed the Jewish tribes of al-Hijāz who had refused to accept his leadership, and their remnants must have brought the news when they drifted north to seek Byzantine protection in 627.[47] In 634, twelve miles east of Gaza, in one of the decisive battles in their conquest of Byzantine Palestine, the Arabs indiscriminately killed four thousand Jewish, Samaritan and Christian peasants.[48] When the Arabs approached the Egyptian frontier, the Jews fled before them, crowding panic-stricken into one of the cities on the road to Alexandria, 'in fear of the Muslim, the cruelties of (their commander) 'Amar and the seizure of their possessions'.[49]

There were, however, respects in which Byzantine fears had some foundation. In other Palestinian battles, for example at Caesarea and Emesa, Jews were to be found in the armies ranged against them. But there were Christians there, too.[50] The population of Palestine as a whole, oppressed by a hundred years of poverty to which the last thirty had added the miseries of war and administrative chaos, was not especially loyal. And once again Jews, as in the guerrilla bands, joined the Christian malcontents. Secondly, the Arab invasion of Palestine nourished the hopes of the militant nationalists. These hopes were reflected vividly, if fancifully, in one piece of Armenian historical tradition. The Jews who were expelled from Edessa demanded Palestine from Heraclius. They together with

> all the remnants of the children of Israel joined the Arabs to form a mighty army. They sent the Greek king the following despatch: 'God gave our father Abraham this land for an inheritance and, after him, to his offspring; as for us, we are the sons of Abraham; you have possessed our land long enough; depart from it peacefully; then we will not invade your land; otherwise we shall seize it from you by force'.[51]

The demand was supposed to have been made immediately after the battle of Gaza; the reference to an Arab alliance was strikingly inappropriate. The real interest of the nationalists, as in the time of the Persians, was in the collapse of imperial rule, not in its substitution by another. After the Arab conquest of Palestine, they prayed for the destruction of both empires. And Byzantine Jewry, as will be discussed in the next chapter, although cut off from the centres of the continuing nationalist struggle, was deeply affected by some of its incidents.

Thus the decree of 632 was an attempt to safeguard imperial security by eliminating the political dangers of religious dissidence, as four years later an attempt was made to avoid the political dangers of the dispute between the Chalcedonites and the monophysites by ordering both sects to accept a doctrinal compromise dictated by the ruling institution. Political loyalty was now to be wholly equated with religious conformity. 'Are you all servants of the emperor?' the governor of Carthage, where the decree was actually promulgated, asked the Jews, 'if you are then you must be baptized'.[52] The Jews must bow to this principle and lose the advantage they had held for centuries over Christian heretics. In his reconstruction of the Byzantine state, Heraclius could afford no exceptions. And yet, despite all these circumstances, despite the events of the past thirty years or more, which convinced the authorities of the risk to security that the Jews particularly constituted, the application of the decree and its consequences were extremely limited. The main effect was in Palestine, but it was not an attempt at forced baptisms. The decree inspired the government to use Justinian's instructions on the correct reading of the scriptures for a campaign of wholesale interference in the service of the synagogue. Weekday services were not to be held. The recital of the Shma‘, one of the most important sections of the liturgy, beginning with the words 'Hear, O Israel, the Lord our God, the Lord is One', was entirely prohibited. The Ḥazān, the precentor who led the prayers, would try and insert this section in an unusual place so that the official often present to see that the imperial orders were obeyed might not notice.[53] These afflictions were the first suffered by Byzantine

Jewry which may have found an echo in Jewish sources. In two apocalyptic texts, *The Book of Zerubabel* and *The Signs of the Messiah*, 'Armilus', the enemy of the Messiah, is identifiable with Heraclius, while the necessary afflictions that Israel must undergo before the final redemption—'the pangs of the Messiah'—are the afflictions of the Jews of Palestine just before the Arab conquest.[54] In a third, *The Sayings of Elijah*, the same period may be referred to in general terms, such as one of 'a king raising his hand against God's children'.[55] However, if the impression was greater than that made by all that Justinian had done, which went entirely unnoticed in the Jewish sources, this persecution, bad as it was in Palestine, did nothing to implement the original intention of the ruling institution.

At Carthage, where the decree was promulgated, its application was perfunctory, and had no effects in the province. The Jewish Berbers knew nothing of it. In 644, they were the best defenders of the province against the advancing Arabs.[56] From 698 to 701, the prophetess Dahiyyā al-Kahīnā led Jews and Greeks together in a fierce and widespread uprising. She captured and held the city of Kairawān which the Arabs had newly built south-west of Carthage, and was officially reported to Damascus as the most serious obstacle to the completion of their conquest. There have been some doubts about the prophetess, but the revolt and its character is vouched for by many Arab sources.[57] Even at Constantinople the decree was not seriously enforced. That recently baptized Jew who had been involved with the factions was permitted to solemnize a commercial contract 'in the name of the God of Abraham, Isaac and Jacob'.[58]

The decree was sufficiently unusual in Byzantium for western historical tradition to link it with the familiar policies of other rulers, or to ascribe to Heraclius an unnecessarily obscure motive. He had been told that a circumcized race would destroy the empire, and had mistaken the Jews for the Arabs. And, accordingly, the equally baseless story took root that there had been a plan against the Jews agreed jointly by him and by Sisibut, king of Visigothic Spain.[59] The contrast between two extremes could not have been more clearly illustrated. During the course of the seventh century the Jews of Spain were steadily deprived of all their rights. It became an offence against Visigothic law to keep the festivals and to celebrate marriages. Finally, all the Jews were declared slaves, and their children were seized from them for conversion.[60] For the same period in Byzantium, the decree was a single violent gesture. It caused no change in the legal status of the Jews. When Palestine had fallen to the Arabs, those Jews who might have been expected to continue to suffer the afflictions of the decree ceased to be imperial subjects. The daily life of the rest was not affected. Contact between Jew and non-Jew, close but not necessarily friendly, continued as before. Some details in the story of a miraculous conversion about the middle of the seventh century give a realistic example from Constantinople.[61] A Christian merchant, ruined by shipwreck and failing to get the help of his friends for a fresh venture, turned to a Jew whose business it was to finance voyages—just as non-Jews did, including dignitaries of the church.[62] The merchant tried to go into partnership with the Jew, but was eventually offered a loan instead. However, his friends, who did not want to do business with a Jew, refused to give the necessary surety. Then it came about that an icon in a church of the Chalthoprateia, the Jewish district, was divinely given a voice to offer its readiness for this responsibility. When the need arose, its surety was lavishly honoured and the Jew forthwith became a Christian. This story illustrates some typical aspects. The Jew was not primarily a moneylender. Nor was his occupation particularly Jewish. And business with Jews was normal, if not welcomed. Neither did the decree inhibit the other aspect of the peculiar relation between urban Jews and their fellow citizens. In 641, Jews were conspicuous among the leaders of a popular uprising which drove out Pyrrhus, the patriarch of Constantinople, a supporter of Martina, the widow of Heraclius, and ensured the crowning of his grandson Constans. The rioters burst into St Sophia, broke benches, defaced icons, tore the altar cloth and carried the keys of the church in a mixture of triumph and mockery through the city streets. And this time immunity from punishment was shared by the Jews among them.[63] In 653, the Jews had influence enough in Syracuse to enlist the advocacy of an important official, perhaps the imperial governor himself, when they wished to rebuild a synagogue destroyed by the Vandals.[64]

At the same time, the attraction of Jews and Jewish customs for the Christians did not wane. Justin II, in his last illness, had had recourse to a Jewish doctor.[65] In 603, the pope Gregory I complained of Christians observing their Sundays in ways reminiscent of the Jewish Sabbath.[66] Similar tendencies persisted after the crisis under Heraclius. In 691, Justinian II, wishing like many other Byzantine emperors to proclaim his unimpeachable orthodoxy before the world, assembled a council of the church. It was nicknamed the 'Quinisext', since its purpose was to codify and strengthen the canon law handed down to it by the sixth Ecumenical Council held in 680 and by the Fifth held in 553. The mass immigration of Slavs and their very recent conversion to Christianity, made the strengthening of the canons dealing with the behaviour of the laity occupy a great deal of the Council's time.[67] But it was not only the risks of paganism and heresy which worried the delegates. In their opening address to the emperor they declared that it was also their purpose to purge the church and the faithful of many Jewish customs in order to save the declining morals of the Byzantine Christians.[68] The thirty-third and the ninety-ninth canons denounced various such customs which, in Byzantine Armenia, had been introduced into the order for the institution of priests.[69] The eleventh was a general warning against the unleavened bread of the Jews, dealing with Jewish doctors, or mixing with Jews in the public baths.[70] The penalties could be exile. But these denunciations and warnings had no more effect than the decree of forced baptism pronounced by Heraclius.

The crisis through which the empire had passed from the seizure of power by Phocas to the conquest of Syria, Palestine and Egypt by the Arabs had sharpened suspicions of Jewish loyalty and had brought suffering to some communities between 629 and 632. But the reconstructed empire of Heraclius and of his successors in the seventh century in its search for security through homogeneity did not proceed to a resolute elimination of the one element which could not possibly fit its concept of unity. The condition of the Jews was not fundamentally altered by the violence against them, any more than it had been by the meddling legislation of Justinian. The same laws continued to protect them. The relation of urban Jews with non-Jews had survived not only the decree of Heraclius, but also the disappearance of the circus parties as the democratic organizations in which that relation had often found its practical expression. So long as Byzantine society remained untouched by hieratic stratification, so long was there an integral place in it for Jews. But, just as the legal and extra-legal attacks under Justinian had significance, so had the Heracleian persecution. If it turned out to be little more than a violent gesture, it was still one which had to be expected and feared in the future.

Notes

1 See the details described by Constantine VII, *Constantini Porphyrogeniti De Ceremoniis Aulae Byzantini* II.77–82, ed. and trans. A. Vogt, *Le Livre des Cérémonies*, vol. 2 (Paris 1939), pp. 112–68; cf. R. Guilland, 'Études sur l'Hippodrome de Byzance', *Byzantinoslavica* 25 (1964), pp. 234–53

2 For references see F. Doelger, *Regesten*, no. 207 in conjunction with his emendation of the date from 634 to 632 in BZ 41 (1941), p. 539

3 *Antonini Placentini itinerarium XXVI*, ed. P. Geyer, *Itinera Hierosolymitana saeculi IV–VIII, Corpus scriptorum ecclesiasticorum latinorum*, vol. 39 (Vienna 1898), pp. 164–5 (= MPL vol. 72, col. 902B); cf. Parkes, *Conflict*, p. 259

4 'τὰ ὁμητήρια 'Ιουδαίων' – 'Jewish lairs', *Antiochi monachi Homilia LXXXIV* (= MPG vol. 89, col. 1692B)

5 John of Ephesus, *Ecclesiastical History* III.27, trans. R. P. Smith, *The Third Part of the History of John of Ephesus* (Oxford 1860), p. 209

6 *Antonini Placentini itinerarium XXX* (= Geyer, pp. 178–9; MPL vol. 72, col. 909C)

7 John of Ephesus, pp. 216–21

8. *S. Eutychii Patriarchae Constantinopolitani Vita VIII.* 73 (= MPG vol. 86.2, col. 2357B)

9 Mahbūb ibn Kustantīn (Agapius of Menbidj), *Kitāb al-'Unwān*, ed. and trans. A. Vasiliev, PO vol. 8, pp. 439–40 (a tenth-century source mainly derived from eighth-century material and usually reliable for events in the eastern provinces); for a parallel allegation at Beirut, see *Le Synaxaire Arménien de Ter Israel*, ed. and trans. G. Bayan, PO vol. 21, pp. 104–6 and cf. Parkes, *Conflict*, pp. 291–3

10 Novel 144 (= Schoell and Kroll, pp. 709–10)

11 John of Nikiu, XCIX. 1–2 (=Charles, pp. 162–3); cf. J. Starr, 'Byzantine Jewry on the Eve of the Arab Conquest', JPOS 15 (1935), p. 263
12 *Kitāb al-'Unwān*, p. 440
13 Starr, *ibid.*
14 Theoph. 248 (5–8); cf. Theoph. 102 (10–12), (Ch. II, note 99)
15 John of Ephesus, ed. and trans. E. W. Brooks, *The Lives of the Eastern Saints*, PO vol. 18, p. 681
16 *Sacramentarium Gelasianum*, MPL vol. 74, col. 1144B and C; trans. Parkes, *Conflict*, p. 401; for the date cf. P. Godet, DTC 6, col. 1186
17 John of Ephesus, *Lives of the Eastern Saints*, PO vol. 17, pp. 90–3
18 Jeffery, p. 204
19 *Gregorii epistolae*, VIII. 25; IX.38; IX.195 (=Ewald and Hartmann, vol. 2), p. 27, p. 67, p. 183
20 Devreesse, *Le patriarcat*, p. 119
21 *S. Isidori Hispalensis chronicon CXIX* (=MPL, vol. 83, col. 1056A)
22 Theoph. 296 (16–21); Michael the Syrian, XX.25 (=Chabot, vol. 2, p. 379)
23 *Doctrina Jacobi nuper baptizati*, Greek text ed. I. Bonwetsch, *Abhandlungen der koeniglichen Gesellschaft der Wissenschaften zu Goettingen*, XII.3 (1910), pp. 38[17]–40[7]; cf. P. Bleik, 'On the Relations of the Jews with the Government of the Eastern Roman Empire 602–34' (in Russian), *Khristyanski Vostok* 3 (1914), 178–82
24 John of Nikiu, CIV (=Charles, p. 166)
25 *Chronicon Paschale*, MPG 92, col. 980A; cf. G. Downey, *The History of Antioch in Syria from Seleucus to the Arab Conquest* (Princeton 1961), pp. 572–3
26 *Kitāb al-'Unwān*, p. 449; *Eutychii Patriarchae Alexandrini Annales*, MPG vol. 111, cols. 1094–5
27 See Y. A. Kulakovsky, 'A Criticism of the Information in Theophanes on the Last Years of the Rule of Phocas' (in Russian), *Vizantiiski Vremenik* 21 (1914), pp. 1–14; R. Devreesse, 'La fin inédite d'une lettre de S. Maxime: un baptême forcé des Juifs et des Samaritains à Carthage en 632', *Revue des Sciences Religieuses* 17 (1937), pp. 25–35; J. Starr, 'St Maximus and the Forced Baptism at Carthage in 632' BNJ 16 (1940), pp. 192–6. Baron, vol. 3, p. 237, note 21, is still prepared to consider the generally rejected opinion of S. Krauss, *Studien zur byzantinisch-juedischen Geschichte*, Leipzig (1914), p. 22, as more definitely is M. Avi-Yonah, *Geshichte der Juden im Zeitalter der Talmud in den Tagen vom Rom und Byzanz*, Berlin (1962), pp. 255–6
28 Procopii *De Bello Persico* II.10.7 (=Haury, vol. 1, p. 194)
29 Zachariae of Mytilene, IX.4 (=Hamilton and Brooks, pp. 225–6)
30 R. Griveau, 'Histoire de la conversion des Juifs habitant la ville de Tomei en Egypte' ROC 13 (1908), pp. 298–313. The sparse and vague references to Tumai in various geographical lists show its unimportance; cf. V. Ermoni, 'Les évêches de l'Egypte chrétienne', ROC 5 (1900), p. 640; H. Munier, 'La géographie de l'Egypte d'après les listes coptes-arabes', *Bulletin de la société d'archéologie copte* 5 (1939), p. 216, p. 219; W. E. Crum, *Catalogue of the Coptic MSS in the British Museum* (London 1905), p. 514 (no. 1250). On the monastery, see H. R. Fedden, 'A Study of the Monas-

tery of St Anthony in the Eastern Desert', *Bulletin of the Faculty of Arts of the University of Egypt* 5 (1937), pp. 30–2

31 John of Nikiu CXX (= Charles, p. 194)

32 F. Macler, *L'Histoire d'Héraclius par l'évêque Sebeos* (Paris 1904), p. 63

33 *S. Georgii chozebitae vita XXXIV*, *Analecta Bollandiana* 7 (1888), p. 134

34 *Doctrina Jacobi*, Ethiopic text ed. and trans. S. Grébaut, *Sargis d'Aberga*, PO vol. 13, p. 63

35 Sebeos, p. 68; cf. Bleik, p. 194

36 cf. his elegy on the fall of Jerusalem, ed. A. Couret, *La Prise de Jerusalem par les Perses* (Paris 1897), p. 16 (59–62)

37 Theoph. 301 (1–3)

38 Sebeos, p. 69; cf. Bleik, p. 198

39 Eustratus of Sabā (or 'Antiochus Strategus'), *Khabar kharābi baiti-l-mukaddasi*, Arabic text ed. P. Peeters, 'La Prise de Jerusalem par les Perses', *Mélanges de l'Université S. Joseph* 9 (1923–4), pp. 12–13; cf. English translation of the Georgian text by F. Conybeare, 'The Capture of Jerusalem by the Persians', *English Historical Review* 25 (1910), p. 503 and the Russian translation by N. Marr, *Texts and Studies in Armeno-Georgian Philology* 9 (1909), pp. 8–9

40 Marr, p. 19

41 Peeters, pp. 36–9

42 cf. e.g. J. Pargoire, *L'Église byzantin de 527 à 847* (Paris 1923), p. 123; S. Vailhé, 'Les Juifs et le prise de Jérusalem en 614', *Echos d'Orient* 12 (1909), pp. 15–17; R. Janin, 'Les Juifs dans l'empire byzantin', *Echos d'Orient* 15 (1912), pp. 126–33. A Couret, *La Palestine sous les empereurs grecs* (Grenoble 1869), p. 211, made the Jews also kill Anastasius I, the Chalcedonite predecessor of Anastasius II. Baron, vol. 3, p. 236 mistook the one for the other, claiming that the former's known oppression of dissident Christians and hellenizers (see Devreesse, *Le Patriarcat*, p. 99) must have included oppression of the Jews and justified his murder by them.

43 Doelger, *Regesten*, no. 195; Sebeos, p. 94; Michael the Syrian, XI.3 (= Chabot, vol. 2, p. 410); for a fuller account, see N. O. Emin, *Researches and Essays in Armenian Mythology, Archaeology, History ond the History of Literature* (in Russian) (Moscow 1896), p. 338

44 Theoph. 328 (15–28); *Eutychii Annales*, MPG vol. 111, cols. 1089–91

45 Theoph. 333 (4–13); Sebeos, p. 95

46 S. Assaf, 'The Beginning of the Jewish Settlement in Jerusalem after the Arab Conquest' (in Hebrew), *Texts and Studies in Jewish History* (Jerusalem 1946), pp. 17–18, 20–2; cf. J. Mann, *The Jews in Egypt and Palestine under the Fatimid Caliphs* (Oxford 1920), vol. 1, p. 43

47 Hitti, p. 117

48 *Chronicon miscellaneum ad annum domini 724 pertinens*, ed. E. W. Brooks, trans. J. B. Chabot, Scriptores Syri, series 3, vol. 4 (Paris 1904), p. 114 (11–17) = J.P.N. Land, *Anecdota Syriaca*, vol. 1 (Leyden 1862), p. 116; cf. Starr, JPOS, p. 289

49 John of Nikiu, 'Enumeration of Chapters' (= Charles, p. 13)

50 Starr, JPOS, p. 290

51 Emin, p. 346

52 *Doctrina Jacobi*, ed. Grébaut, PO vol. 3, p. 556; cf. Starr, JPOS, p. 288

53 J. Mann, 'Changes in the Divine Service of the Synagogue due to Religious Persecution', *Hebrew Union College Annual*, 4 (1927), pp. 252–9

54 I. Levi, 'L'Apocalypse de Zerubabel', REJ 68 (1914), pp. 136–7 (text) REJ 69 (1920) pp. 108–15 (commentary); L. Marmorstein, 'Les Signes du Messie', REJ 52 (1906), pp. 181–6

55 *Perek Eliyahū*, ed. Y. Even-Shmuel (in Hebrew), *Midrashei-Geulā*, Tel-Aviv (1954), pp. 49–54

56 H. Fournel, *Les Berbers, Études sur la conquête arabe de l'Afrique par les Arabes d'après les textes arabes imprimés*, vol. 1 (Paris 1875), p. 109

57 Fournel, pp. 215–14; cf. Baron, vol. 3, p. 90, p. 272

58 *Doctrina Jacobi*, ed. Bonwetsch, p. 90 (5–11)

59 Starr, BNJ, p. 196

60 *Leges Visigothorum*, ed. K. Zeumer, MGH: Legum sectio 1; *Leges Nationum Germanicorum*, vol. 1 (Hanover and Leipzig 1902), pp. 426–56; cf. J. Juster, 'La condition légale des Juifs sous les rois visigoths', *Études d'histoire juridique offertes à Frederic Girard* (Paris 1913), vol. 2, pp. 279–98

61 B. N. Nelson and J. Starr, 'The Legend of the Divine Surety and the Jewish Moneylender', *Annuaire de l'Institut de Philologie et d'Histoire Orientales et Slaves*, 7 (1939–1944), pp. 289–338

62 cf. H. Delehaye, 'Une vie inédite de Saint-Jean Aumonier', *Analecta Bollandiana*, 45 (1927), pp. 30–2

63 *Nicephori opuscula historica*, ed. C. de Boor (Leipzig 1880), pp. 30^{26}–31^3; cf. J. Starr, *Jews in the Byzantine Empire 641–1204* (Athens 1939), no. 2

64 S. *Zosimi Episcopi Syracusani vita III* (= *Acta Sanctorum Martii*, vol. 3, col. 839C); cf. Starr, *Jews in the Byzantine Empire*, no. 4

65 S. *Symeonis Junioris vita XXIV*. 190–1, ed. H. Delehaye, *Les Saints Stylites, Analecta Bollandiana* (Subsidia Hagiographica) 14, Brussels (1923), pp. 266–267^{19} (= MPG vol. 86.ii, cols. 3160D–3161C)

66 S. *Gregorii magni epistolae XIII*.3 (= Ewald and Hartmann, vol. 2, pp. 367–8); cf. Katz, JQR, p. 120

67 cf. V. Laurent, 'L'Oeuvre canonique du concile in Trulo (691–692)', *Revue des Études Byzantines*, 23 (1965), pp. 7–41

68 Mansi, vol. 11, col. 933E

69 Mansi, vol. 11, cols 957D; 985E

70 Mansi, vol. 11, col. 945E

CHAPTER IV

The Jews and the
Iconoclasts

The first emperor to follow the precedent set by Heraclius was Leo III. He, too, would not accept the peculiar status enjoyed by the Jews, the status accorded them by the twin principle of Jewish legislation in the Codes—Roman juridical theory and the theological concept of the 'living testimony'. He, too, felt that this status directly contradicted the sort of loyalty demanded by the reconstructed Byzantine state. And so, in 721 or 722, he attempted to end the anomaly at one blow as Heraclius had, by ordering all his Jewish subjects to be baptized.[1] Some circumstances were similar. For twenty years before Leo's reign the empire had been beset by internal upheavals and external dangers. It was noted in the first chapter how Leo established himself in power only after six emperors had tried and failed. Thus, for the same reasons as in the time of Phocas, there was no effective defence of the frontiers. The yearly raids of the Arabs into Asia Minor, which, even when they reached Constantinople had been no more than a serious nuisance to his predecessors, now became a test of survival, culminating in the great siege. His success there helped him to the throne, but it was only the beginning of his task. The Heracleian system had finally stood the test, but confidence in the ruling institution, its basis, had dwindled because of its rapid passing from hand to hand. Now it had passed to Leo. However, without a clear rule of succession, he had no special claim to the continued support of its constituent elements—the heads of the church, the senior administrators and the army command—which he had gained through his victories over his rivals and over the Arabs. He had to ensure that in himself, as in Heraclius, the complete unity of Byzantium was again unchallengeably made manifest. In the context of a problem of such magnitude, that of integrating the Jews into the all-embracing pattern was a small enough matter. In 721, the empire was not being threatened as in 632. Supposed sympathy of the Jews with its enemies was not the immediate threat it had been in the eyes of Heraclius. Leo's particular suspicions of Jewish loyalty had a different cause. They were the result of events primarily affecting communities not under his rule.

The Arab conquests had been a severe setback to Jewish nationalism, snatching away the golden opportunity seemingly promised when a century of mutually destructive conflict had ended the effectiveness of both Byzantium and Persia throughout the lands between the Nile and the Euphrates. However, sporadic risings continued to occur, serious enough to trouble the Arabs and to make an impression on the chronicles. These risings had characteristics which eventually gave them significance beyond the borders of Islām. The messianic aspect, always present, became predominant as real political prospects grew remote. But now this aspect tended to be markedly heretical. Disappointment bred reaction against traditional religious authority. The militant nationalists of the seventh and the eighth centuries minimized, or wholly denied, the value of the rabbinical interpretation of the scriptures.[2] Most strikingly, these risings had a characteristic in common with previous examples—they attracted noticeable non-Jewish participation.

In 645, there was such a rising in Mesopotamia.

That year there appeared a certain Jewish man from the village which is called Pallughthā—the place where the waters of the Euphrates are divided to irrigate the soil—a native of Beth-Arāmāye, who claimed that the Messiah had come. He gathered around himself a vile crowd of weavers, barbers and fullers, about four hundred strong, who burned down three sacred edifices and killed the local governor. But there came soldiers from the city of 'Akūla and slew them, their wives and their children, while their leader was crucified in his own village.[3]

Pallughthā has been identified with Pumbedītā.[4] The leader of the rising left this centre of Jewish learning to put himself at the head of the working population of the district. He was clearly distinguished from his followers, who were not called Jewish. And his birthplace was relevant. Beth-Aramāyē was another name for Samaria.[5] Thus his origins were among people noted both for their militancy and their heresy. In the reign of the Caliph 'Abd al-Malik (685–705), the Persian Jew Abū Isa al-Ispahāni announced the Messiah and led a revolt which was quickly crushed.[6] But his influence was wider. He founded a sect which spread to Syria and Palestine where it continued to be a source of irritation both for the Islāmic authorities and for the rabbis. It preached a militant, Palestinian-centred nationalism. It also 'acknowledged the prophecy of Jesus, son of Mary, and of the master of the Muslims'.[7] Even in the tenth century, its members were still active at Damascus.[8]

Finally, in the year before Leo's decree, a certain Severus or Serenus led a rising in Syria of sufficient consequence to earn repeated mentions until the fourteenth century. He was variously described in Greek, Arabic, Syriac and Latin sources. He had claimed to be the re-incarnation of Moses, who would lead the Jews back to the promised land.[9] 'He cheated the Jews, saying that he was Christ, the Son of God'.[10] Perhaps it was this particular description which was eventually responsible for the otherwise inexplicable and completely unsupported assertion that some years before Leo's decree 'many Jews converted and became Christians'.[11] He was a Christian converted to Judaism. He went everywhere looking for Jews to join him and even acquired disciples in Spain.[12] But, while for the Jews he was Moses or the Messiah, for others he only claimed to be the messenger of the Messiah.[13] His contemporaries thought him very dangerous. When his rising was crushed his punishment, according to the earliest source, was death by torture.[14] As time went on, and the fears he had aroused declined, so did the accounts of the severity of his punishment,

63

until it was only remembered as the return of the money he had collected from his disciples.[15] All those pieces of information, contradictory as they were, together pointed to an episode of militant messianism spreading, if not to Spain, at least west of Syria.[16] The strength of the influence that Severus had on Jews can be gauged from the fact that the gaon, or teacher of the Talmudic academy, Naṭronai bar Hilai found it necessary to rule, one hundred years later, on the correct procedure for receiving still active followers back into the field of orthodox Judaism.[17] But the information that Severus told 'others' that he was the messenger of the Messiah indicated that he, like the rebel of Pallughthā, also influenced non-Jews, whether Muslims or Christians. And it was the same interest in non-Jews which caused al-Ispahāni to make his respectful allusion to Jesus and Muḥammad.

The three risings had another characteristic in common. Their messianic hope was not only the result of disappointment with the failure of nationalism in Palestine, whether Jewish or Samaritan, during the sixth and the early seventh centuries. It was also engendered by the growing belief that the struggle between Byzantium and the Arabs was itself a sign of the Last Days. The attacks on Constantinople from 674 to 678 and the siege of 715–716 emphasized that these days were at hand. It was at Constantinople that the Messiah would appear, to witness the mutual destruction of Esau and Ishmael—of the Christian and of the Islāmic powers. The concept in itself was not new; it had inspired themes in Jewish apocalyptic writing at various moments of the struggle between Rome and Persia. But it was most forcibly expressed at the end of the seventh and at the beginning of the eighth century.[18] How could movements so inspired attract Christians and Muslims? This was no paradox. The Messiah was the bringer of salvation to all mankind. Jewish nationalists naturally welcomed the imminent end of two empires which between them decided the politics of the Mediterranean world. But the messianists of all three religions as naturally welcomed the end of any secular government, their own included, as the necessary prelude for the establishment of the kingdom of heaven on earth. And Byzantine Christians had followed Jewish messianic claimants. In the fourth century, for example, on the island of Crete, they, together with Jews, had been persuaded to throw themselves off a cliff, in the faith that the Messiah had given them wings.[19] In the year 593 in Sicily, a Jew proclaimed himself to be the prophet Elijah, one of the traditional precursors of the Messiah. Many Christians came to do him reverence as his willing disciples and personal servants.[20] Such were the reasons why these risings, although they took place beyond the frontiers of Byzantium, could not be ignored by its ruling institution. And because they were led by Jews, they gave new grounds for suspicion of Byzantine Jewry. Even had there been no echoes of the last rising in lands west of Syria, it was this new Jewish nationalism with its universal message for Jew and non-Jew alike, directly inimical to the state, which was one cause for the action that Leo took against his Jewish subjects. That this action was meant to ensure political loyalty was as clear as the motive of Heraclius had been in 632: Leo's baptized Jews were to be given the title of 'new citizens'.[21]

Did messianic nationalism actually win any disciples among Byzantine Jews? It is impossible to say with certainty, but in a comparison of three accounts of Leo's decree there is indirect evidence that it did. The principal source for the period relates the circumstances thus:

> That year the king compelled the Jews and the Montanists to be baptized. The Jews did so without protest and afterwards washed off the baptism, annulling the sacrament by eating beforehand, thus scorning the (Christian) faith. But the Montanists . . . chose a day, went inside houses allotted for the purpose and, in their own sin, set fire to themselves.[22]

Now, the Montanists here were very much out of place. They had been heretical Christian mystics, often fiercely persecuted, but the last occasion had been in the time of Justinian.[23] Towards the end of the sixth century they had virtually disappeared as a sect and there was no reason why, over a hundred years later, Leo should have given them particular attention in his efforts to restore imperial unity. Secondly, it was quite contrary to ecclesiastical law and custom for heretics, once baptized in the name of the trinity, however incorrectly understood, to be baptized again in order to be received into the church.[24] It was particularly strange that baptism should have been mentioned here, since the Montanist rite in this respect was very nearly orthodox.[25] Thirdly, it was equally strange that their heroic decision to die rather than submit closely coincided in its details with what was said of their reaction to Justinian's persecution.[26] Finally, an immediately subsequent reference to them by the patriarch of Constantinople says nothing at all about Leo's decree.[27]

Who these Montanists whom Leo persecuted may really have been can be learned from the second account according to which he 'forcibly baptized the Jews so that henceforth the Jews were known as Montanists'.[28] It was not in itself unnatural for a Christian source to connect Montanists with Jews. The original Montanists had been accused of Jewish sympathies.[29] However, in the present context, the terms were not vaguely synonymous. The first account of the persecution clearly distinguished between them. There is reason to suppose that not Jews in general but a particular Jewish sect came to be so described. A marginal comment to the text of a baptismal formula for Jewish converts to Christianity explains that 'the Montanists are separated from Hebrew customs and are to be found, for certain reasons, outside the synagogue. But, if they repent, they are received as fellow believers'.[30]

There is reason to suppose that this sect consisted of militant messianists. For the real Montanists had preached the physical establishment of a messianic kingdom on imperial territory, rising in revolt more than once in pursuance of their aim.[31] And the third account of Leo's persecution told how he had ordered the conversion of all those professing a religion not his own—in particular of the Jews and of a sect not called 'Montanists' but 'rebels'.[32] It may be that these 'Montanists henceforth known as Jews', these 'Montanists separated from Hebrew custom,' these 'rebels', were all references to the disciples whom Severus managed to attract in Byzantine territory. His militant messianism also needed rabbinic sanction for acceptance by the synagogue. And his Christian associations, the possibility that he might attract

Christians as well as Jews, acquired for his disciples the name of the Christian messianism which had troubled Justinian, just as they themselves were troubling Leo.[33] It was their existence within Byzantine Jewry which impelled him to take the action he did. It was they, as distinct from the community as a whole, who bitterly resisted. It was their resistance which the first account confused with the fate of the real Montanists. And it may be because Leo's decree was mainly directed against dissident Jews that there is no word of it in Jewish sources.

It is possible that Leo continued to persecute these militants. In 726 he published a compendium of laws called the *Ecloga*, or selections.[34] It thus did not pretend to the completeness of a Code but only dealt with subjects of contemporary importance. In the sections prescribing the penalties for the principal offences against the state, the Montanists were singled out for 'death by the sword'.[35] However, whether a militant movement which came to be called Montanist existed among Byzantine Jews or no, the majority remained as unaffected as they had been by the persecution of Heraclius. The picturesque language of the first account of Leo's decree made at least that clear enough. The *Ecloga* did not mention the Jews at all. Some years later, an appendix to it merely repeated passages from Justinian's legislation: The Jews could hold no government posts. They were forbidden to own Christian slaves. Proselytizing was punishable by death and by confiscation of property.[36] There was nothing about compulsory baptism. Despite the decree, Judaism had not been proscribed. The Jews remained recognized as inferior citizens, while the re-affirmation of these disabilities showed that their ambivalent relations with non-Jews were also unchanged—and were still considered dangerous.

These relations were a factor in Leo's better-known act as spiritual head of the ruling institution. In 726, he began a personal campaign against the honoured place that the icons were accorded by Christian custom. In 730, he ordered their wholesale destruction.[37] The peace of the church was once more broken, and Byzantine opinion was divided for over a hundred years. The opponents of iconoclasm had no doubts about the Jewish part in these

6

events. They were a fruit of the long supposed Jewish conspiracy with the Muslims against the Christian state. A Jew from Laodicea had prophesied to the caliph Yazīd II (720–724) forty years of power over all the Arabs if he would destroy the icons in the Christian churches.[38] This he did, and it was then that the evil spread to imperial territory—it was his lead that Leo followed.[39] Or Leo himself was also approached by a Jew, who had similar magical pretensions and had offered a similar bargain; perhaps it was a Christian convert to Islām who had been the tempter.[40] The legendary qualities of this story in its different versions are in themselves no objection to its usefulness as a source. Genuine information was often conveyed in this way; examples have already been given from stories of miraculous conversions of Jews to Christianity. This story has other difficulties. The first is its assertion that Leo in his campaign against the icons had, with Jewish encouragement, copied what the Muslims were doing. This was unlikely. Not long before, Yazīd's predecessor ʿUmr II had been especially anxious to insist on Islām's superiority over Christianity in its rigid application of the scriptural prohibition on the making of images. In a curious diplomatic exchange with Leo during a period of truce, he accused the Christians of idol worship because of their use of icons.[41] Leo's reply had been not only to defend the icons but also to express his strong distaste for any theological discussion with Muslims: negotiation over secular matters was possible, but the divine was not for the profane, since Muḥammad's own blasphemies were unpardonable.[42] At the same time, he took the opportunity to emphasize 'the enmity that exists between us Christians and the Jews'.[43] The second difficulty was that, so far as Muslim rulers were concerned, Yazīd was not the initiator of a campaign against the icons. He got a bad name because he had haphazardly punished Christians for allegedly hiding their wealth from his tax-collectors.[44] His caprices in this line had produced stories more fanciful than those told of Leo: for example he had caused a fearful stench throughout the lands of Islām by killing all white dogs, pigeons and roosters.[45] It was ʿAbd al-Malik, the first caliph with a stable enough position to reflect on such questions, who, about the year 700, issued prohibitions against icons and other outward symbols of Christian worship—a quarter of a century before anything similar happened in Byzantium.[46] But even these prohibitions only applied to their display in places where they might offend the eyes of the faithful.[47] Thus, the ostensible point of the story about Leo, apart from its magical decoration, was inherently improbable. He had not been directly influenced by Jewish advice to follow the example of a Muslim caliph.

For all that, the story has some substance. It refers, although in a highly enigmatic and simplified fashion, to a real relation between the Jews and iconoclasm. Icons began to play a noticeable part in Christian worship during the fourth century.[48] From then on, both those theologians who supported their use and those who had doubts, naturally included arguments from their interpretation of the Second Commandment in relation to the use in worship of man-made ritual objects.[49] Such arguments, for example, were advanced by both sides when a dispute about icons broke out in Armenia at the beginning of the seventh century.[50] They appeared in the official statement of the iconoclasts at the council of the church called by them in 754.[51] It is true that these arguments were secondary. The main subject of the dispute was the essential nature of the icons. The iconodules, 'the slaves of the icons'—the contemptuous epithet the defenders of the icons eventually accepted as their own—claimed for them an incarnate holiness transcending their material qualities, by an analogy from the doctrine of the incarnation of the Deity in the material person of Jesus. The iconoclasts replied that their use, however subtly they might be defined, must necessarily derogate from the spirituality of the act of worship. But the appeal to the Pentateuch was never abandoned. So far as the iconodules were concerned, this was not solely because Christian theologians could hardly ignore the authority of their 'old testament'. Theirs was a more immediate need.

The Jews of the Christian Roman period had had no marked objection to the portrayal of living creatures for the ornamentation of the synagogue. In the mosaics at Dura-Europus on the Euphrates, at Beit-Alpha in Palestine, in other synagogues in

North Africa and Spain, there appeared not merely figures of birds and animals but even persons from the scriptures. However, from the end of the fifth century, the attitude became stricter. At Naʿarā, for example, and at Kfar Naḥum (Capernaum) such figures were deliberately destroyed, while floral patterns were left untouched.[52] It was the fear that Jewish influences were widespread enough for this new attitude to strengthen existing Christian scruples which necessitated continual recourse to the Pentateuch for arguments to defend the icons. 'The Jews frequently reproach us in this matter', complained the patriarch of Constantinople not long before the edict of 730.[53] And his complaint was judged significant enough to merit quotation at the Council of Nicea in 787, when the iconodules had won a temporary victory.[54] For, just as according to the iconodules it was the Jews who were directly responsible for Leo's decision, so it was they who were also to blame for the spread of iconoclast ideas which encouraged him to make it. How seriously this was believed was apparent from the frequent repetition of the same arguments in Christian apologetics supposedly addressed to the Jews. Again and again, the chief objection of the Jews to Christianity was stated to be the use of icons; again and again its refutation was confined to answers from the Pentateuch. This was the context of a late sixth-century exposition of the subject. Although the author, the bishop of Cyprus, was acquainted with actual Jews both there and in Alexandria, it was not in them that he was interested. It was for the benefit of Christians that he expounded how the reverence enjoined for the Scroll of the Law did not mean the worship of its leather and ink, any more than the reverence of the Christian for his icon meant the worship of its wood and colours.[55] The Jews prostrated themselves before the Ark of the Covenant, argued the author of the so-called 'Trophies of Damascus' (about the middle of the seventh century), they revered the Tablets of the Law and the Cherubim on the Ark which were carved in a human likeness. Aaron's Rod and a piece of manna were preserved as reminders of the miracles the Lord had performed for Israel. So did the Christians revere the icons, reminders of God and of the saints.[56] The honour that the Christians paid the icons was like the honour that Jacob paid to Joseph's staff, asserted a similar text of that period.[57] At Nicea, it was related how a Jew who actually believed in Christ but could not accept Christianity because of the icons, was eventually persuaded by miscellaneous instances of such Jewish usages.[58]

However, the intention was never to persuade the Jews by arguments from their own scriptures. It was to persuade Christians who had been influenced by the arguments of Jews drawn from the same source. This intention received its clearest illustration in an eighth-century example of a set debate on the icons. 'How shall we persuade the Jews?' the iconodule began by asking in despair. What he succeeded in doing was not to persuade the Jews, but a puzzled Christian—in front of an audience of Christians and Jews.[59] The same intention inspired another approach: tales of how it happened that the icon itself miraculously converted the Jew to Christianity. The icon that stood surety for a debt was one example, and there was a host of others. The iconodules hoped that they would be particularly convincing precisely for Christians, since they fitted into a Christian tradition of the icons' miraculous powers established long before their place had been called into question.[60] Thus, the icon of our example had already acquired this reputation in the time of the Emperor Maurice, to whom it had given some useful advice at a critical moment.[61] This preoccupation with Jewish influence had a wider significance. It was yet another instance of ecclesiastic reactions to the potential attractiveness of Judaism in Byzantium, a society where Christians and Jews could freely mix. It was a parallel to the warnings of the 'Quinisext' Council. Its very existence was additional evidence that Leo's decree of forced baptism had not altered the situation.

At the same time, there was a basis for these fears in the particular context of iconoclasm. Leo had genuinely resented 'Umr's intrusion into Christian theology. And he defended the icons to him—but his defence was far from enthusiastic: the scriptures did not prohibit human likenesses, the Cherubim on the Ark had been made by divine command. On the other hand, there was no command to respect the icons; this he did because they were the traditional representations of the disciples of Jesus and of the saints because, as he put it, 'their presence charms us'.[62] He used a standard argument from the refutations of the iconodules, but his language was even more reserved, although those arguments deliberately omitted most of what a true iconodule believed. For Leo, the value of the icons was purely educational—or sentimental. He went on to underline the ambiguity of his attitude by a completely unreserved justification for the reverence given to the cross, a custom which 'Umr had also attacked, but which Christian iconoclasts always accepted. When Leo wrote that letter, he was already half way along the road to iconoclasm.[63] He had not been influenced by any Muslim caliph, with or without the help of Jewish magicians. But he had been influenced by a certain climate of opinion which included a Jewish element.

Leo came from a village in northern Syria. He had been brought up in a culture which, long before the coming of Islām, had been only superficially Byzantine. Its substance was semitic, whether Arab or Jewish. Its language was likely to be Aramaic rather than Greek.[64] The complex elaborations of Byzantine Christianity were alien to its religious outlook. It was inclined to a simple monotheism, unwilling and unable to draw the kind of distinctions required if the conception of the icons taught by the iconodules was to be clearly differentiated from mere idolatry. Leo's military career brought him to the command of the Anatolic Theme. It was its soldiers who helped him to defeat his rivals to the throne; it was on them that he relied during the difficult first years of his reign. And they were as pre-disposed to simplicity in belief or ritual as the people of his birthplace. The reasons were similar. The Anatolic Theme was roughly co-terminous with the old province of Phrygia, a part of central Asia Minor where marked traces of Syriac culture were to be found.[65] During its long history, Phrygia had nurtured innumerable sects hostile to whatever orthodoxy was being proclaimed by the government of the day. For example, it had been the home of Montanism which was, indeed, often called 'the Phrygian heresy'.[66] In particular, it was noted as a centre of Jewish influence. The chief Jewish communities were there, established centuries before Byzantium had inherited the empire from Rome, stretching from Amorium in the north, almost to the coast of the Mediterranean. For at least its first two hundred years, Christianity had had to fight a hard struggle against beliefs which it had found as a mixture of Judaism and Hellenism, but which it itself, against its own intentions, turned into a mixture of Judaism and Christianity.[67] It was in Phrygia that those 'God-Fearers' originated who troubled the authorities at Antioch.[68] Towards the beginning of the fifth century, at Laodicea, the town whence had come Yazīd's Jewish magician, there had arisen a Judaeo-Christian sect, similar to the North African Caelicoli, but with greater influence. It was called 'hypsistarian', from the Greek 'hypsistos'—'most high'. The reason was that its members prayed to the 'most high God who possessest all things', a form which they borrowed from the Jewish prayer of the Eighteen Benedictions, in order to stress God's unity and to dissociate themselves from trinitarian doctrine.[69] It spread to other parts of Phrygia, and was still to be found in Cappadocia, the eastern district of the Anatolic Theme, in the ninth century.[70]

The militant movement into which iconoclastic ideas crystallized arose in Phrygia. The leader was Constantine, Bishop of Nacoleia, not far from Amorium. He explicitly asserted that the use of the icons was contrary to the commands of the Pentateuch. The iconodules accused him of introducing 'this alien innovation' in conspiracy with 'the hated Jews and the unholy Arabs'.[71] But this accusation, as others of such Jewish responsibility, was a great over-simplification. The Jews of Phrygia were not the cause of iconoclasm. Nor were its Judaeo-Christian sects. Constantine was merely giving expression to purely Christian iconoclastic ideas, which had existed as long as icons had, but which had found a fruitful field in his diocese and in the province where they were encouraged to grow both by a non-Byzantine, semitically oriented cultural background as in Syria, and by positively Jewish elements, whether working through the sects or through the Phrygian Jewish communities. It was thus that Leo, already predisposed in that direction and anxious to keep the loyalty of his Anatolic soldiers, came to give Constantine the support of the ruling institution and then to publish his edict. The struggle, once begun, became for Leo and for his son Constantine V certainly a struggle against the predominantly monastic party of iconodules—but fundamentally a struggle to re-affirm the indivisibility of a supreme ruling institution against excessive influence by any sort of church party, as Heraclius had re-affirmed it against the excesses of the parties of the hippodrome. In this respect, the fact that the choice of the actual issue had been in some degree determined by Leo's own origins and by those of the troops on whom he depended, was entirely irrelevant. It is a serious misreading of the situation to suppose, as some historians have done, that this choice indicated the sympathy of the ruling institution, when in iconoclastic hands, for Byzantine Jews.[72] Leo's anti-Jewish decree was published at precisely the time when he was taking the road to full iconoclasm. It was rather the permanent ambivalence of the Jewish–Byzantine relationship that was once again illustrated. The free mingling of Jews with Christians had enabled the spread of ideas which helped the iconoclasts in their propaganda. But no one was going to thank the Jews for its success. On the contrary, this very evidence that they so indisputably continued to form an integral element within Byzantine society, if not fears of their messianic nationalism, was enough to cause an iconoclastic emperor to repeat the violent gesture against them first made by Heraclius.

These close relations were particularly noticeable in the last years of iconoclasm. At Amorium, during the first half of the ninth century, there were Christians who, while still not renouncing baptism which they continued to consider necessary for salvation, had come nearer to Judaism than the Hypsistarii, nearer than the half-converts at Antioch or in Egypt, nearer than the Phrygian 'God-Fearers'. Not only did they stress the unity of God and keep the Jewish Sabbath. They kept the whole of the Jewish Law with the exception of circumcision. They often went to live in Jewish families in order to learn their customs, and readily accepted their guidance in business as well as in religious affairs.[73] From Amorium they spread throughout Phrygia and to neighbouring provinces. Their beliefs and practices had a serious result for the empire. They inspired the emergence of a new sect—

the Athinganians. More radical than the iconoclasts in their un-compromising opposition to elaborations in doctrine and material objects of reverence, their aim was to turn Byzantine Christianity into the simplest and purest kind of monotheism.[74] It is not sur-prising that they clashed with the Emperor Michael I (811–813). Times were changing. Michael was personally already an iconodule, although his reign was too short to reverse general policy. He confiscated Athinganian property, sentenced some to death and exiled others. And the Athinganians were such extrem-ists that his orders were readily carried out by the troops of the Anatolic Theme under their commander, the future Emperor Leo V (813–820)—a convinced and militant iconoclast.[75] How-ever, the Athinganians remained undaunted. Later in the century, they joined with other sects, often not easily distinguishable from them, who took up arms in a similar cause and were only sup-pressed with great difficulty. The significance of these conflicts for Byzantine Jews will be discussed in the next chapter. The fear and hatred which the Athinganians inspired was reflected in an accusation against Michael's predecessor, Nicephorus I (802–811). His method of raising money for the Bulgarian wars infuriated the chronicler, who could find nothing worse to say than that Nicephorus 'was a friend of the Athinganians and an initiate in their mysteries'.[76]

Meanwhile, the relations of Jews and Christians in Amorium had a seemingly characteristic climax. In 838, the city was tem-porarily occupied by the troops of the Caliph M'utāsim after a long siege.[77] M'utāsim had been helped by a traitor with the nickname 'ox' or 'ox-like', a nickname which was somehow supposed to be connected with his participation, shortly before his treachery, in a quarrel between Christians and Jews. These circumstances in the fall of Amorium to the Muslims recalled the fall of Jerusalem to the Persians. On both occasions, there had been a long siege. On both occasions, the event immediately prior to the final disaster was a quarrel involving Christians and Jews, against a background of close relations between the two communities. But there was an interesting difference. Whatever the traitor's nickname may have meant—perhaps it was an obscure joke whose point has since been lost—there was not the slightest hint that it meant the traitor was Jewish.[78] Nor was it suggested that any other Jew in Amorium was responsible for his treachery. The absence of such suggestions is most striking in a nearly contemporary account of the deaths and posthumous miracles of forty-two prisoners, who preferred martyrdom to accepting Islām.[79] Their end was described in every detail, both in a Greek and in a Slavonic version, as was the siege, the treachery, the fall of the city and all the casualties on the Byzantine side. This account was a close parallel, both in style and content, to the eye-witness account of the fall of Jerusalem quoted in the previous chapter. But the Jews of Amorium, unlike the Jews of Jerusalem, were nowhere mentioned. This time, the usual allegation of a Jewish plot with the enemies of the empire against Byzantine Christians was not made.

It was the exceptional position of the Jews of Amorium during those years that resulted in the conferment of an unusual imperial favour. Michael II (820–829) relieved Byzantine Jews of certain financial burdens. Their nature will be discussed together with the general question of whether Byzantine Jews were normally subject to any special Jewish tax. This concession, whatever its nature, gave rise to stranger stories about Michael than that told of Nicephorus I and the Athinganians. It was no wonder that he was friendly to Jews. He was one of the Amorian half-converts, brought up in a Jewish household; perhaps he was himself of Jewish or of semi-Jewish origin.[80] In recent times, the possibility was even seriously considered that not only was he a full proselyte but actually the author of a liturgical hymn in praise of the unity of God sung in the services for the Jewish New Year and the Day of Atonement.[81] These stories were, in the first place, the result of a particular hostility to Michael. It became necessary to discredit him and the dynasty which he founded for reasons discussed in the next chapter, which had no more to do with his alleged Jewish sympathies than dislike for the financial policy of Nicephorus I was evidence of his sympathy for the Athinganians. However, the stories about Michael contained one important grain of truth. He was born and brought up in Amorium. For most of his life he was a serving soldier of the Anatolic Theme, and it was a soldier he primarily remained when he came to the throne. He was probably affected by the climate of opinion most familiar to him, and did not see the need for excessive discrimination between his Jewish and his non-Jewish subjects.

Michael was the last of the iconoclasts, and his iconoclasm was purely formal. In any event, unlike the majority of Byzantine emperors, he showed not the least enthusiasm for theological questions. The influences of his Phrygian background no more indicated any sympathy by iconoclastic rulers for Judaism than had Leo's. With both, this background was significant in the history of Byzantine Jewry. But iconoclasm itself ended as it had begun: it was the issue over which the ruling institution had chosen to affirm the supreme authority belonging to its theological, no less than to its political, prerogatives. The final restoration of the icons in 843, the rejoicings at the so-called Feast of Orthodoxy celebrated that year and to this day a feast in the calendar of the Greek and Russian churches, did not mean the end of the struggle. The emperors continued to intervene, with the same purpose, in the disputes of the strict and the moderate church parties, but the iconoclast issue was replaced by others. And some of those new issues, too, had Jewish significance.

Notes

1   Doelger, *Regesten*, no. 286. The notice is for 'the year of the world' 6214, which fell partly in the year 721 and partly in the year 722 of the present era
2   See Ankori, pp. 7–8
3   *Chronica Minora*, trans. I. Guidi, Scriptores Syrii series 3, vol. 4, fasc. 1 (Paris 1903), pp. 27–8; cf. J. Starr, 'Le mouvement messianique au début du viii-ième siècle', REJ 102 (1937), pp. 81–92
4   J. Obermayer, *Die Landschaft babylonien* (Frankfurt 1929), pp. 220–3
5   Starr, REJ 102, p. 84
6   L. Nemoy, 'Al-Qirqisāni's Account of the Jewish Sects and of Christianity', *Hebrew Union College Annual* 7 (1930), p. 328; cf. W. Bacher, 'Qirqisāni the Karaite and his work on the Jewish Sects', JQR (old series) 7 (1895), p. 705
7   Nemoy, p. 382

8 Ankori, pp. 214–15 (note 22), cf. J. Mann, *Texts and Studies in Jewish History and Literature*, vol. 2 (Philadelphia 1935), p. 303 (note 6)

9 *Le Chronique de Denys de Tell-Mahré*, 4th part trans. J. B. Chabot, *Bibliothèque de l'école des hautes études*, fasc. 112 (Paris 1895), pp. 25–7 (a mid-eighth-century source)

10 Theoph. 401 (19–20)

11 Michael the Syrian, XI.12 (= Chabot, p. 453)

12 *Kitāb al-'Unwān*, p. 504; *Anonymi auctoris chronicon ad annum christi 1234 pertinens*, trans. J. B. Chabot, Scriptores Syrii series 3, vol. 14, fasc. 1 (Paris 1920), p. 308; a fourteenth-century interpolation in *Continuationes Isidorianae*, ed. Th. Mommsen, MGH, *Auctores Antiquissimi* XI, *Chronica Minora*, vol. 2, Berlin (1894), p. 359, note 1

13 Michael the Syrian, XI.19 (= Chabot, vol. 2, p. 490)

14 *Denys de Tell-Mahré*, p. 27

15 *Anonymi auctoris chronicon*, p. 308

16 Starr, REJ 102, pp. 88–9

17 *Teshuvot ha-Geonim, Sha'arei-Tsedek* (Responsa of the Gaons—Gates of Righteousness) (in Hebrew), Salonika (1792), p. 24 (no. 7, no. 10). On the relevance of this ruling to Severus/Serenus, see L. Ginsberg, *Geonica*, vol. 2 (New York 1929), pp. 50–1 (note 1); Starr REJ 102, p. 91. On Naṭronai, see J. Rosenthal 'Heresies in the time of Sa'adiah' (in Hebrew), Ḥoreb 9 (1946–1947), p. 21; cf. Baron, vol. 5, pp. 380–2 (note 58) who is inclined to ascribe the ruling to Naṭronai bar Nehemiah (about the year 739) and generally to minimize the influence of Severus/Serenus

18 J. Mann, *Journal of the American Oriental Society* (communication to its Congress) 47 (1927), p. 364; cf. Baron, vol. 5, pp. 142–4; Starr, *Jews in the Byzantine Empire*, no. 11c. In the Babylonian Talmud, *Tractate Sanhedrin*, 106A, there may be an eighth-century interpolated passage expressing this theme; see I. Epstein, *The Babylonian Talmud, Seder Nezikin, Sanhedrin* II (London 1935), p. 722 (note 12); p. 723 (notes 1 and 2)

19 *Socratis Historia Ecclesiastica* VIII. 38 (= MPG vol. 67, cols. 825B–828A)

20 *S. Gregorii epistolae* III.37 (= Ewald and Hartmann, vol. 1, p. 195)

21 Michael the Syrian, XI.19 (= Chabot, vol. 2, p. 490)

22 Theoph. 401 (21–7)

23 C.I. 1.5.20 (3–7) (= Krueger, p. 59)

24 See G. Bareille, 'Baptême des Hérétiques', DTC vol. 2 (1910), cols. 228–9

25 *S. Epiphanii Adversus Haereses XLVIII* (= MPG vol. 41, col. 856B)

26 *Procopii historia arcana XI.23* (= Haury, p. 74)

27 *S. Germanii Patriarchae Constantinopolitani de haeresibus et synodis* 4, 5 (= MPG vol. 98, cols. 41C–44B); cf. P. Labriolle, *Les Sources de l'histoire de Montanisme* (Paris 1913), pp. 246–7

28 *Leonis Grammatici chronographia*, ed. B. G. Niehbur, CSHB (1842), p. 179; cf. Starr, *Jews in the Byzantine Empire*, no. 12

29 *Eusebii historia ecclesiastica V. 16* (= MPG vol. 20, col. 469B); cf. Parkes, *Conflict*, p. 126

30 Beneshevitch, p. 318; trans. Starr, *Jews in the Byzantine Empire*, pp. 177–8

31 See P. Labriolle, *La crise montaniste*, Paris (1913)

32 *Kitāb al-'Unwān*, p. 504. For an elucidation of the word used, see pp. 492–3

(note 4). Neither Baron, vol. 3, p. 176, nor Starr, *Jews in the Byzantine Empire*, no. 11[b] suggest who these 'rebels' were

33　For a fuller discussion, see Beneshevitsch, pp. 215–17; cf. A. Sharf, 'The Jews, the Montanists and the Emperor Leo III', BZ 59 (1966) pp. 37–46

34　On the composition and date, see Ostrogorsky, p. 134 (note 6)

35　*Ecloga* XVII.*52*, ed. J. and P. Zepos, *Ius Graecoromanum*, vol. 2 (Athens 1931), p. 61; trans. E. H. Freshfield, *A Manual of Roman Law* (Cambridge 1926), p. 113

36　*Ecloga Leonis et Constantini cum appendici* IV.6, 24; VI.26, 28, 30, ed. A. G. Monferratus (Athens 1889), pp. 64–5, p. 67, pp. 72–3; trans. Freshfield, p. 130

37　Ostrogorsky, pp. 143–5

38　Theoph. 401[29]–402[2]

39　*S. Nicephori antirrheticus adversus Constantinum Copronymum* III (= MPG vol. 100, cols. 529 B–C)

40　*Georgii Monachi Hamartoli Chronicon*, ed. C. de Boor, vol. 2 (Leipzig 1904), pp. 735–6; *Martyrorum Constantinopolitanorum Vita, Acta Sanctorum Augusti*, vol. 2, pp. 435–6; *Georgii Cedreni Historiarum Compendium*, MPG vol. 121, col 864D; *Joannis Zonarae Epitome Historiarum XV.2*, ed. C. de Boor, vol. 3 (Leipzig 1870), pp. 338–9

41　*Kitāb al'Unwān*, pp. 502–3; cf. A. Jeffery, 'Ghevond's Text of the Correspondence between Omar II and Leo III' *Harvard Theological Review*, 37 (1944), pp. 269–332

42　Jeffery, *ibid.*, p. 282, p. 294

43　Jeffery, *ibid.*, p. 288

44　*History of the Patriarchs*, PO vol. 5, pp. 326–7

45　*Denys de Tell-Mahré*, pp. 17–18; cf. O. Grabar, 'Islamic Art and Byzantium' DOP 18 (1964), pp. 83–4

46　*History of the Patriarchs*, PO vol. 5, p. 279; pp. 306–8

47　A. S. Tritton, *The Caliphs and their Non-Muslim Subjects* (London 1930), pp. 105–6

48　See E. Kitzinger, 'The Cult of Images in the Age before Iconoclasm' DOP 8 (1954), p. 86 and note 5

49　For examples, see N. H. Baynes, 'Idolatry and the Early Church', *Byzantine Studies and other Essays* (London 1960), pp. 118–19

50　S. de Nersessian, 'Une apologie des images du septième siècle', BYZ 17 (1944–1945), pp. 70–3

51　M. V. Anastos, 'The Argument for Iconoclasm as presented by the Iconoclastic Council of 754', *Late Classical Studies in Honour of A. M. Friend, Junr.* (Princeton 1954), pp. 179–84

52　J. B. Frey. 'La question des images chez les Juifs à la lumière de récentes découvertes', *Biblica* 15 (1934), pp. 290–8

53　*S. Germani Patriarchae Constantinopolitani epistolae* IV (= MPG vol. 98, col. 168B)

54　Mansi, vol. 13, col. 109 B–E

55　*Leontii Neapolitani episcopi sermo contra Judaeos*. MPG vol. 93, cols 1597B–1609A; extract trans. Starr, *Jews in the Byzantine Empire*, no. 1; cf. N. H. Baynes, 'The Icons before Iconoclasm', *Byzantine Studies*, pp. 230–7

56 G. Bardy, *Les Trophées de Damas*, PO vol. 15, pp. 245–7; cf. Williams, pp. 162–3

57 *Anastasii Abbati adversus Iudaeos disputatio*, MPG, vol. 89, cols. 1233C, 1235B; cf. Williams, pp. 175–80

58 Mansi, vol. 13, p. 166

59 *Quaestiones ad Antiochium Ducem*, MPG, vol. 28, col. 621; col. 709; cf. Williams, pp. 160–2

60 Parkes, *Conflict*, pp. 291–4

61 Theoph. 285 (5–17)

62 Jeffery, *Harvard Theological Review*, p. 322

63 cf. J. Meyendorff, 'Byzantine Views of Islām', DOP 18 (1964), pp. 125–7

64 P. Peeters, *Le Tréfonds oriental de l'hagiographie byzantin* (Subsidia Hagiographica No. 26), (Brussels 1950), pp. 141–2; p. 175

65 *Ibid.*, p. 90, p. 102

66 H. Grégoire, 'Épigraphie chrétienne—les inscriptions hérétiques d'Asie Mineure', BYZ 1 (1924), pp. 693–710

67 See A. Reinach, 'Noe Sangariou. Étude sur le déluge phrygien et le syncrétisme judéo-phrygien', REJ 67 (1913), pp. 213–45

68 W. R. Ramsay, 'The Jews in Greco-Asiatic Cities', *Expositor* 5 (1902), pp. 97–100

69 ὕψιστος=אל עליון; cf. παντοκράτωρ=קונה שמים וארץ; see *Gregorii Theologi orationes XVIII*. 5 (=MPG, vol. 35, cols. 989D–992B); *S. Gregorii Nysseni contra Eunomium II* (=MPG vol. 45, col. 484A); cf. G. T. Stokes, *Dictionary of Christian Biography*, vol. 3 (1882), pp. 188–9. On the rise of this sect at Laodicea (Lādik in north-eastern Phrygia), see W. M. Calder, 'Epigraphy of Anatolian Heresies', *Anatolian Studies Presented to Sir William Mitchell Ramsay* (Manchester 1923), pp. 88–9

70 *S. Nicephori antirrheticus adversus Constantinum Copronymum I* (=MPG vol. 100, col. 210D)

71 Mansi, vol. 12, col. 200A; cf. G. Ostrogorsky, 'Les débuts de la Querelle des Images', *Mélanges Diehl*, vol. 1 (Paris 1930), p. 236; G. B. Ladner, 'Origin and Significance of the Iconoclastic Controversy', *Medieval Studies* 2 (1940), p. 129. On Nacoleia, see W. M. Ramsay, *Cities and Bishoprics of Asia Minor* (Oxford 1895), p. 144

72 E.g. Pargoire, pp. 282–3; Janin, p. 126

73 *Theophanis continuator*, ed. I. Bekker, CSHB (Bonn 1838), pp. 42–3; trans. Starr, *Jews in the Byzantine Empire*, no. 20

74 Cf. J. Starr, 'An Eastern Christian Sect; the Athinganoi', *Harvard Theological Review*, 29 (1936), pp. 93–106

75 Theoph. 494³³–495³; 497 (4–6); cf. Ostrogorsky, *History*, pp. 178–80

76 Theoph. 488 (22–5)

77 *Tafsīr al-Tabāri III.1236*, trans. A. A. Vasiliev, *Byzantium and the Arabs* (in Russian) (St Petersburg 1900), Appendix IV, p. 30

78 *Genesii de rebus Constantinopolitanis III.65* (=MPG vol. 104, cols. 1027C–1073A); *Joannis Zonarae Annales XV.24* (=MPG vol. 134, col. 1412C); *Georgii Cedreni Historiarum Compendium*, MPG vol. 121, col. 1020; cf. J. B. Bury, *A History of the Eastern Roman Empire 802–867* (London 1912), pp. 268–70

79 *Acta 42 martyrum Amoriensium*, ed. V. Vasilievsky & P. Nikitin (Greek and Slavonic texts with Russian commentary), *The Tale of the 42 Amorian Martyrs and the Order of Service for them* (Mémoires de l'Académie Impériale des Sciences de S. Petersburg, VIII-sèrie, classe historico-philologique, vol. 7), St Petersburg (1905), pp. 40–3; cf. p. 71, 193 and for probable date of composition, pp. 272–9

80 Theoph. Cont. p. 48; cf. Doelger, *Regesten*, no. 414

81 Krauss, *Studien*, pp. 41–2; cf. G. Care, 'Ein juedischer Proselyt (?) auf dem Thron vom Byzanz', MGWJ 53 (1909), pp. 576–80. For the most extreme and uncritical version of these stories, see Galanté, p. 17: Michael kept the Sabbath on Saturdays, Easter on the date of Passover, denied that Christ was the Messiah and placed Judas among the saints. He also encouraged the building of numerous synagogues. Galanté gives as his source B. Poujoulat, *Histoire de Constantinople* (no place or date of publication)—which it has not proved possible to trace.

CHAPTER V

The Macedonian
Persecutions

The next emperor to try his hand at eliminating the Byzantine Jewish anomaly by mass conversion was the founder of the Macedonian dynasty, Basil I. Unlike the attempts of Heraclius and of Leo, his was more than a single violent gesture. Both for Heraclius and for Leo, the Jews had constituted an immediate danger to the state, calling for quick and decisive action. The circumstances of Basil's attempt were different. His was part of a general missionary endeavour. One fundamental duty of the ruling institution in its theological function was the crushing of heresy, and the preservation and expansion of orthodox Christianity. It was in order to fulfil this duty, quite as much as for the furtherance of the secular interests of his empire, that Basil extended Byzantine ecclesiastical domination to Bulgaria, to the southern Balkans and to the Dalmatian coast. It was true that the privileges enjoyed by Byzantine Jews, first and foremost their privilege to exist at all as the sole legal non-Christian sect, had specific theological sanction. But this was looked upon as a temporary contradiction whose removal it was the duty of every conscientious Christian to hasten. And Basil had a particular reason for being keen to do so. He had to deal with the Paulicians, which in his day was the chief Christian sect to express the syncretic elements we have noted. It, too, had arisen in Phrygia, and its doctrine, too, was a fanatically puritan monotheism close to that of the Athinganians, with whom the

Paulicians were often confused. But the Paulicians were more dangerous. Their adherents were recruited from the same sort of theme militia men whose ancestors had been drawn to iconoclasm. They fought, and sometimes defeated, the regular troops sent against them. They succeeded in establishing a virtually independent frontier state half in Byzantine, half in Arab territory which became the centre for a wide interpenetration of Christian and Muslim traditions. At the beginning of Basil's reign, they allied themselves with the Arab governor of Melitene in northern Syria, and a joint Arab-Paulician army marched through the length of Asia Minor before its destruction at the end of a long and bloody campaign.[1] These events were certainly enough to revive the old idea of the Muslims and the Jews acting in common to the detriment of the empire, through the agency of a Jewish-inspired heretical sect.

However, although the crushing of the Paulicians was as much a part of Basil's missionary duty as of his duty to defend the frontiers, and although the Paulicians focused his attention on the Jewish question, he distinguished between the two and, unlike Heraclius and Leo when faced with an alleged conspiracy of this kind, did not immediately proceed to a violent solution. He began by accepting that the anomaly could not be removed by force. The church had repeatedly commanded that the Jews must be encouraged, not forced into conversion. Besides, he had learned from the experience of Heraclius and Leo that a violent solution was no solution at all. A simple imperial decree was not enough. Accordingly, his tenth century biographer described how (in the year 873 or 874),

> Seeing that there was nothing so pleasing to God as the saving of
> souls, and not neglectful or idle in this apostolic labour, he first
> drew into his net for submission to Christ the uncircumcised (i.e.
> in their hearts) and stubborn Jewish people. First he ordered them
> to come to disputations, bringing proofs of their faith if it was in
> their eyes strong and irrefutable but, if they became persuaded
> that Christ stood higher than the Law and the Prophets, he ordered
> them to go over to the teaching of the Lord and to be baptised.
> He offered high appointments to those who so came forward,
> and promised them exemption from the burden of former taxes.

He also announced that he would grant official rank to men of no standing. He thus freed many from their cloak of obstinacy and brought them to faith in Christ. But most of them, when the king no longer lived, returned like dogs to their vomit. However, if the Jews, or rather some of them, turned out to be 'as changeless as the Ethiopian', the pious king is likely to have been requited by God for the enthusiasm he brought to his difficult task.

Then the biographer made it clear how this task was part of a wider missionary enterprise by straightway describing Basil's successes in Bulgaria.[2]

It is true that this method of Basil's brought results. The authorities did manage to bribe or badger some Jews into temporary professions of Christianity. But Basil did not gain an incontestable reputation for piety thereby, as his biographer implied. He was uncompromisingly, if anonymously, attacked in a contemporary polemic entitled 'A word on how one must not baptize Hebrews hastily if they have not been strictly examined beforehand.'[3] To bring Jews to baptism by gifts or by promises of money was a betrayal of Christ. And to become fit for baptism, even for a better motive, was not merely a matter of professing a belief. It was necessary to understand and to take up material and spiritual burdens, while sincerely and explicitly rejecting past errors. But, because the authorities were now more concerned with the quantity of so-called converts than with their quality, they had no scruples in ignoring these essential principles. Indeed, so far had this laxness gone that, instead of a properly qualified member of the clergy pronouncing on the fitness of a candidate for the privilege of baptism, it was common talk at court, even among the women, how a renunciation of Jewish customs by means of a simple declaration in front of the emperor had become sufficient. And this laxness had come about because the church was plagued with too many accommodating priests willing to acquiesce in this, as in other harmful innovations, ready to jettison any canon thought inopportune by the authorities—such as that particularly unambiguous one proclaimed by the Seventh Ecumenical Council at Nicea which demanded proofs of sincerity before permitting the baptism of a Jew. The real intention of this polemic was not only to attack Basil for his method but also to cite it as an outstandingly outrageous example of a general laxness in observance encouraged by certain policies of the ruling institution. In other words, it was yet one more expression of the standard accusation that the strict were wont to levy against the moderates. This was no accident. The conflict between the two parties had once again become acute.

The Feast of Orthodoxy had brought only temporary peace to the church. In 858, in pursuance of a palace intrigue, Michael III, Basil's predecessor and the last of the Amorian emperors, had demoted the strictly observant patriarch Ignatius, putting in his place Photius, a sophisticated layman and a scholar of note, who was raised through the necessary ecclesiastical degrees in a few days, some said in a few hours. His uncanonical ordination, as his character, infuriated the strict party. Basil could not afford dissensions at the outset of his reign. His path to the throne had not been smooth. He had begun his career in Michael's stables, had gained his affectionate trust and had treacherously murdered him. He badly needed all the support he could get and, for the sake of a united church, he reinstated Ignatius. But the opponents of Photius were not appeased. He had only been an excuse to reopen their old campaign, and his abandonment proved worse than useless for Basil. The strict party, following an old iconodule precedent, continually irritated him with appeals to the pope. In 870, when the Bulgarians finally rejected the western church in favour of the patriarchate, it became obvious that Ignatius with his pro-papal followers could no longer be relied upon. Photius gradually came back into favour. In 875, he was appointed tutor to Basil's children. In 877, Ignatius was dead and Photius was patriarch. Thus, the period when Basil was embarking on his Jewish policy was the period when he was drawing closer to the moderates. There is no evidence that he was influenced by them in the method which he chose, but he was linked with them because of the direction he was taking, and his method was attacked on that score. In the enthusiasm which he brought to his task, if not in his method, he might, indeed, have been influenced by Photius himself. For Photius placed much stress on the missionary aspect of

Christianity whose greatest glory, he once wrote, was the bringing of Jews to baptism.[4] This, then, was the way in which the conflict between the two parties within the Byzantine church had its links with the Jewish question under Basil I—just as there had been similar links under other emperors.

There was a reason why Basil's biographer chose to ignore the fact that Basil's Jewish policy was controversial. He may have been Basil's own grandson, Constantine VII. He was certainly someone who had Constantine's direct instructions to exaggerate the achievements of the founder of the dynasty, so that the lowly usurper might be made respectable and his victim discredited. Thus it was thought necessary to exaggerate Basil's undoubted military achievements by insisting that it was he, and not Michael, who began the successful counter-attack against the Muslims, after their victories on the eastern front which had culminated in the capture of Amorium. Similarly, it was exaggerated how badly Michael had behaved to the church and how unimpeachable, in contrast, was Basil's own piety. In this context it was natural enough to expatiate on the willing acceptance of Christianity by a number of Byzantine Jews which, even if it was admitted to have been an impermanent achievement, was nevertheless truly one which no other emperor could claim. But the only account which rivalled the biographer in its praises of Basil was, not surprisingly, that of his son, Leo VI. It was contained in the preamble to a novel which he published on the Jews and which we shall consider later. It is remarkable how other accounts merely stated the bare fact, even when it was claimed that all the Jews under Basil's rule, and not only some of them, acceded to his persuasive encouragements.[5] No one thought it necessary to praise him. On the contrary, in an instance when more than the bare fact was stated, it was implied that Basil's success had something to do with a fondness for Jews.[6] The existence of a special 'Macedonian' version of history had itself a Jewish interest, and to this point, too, we shall return.

Yet, however much Basil's achievement merited the praise of his descendants, he himself was not satisfied. It was not long before he reverted to the method of Heraclius and of Leo III, abandoning his method for theirs of baptism by force. The chief evidence for its use, after attempts at persuasion by arguments and inducements, is to be found in Italian Jewish sources. Towards the year 1054, Aḥima'atz of Oria in Byzantine Italy, compiled in rhymed couplets the story of his family from about the middle of the ninth century to his own day. He related how Rabbi Hananel, a son of Amittai, its founder, was challenged by the bishop of Oria to prove the superiority of Jewish calendrical calculations over Christian by foretelling the day and the hour of the next appearance of the new moon, how Hananel agreed to accept Christianity if he was worsted in this test, and how he was saved from these consequences when he made a mistake in his calculations by the moon nevertheless miraculously appearing exactly at the time which he foretold.[7] Aḥima'atz then related how Hananel's elder brother, Rabbi Shefatiyā, the leader of the Oria community, was commanded to go to Constantinople for a disputation with Basil himself. This time, the question was which of the two buildings, sacred to Judaism and to Christianity respectively, was the costlier—the Temple of Solomon or the great church of St Sophia which had cost Justinian, so it was said, three hundred and twenty thousand gold pieces—about £14 million sterling in pre-1939 values—perhaps because it was well known that Justinian himself had exclaimed at its completion, 'Solomon, I have surpassed thee'.[7a] And Shefatiyā was able to prove that it was the Temple. Basil was very friendly. He saw to it that food was served to the rabbi in such a way that his stay would not be marred by fears of breaking the Jewish dietary laws. And when he was worsted in the argument, he offered Shefatiyā not only money and other gifts but also a position of power in the imperial bureaucracy—if only he would consent to be baptized. When Shefatiyā refused, 'the wicked man sent messengers everywhere to convert the Jews by force . . . and the light of the sun was hidden'.[8] Shefatiyā's son, who again bore the family name of Amittai, broke his heart over the disaster that followed, and loudly bewailed it all the days of his life.[9] He perpetuated its memory in two liturgical poems. He spoke of a 'Sinful king, eager to defile the old and to annul the circumcision of the infant young, by ordering the joining of three deities in place of the Divine Unity of the faithful,'[10] and of how, as a result of this order 'an exhausted and feeble congregation mourned the befouling waters (i.e. of baptism), pronouncing with weak lips 'Lord' but adding two others.'[11]

The persecution was also remembered in a penitential prayer composed by Rabbi Silano of Venosa, who was a contemporary both of Amittai ben Shefatiyā and of his father, and had visited Oria. The sorrows and tribulations whose mention is obligatory in this kind of prayer, which is recited in the period of semi-mourning before the Jewish New Year, have a factual and vivid air about them which leaves little doubt that they are meant to be the sorrows and tribulations visited upon Oria by Basil.[12] Yehudā ben David Ḥayyūj, the great Hebrew philologist and grammarian who flourished at Cordova in the early years of the eleventh century, in a commentary to a penitential prayer which he ascribed to Shefatiyā, told how Basil's agents used physical torture to compel conversions: 'How did they force them? Anyone refusing to accept their error (of Christianity) was placed in an olive mill under a wooden press, and squeezed in the way olives are squeezed in the mill.'[13]

However, Aḥīma'atz did not want to leave the impression that his community, still less his own forefathers, had been forced to a show of Christianity. And so, in his story of Shefatiyā's visit to Constantinople, he told how Basil's daughter fell seriously ill, how no doctor could do anything for her, and how Shefatiyā cured her by 'exorcising the demon'. Basil rewarded him with a 'chrysobull'—an imperial rescript sealed with the emperor's golden seal—which exempted Oria from the attentions of the imperial agents. This exemption was noted by Yehudā ben David in his commentary, where the story of Basil's daughter immediately followed the story of the olive press. Another tradition combined the story of the olive press and of the exemption in a different way. When a rabbi was brought to the torture, the press got out of hand and destroyed everything around it. This was why the persecution was stopped. Both these traditions asserted that four other Italian communities benefited (which were not named) —as well as Oria.[14]

The poetic and picturesque character of all this evidence does not detract from its essential reliability. Ḥananel need not have disputed with a bishop (Oria did not have one at the time), and Shefatiyā need not have met Basil face to face. But calendrical questions were accepted by both Christians and Jews as of fundamental religious importance for the obvious purpose of the correct fixing of festivals. The Jews prided themselves on being experts and were recognized as such by Christians. At the end of the reign of Justinian, Phineas of Tiberias had participated in a discussion on the date of Easter.[15] We shall notice later that a learned Jew from Cyprus was asked for his opinion on another calendrical question. Similarly, Basil's behaviour according to Aḥimaʿatz, even if the care for Jewish dietary laws was a dramatically appropriate invention, was in general consonance with what Basil's biographer had to say of his first method for converting the Jews, and agrees with what the other source we quoted alleged about his peculiar friendliness to them. The story of Shefatiyā and the demon who troubled Basil's daughter, in the form that Aḥimaʿatz told it has, indeed, the characteristics of a pious legend. But there is nothing inherently improbable in her being cured by a Jewish doctor. As we have seen, they were much in request—by an emperor as well as by ordinary citizens. Basil may then have been moved to make the gesture of gratitude recorded by Aḥimaʿatz, but it is probable that it remained no more than a gesture. The evidence, particularly that of Aḥimaʿatz himself, is against the reality of an exemption. Basil's agents used compulsion against the Jews of Oria which some of them were unable to withstand. And the story of the olive press, again legendary in form, is a strong indication that physical force was included.

The decision to persecute instead of to persuade was not confined to Oria. It applied to the whole empire. The statement by Aḥimaʿatz that 'the wicked man sent messengers everywhere to convert the Jews by force' was amplified by Yehudā ben David in his commentary immediately before he spoke about the olive press:

> The wicked Basil ordered the persecution throughout the whole land of Greece (i.e. Byzantium), and forced more than a thousand communities to err. There was not a province nor a city which he did not bring to sin.

Once more, allowance must be made for rhetoric. The thousand communities had no demographic significance. But the gist of his information was supported by non-Jewish sources. About the year 912, the Frankish monk Auxilius who had spent many years in Italy, in a defence of the ordinations and sacraments administered by the pope Formosus which had been the subject of controversy, instanced the persecution as a well known event in order to show that the sacrament of baptism, however administered—even by force—was eternally valid.[16] And a chronicle of dates and events affecting Sicily and south Italy, written at the beginning of the eleventh century, baldly stated that in the 'year of the world' 6382 (= A.D. 873-874) the Jews were baptized—a statement from which no implication of persuasion or encouragement can be derived.[17] On the other hand, Basil's biographer said nothing about his abandonment of persuasion. It is possible that this omission was deliberate: in order not to derogate from the uniqueness of Basil's achievement. Leo VI also said nothing about force in his account of how his father dealt with the Jews. But these omissions were not merely further examples of Macedonian historiography. None of the sources we quoted which spoke of Basil's first method went on to speak of force. The reason probably is that Basil, unwilling to confess officially his dissatisfaction with his own method, never issued a formal decree of forced baptism. He made his decision clear enough; but the fact that its results were only mentioned in Italian and western sources, whether Jewish or non-Jewish, suggests the conclusion that it was mainly his Italian Jewish subjects who suffered. The military and political situation in the extreme south-west of Italy, where the most important Jewish communities lay, made such a singling-out highly probable. For more than thirty years, Bari and Taranto had been in Muslim hands and many other cities the object of continuous raids. During the last years of his reign, Basil succeeded in re-establishing Byzantine rule over the whole area. But the beginnings of his task had been difficult and complicated. For he not only had to fight the Muslims but to deal with the territorial claims of the Western powers—of the pope and of the German emperor. Between 871 and 876, for example, he spent much energy in regaining Bari not from the Muslims, but from the troops of the German Louis II who had occupied it under a temporary agreement with the Byzantines. It was in this context that the Jews were an additional problematic element. When Oria was attacked in 856, Aḥimaʿatz claimed that Shefatiyā was sent to treat with the Muslim commander.[18] Whether this was so or not, the story illustrated that Jews were the natural intermediaries for this purpose. But their loyalty in Byzantine eyes was no more than doubtful—particularly if they had for some time lived under the Muslims. Thus, the suffering of the Italian communities was yet another instance of the old Byzantine suspicions. And, while these suspicions were not the cause of Basil's general Jewish policy, they played a part in the second stage of its application.

The persecution went unnoticed by the imperial legislation of the period, a recurrent peculiarity this time partially explicable by the absence of a formal decree. The *Procheiron* or handbook, a legal text-book for everyday use which was published between 870 and 879, merely repeated the penalties decreed by Justinian for a Jew who bought and circumcised a Christian slave, or who was convicted of any attempt at proselytization.[19] The *Epanagogē*, or introduction (i.e. to the *Basilica* Code completed by Leo VI), was published a little after 879 and repeated the prohibition on Jews serving in the army or holding any public posts or official positions.[20] Basil explicitly intended the *Procheiron* and the *Epanagogē* to be the basis for a re-codification of all Byzantine and Roman enactments, for a thorough 'purification of the old law'.[21] And while too much should not be read into the lack of references to his new and enthusiastically pursued Jewish policies, the old pieces of Jewish legislation which he did see fit to repeat indicate that the general social position of the Jews had not changed. This is strikingly confirmed by a book of canon law which appeared about the year 883 and which consisted of selected rulings considered suitable for contemporary use, beginning with the Quinisext Council and ending with those pronounced by the patriarch Photius. Once again the Byzantines were told to respect the inviolability of the synagogue, to allow the Jew his rest on the Sabbath and Festivals, to see to it that the unoffending Jew was not insulted. Once again, the Jews were warned not to interfere with the reading of the Law in Greek—either the Septuagint or the Aquila version—or in any other language, depending on the locality.[22] The contrast between these exhortations and the policy which the authorities were actually pursuing—at least in Byzantine Italy—was strange indeed. But it expressed in the clearest manner possible the unchanging ambiguity of the Byzantine Jewish situation.

How long did the persecution continue? The substance of the elegant comment by Basil's biographer that the dogs returned to their vomit after his death, was supported by Aḥima‘atz:

> And after his (Basil's) generation, there arose another; Leo the king, his very own son; he annulled the evil decree proclaimed in the days of his father, and allowed the Jews to return to the worship of their God as in the days of old.[23]

There could hardly be a plainer statement that Leo stopped the persecution. But Leo himself, in his novel on the Jews, said something different. Past imperial legislation, he recalled, had always recognized Judaism, and had ensured its perpetuation by allowing the children to follow the religion of their fathers. Basil, more concerned to save Jewish souls than other emperors had been, brought many Jews to Christianity by teaching and persuasion—but he did not annul the laws which recognized Judaism. The time had come to set right this shortcoming. The old laws were hereby null and void: henceforth the Jews had to live according to the ceremonies and customs of Christianity. If they disregarded them and returned to their own, they would be punished as apostates.[24] And in another novel it was made clear that this punishment was death—not the confiscation of property or the impairment of testamentary rights decreed by the Theodosian Code and confirmed by Justinian.[25] Leo made the distinction between a novel and a code—the distinction that can be likened to that between a specific enactment and a constitution—much more explicit than had Theodosius and Justinian. In Leo's eyes, his novels had an immediate and practical purpose. While a code embodied the principles of imperial legislation and could copy earlier codes, a novel was an imperial instruction for dealing with a problem of everyday life.[26] Thus Leo, out of his own mouth, contradicted both the good opinion that Aḥima'atz was to form of him and the regrets to be expressed by Basil's biographer.

This contradiction has remained a puzzle.[27] However, it is not wholly inexplicable. In one important respect, Leo did not alter Basil's policy. Although he ordered the Jews to live like Christians, he did not issue a decree of forced baptism any more than had Basil. On the other hand, in contrast to the second stage of Basil's policy, there is no record that any Jews in Leo's reign were forcibly baptized without the formality of a decree. And there is reason to believe that, whatever the novel said, they did not lose the protection of the legislation they had always enjoyed. There was scarcely a sign in the *Basilica* that their condition differed from what it had been at the time of the *Epanagogē*. The privileges and the restrictions of the codes were exactly repeated. The punishment for apostates remained unchanged. The only possible echo of Leo's ideas was that Justinian's regulation on the reading of the scriptures was made compulsory instead of permissive: the locally spoken language had to be used, the alternative of Hebrew was omitted.[28] This silence is extraordinary. Neither the absence of a formal decree of forced baptism, nor Leo's concept of the novel as specifically an instrument of day-to-day legislation is sufficient to explain it. Whether Leo's novel on the Jews ante-dated the *Basilica* or whether, as is sometimes supposed regarding his novels as a whole, it constituted an addition to it, it is extraordinary that what amounted to an instruction for the obliteration of a considerable number of sections should never have been implemented, either during the completion of the *Basilica* or in the form of an amendment. Neither was Leo's concept of a code as an instrument of juridical principle likely to have made him hesitate. He meant, after all, to jettison a principle which had been a part both of Byzantine and of pre-Christian Roman jurisdiction. And all his legislative work showed him to be a ready innovator not in the least inhibited by precedent, in contrast to most Byzantine emperors, if he thought that the needs of the State demanded radical alterations.[29] The reason for the silence of the *Basilica*, the reason for the absence of compulsory baptisms whether 'official' or 'unofficial', was probably that Leo's novel was never enforced. Its existence conclusively disproves that he explicitly reversed his father's policy: that 'he annulled the evil decree'. On the contrary, his declared intention was to supply its omissions. Thus, for a time, the attempt continued to compel the Jews to a show of Christianity—to a life according to its ceremonies and customs. But Leo found that the Jews were indeed 'as changeless as the Ethiopian'. In spite of the weakness of some, the tenacity of most proved too much for their persecutors as it had in the past and would do in the future. So Leo quietly abandoned his attempt, as had Heraclius and Leo III before him. The novel remained, but the rest of imperial legislation was not affected. Aḥima'atz himself may have indicated when the persecution actually ended. When he said that the light of the sun was hidden, he added that it remained hidden for twenty-five years. This could have been a simple chronological error (there are others in his story), since Basil was dead twelve years after the persecution had begun, or the Hebrew word for twenty-five might have been necessary so as to rhyme that couplet.[30] But it might have meant that the persecution actually ended in 899. Of course, Aḥima'atz thought it dramatically more appropriate to make this date coincide with the change of emperors. For what was remembered in his day was that it was under Leo that the Jews had been allowed 'to return to the worship of their God as in the days of old'.

However, this freedom to enjoy the privileges granted by the Codes did not last for very long. Leo's abortive attempt to complete his father's work was renewed by Romanus I. How this came about was described by the Doge of Venice, Peter II, in a letter to the German emperor, Henry I, a copy of which was read to a council of the western church held at Erfurt in 932. Certain

94

Jews of Jerusalem, who had prematurely boasted of their victory in a Jewish-Christian debate, had suffered miraculous punishment. And mass conversions had followed:

> Then the patriarch of Jerusalem sent his representative to Constantinople with letters for the emperor Romanus, wherein he related all that God had deigned to make manifest, exhorting the emperor, in as much as all the Jews of Jerusalem had become Christian, to convert all the Jews of his realm to faith in Christ. Whereupon the emperor ordered all the Jews to be baptised. Yet the Jews themselves, hearing of the divine miracle, freely and of their own accord believed, and accepted baptism.[31]

This description cannot be accepted as it stands. It is very difficult to believe that Christians under Muslim rule were allowed to proselytize—with or without divine intervention to make their efforts successful—on the scale that it implies. But it is not impossible that some conversions were made. Christian influence in Jerusalem was exceptional. In the second half of the century a Jewish scholar there complained how 'the uncircumcized had reached such a position that they attack us to drive us forth from the holy city and separate us from it'.[32] This complaint was echoed in Muslim sources which bemoaned the decline of Islāmic culture in Jerusalem, and spoke of a Christian community strong enough to levy taxes on the sale of goods and to hold various trading monopolies, oppressing the poor and making the rich envy them.[33] Of course, Peter was not an unprejudiced reporter. His hope was that the German emperor with other western rulers would be inspired to follow the example of the patriarch and of Romanus. That is why he caused an exaggerated version of events to be read out at Erfurt. The whole circumstance inevitably recalls the legend that Heraclius persecuted the Jews as part of a joint campaign agreed with the Franks and the Visigoths. But these reservations do not invalidate the substance of Peter's information: that shortly before the year 932 Romanus ordered the conversion of the Jews.

His reasons can only be guessed at. They were probably political and had nothing to do with the immediate Jewish situation. Romanus, like Basil, was an interloper and a usurper. The son of an Armenian peasant, he had risen to be a naval commander with victories to his credit. After the short and undistinguished reign of Leo's brother, Romanus, by force and by fraud, managed to outwit the various magnates struggling for control over Leo's only son, the fourteen-year old Constantine VII. In order to give himself Macedonian authority, he married Constantine to his daughter Helena. But his ambition was to found a separate, if allied dynasty. In the last days of the year 919, he had himself crowned emperor, with his own son, Christopher, as 'co-emperor' (a normal Byzantine custom for the ensuring of a peaceful succession), taking precedence over Constantine. It was not long before Romanus, like Basil, had overcome the handicap of his path to the throne and was adequately fulfilling his duties as head of the ruling institution. He dealt effectively with his remaining rivals. He proved himself a good administrator, particularly in his choice of senior officials. By 934 he was strong enough, as we noted in the first chapter, to challenge the encroachments of the provincial landowners on the smallholdings of the themes. He was equally fortunate in foreign affairs. In 927, by adroit diplomacy, he virtually ended the long-standing threat of Bulgaria, grown no less after the acceptance of Byzantine Christianity, and thus was able to expand and consolidate the Byzantine penetration of the Balkans begun by Basil. A few years later, he began to turn Basil's counter-attack against the Muslims in the east into an actual conquest of Muslim territory while, by 936, he stabilized, if he did not improve, the Byzantine position in Italy. If judged against the background of his dynastic ambitions and of these events, it is possible that his decision to return to Basil's policy on the Jews, to the principles enunciated in Leo's novel, was taken to show that in this respect too he was no worse than a true Macedonian.

His decision may also have been prompted by ecclesiastical considerations, if not precisely those which Peter conveyed in his letter. Constantine had been the fruit of Leo's fourth marriage, over the canonical legality of which there had been a prolonged and violent quarrel between the strict and the moderates. When Romanus was climbing to power the strict party had been victorious, and he naturally worked in close co-operation with their patriarch, Nicholas Mysticus, in whose eyes Constantine was automatically illegitimate. But Romanus was then genuinely uninterested in religious questions, he was concerned only to extend the control of his family over organs of government. Christopher was senior co-emperor. When Nicholas died in 931, another son, Theophylact, was made patriarch. Even after allowance has been made for the prejudices of the same historian who was Basil's biographer, it is clear that Theophylact was a thorough 'moderate' in so far as he was totally indifferent to everything but the welfare of his pedigree stables. Although by then Romanus had little to fear from any opposition whether ecclesiastical or secular—even the pope readily sent his legates to Theophylact's installation—it is possible that he wished still further to enhance his standing by an act which would be popular both with the strict and the moderates. Besides, it was an act which happened to fit in very well with his foreign policy. He saw how his enterprise to re-conquer Muslim held territory might be greatly helped by strengthening the intermittent contacts that existed with the patriarchates under Muslim rule. In 937, friendly letters were exchanged with Antioch and with Alexandria.[34] Thus, it was in order to establish similar relations with the patriarch of Jerusalem that Romanus was ready to listen to his story of miraculous conversions and to obey his exhortation to order the conversion of his own Jewish subjects. And it may be that the story of Byzantine Jews freely and of their own accord accepting baptism had this much basis in fact: Romanus may have begun as Basil had—by persuasion and bribery. At any rate, for some time there was no record of any persecutions. At first his order essentially remained what it was meant to be—a formal gesture intended to meet purely political needs, without the motivation of a missionary ideal. Of course, from the Jewish point of view, there was nothing formal about it. Whether some were once again badgered into baptism or no, the order was the renewal of an explicit threat to their existence.

Towards the end of the reign of Romanus, the threat became a reality. He finally understood that he would never supplant the

97

Macedonians despite all his military and political achievements. Disappointed in his dynastic hopes, he was aware of the growing support for Constantine. Fear of what awaited him drove him into remorse for his crimes and into hysterical repentance. He became a prey to a gloomy and superstitious religion, and passed his days with the extremest of the strict.[35] It was then that he seriously applied what had been a mere tactic and began to persecute the Jews. And just as the original inception of his decision had been connected with his foreign policy, so its application produced international repercussions. The first of these had to do with the Khazars. Their full story cannot be re-told here. Their territory, north of the Caucasus, stretched when at its greatest extent from the Volga to the Crimea. Its importance for the Byzantines was that it lay, together with territory of other tribes, between the probable line of advance to the north-east and the new element of a rapidly crystallizing and frequently hostile Russian state. At the end of the eighth, or at the beginning of the ninth century, the rulers of the Khazars were converted to Judaism. This is how these Jewish Khazars and the persecution of the Jews by Romanus were described by the contemporary Arab historian and geographer 'Ali al-Mas 'ūdi:

> The king of the Khazars had already become a Jew in the caliphate of Hārūn al-Rashīd (i.e. between A.D. 786 and 809) and there joined him Jews from all the lands of Islām and from the country of the Greeks. Indeed, the king of the Greeks at the present time, the Year of the Hegīra 332 (= A.D. 943–944), has converted the Jews in his kingdom to Christianity and has coerced them ... so many Jews took flight from the country of the Greeks to Khazaria, as we have related.[36]

In spite of these influxes, which originally may even have included refugees from the persecutions of Leo III, the Jewish Khazars remained in a minority among a mixed population of Muslims and Christians.[37] When they heard of the new persecution, it was on the latter that they turned and 'slew many of the uncircumcized', in the hope that this threat to the rest would help their brothers in Byzantium. But Romanus sent rich gifts to the Russian Oleg who attacked Khazaria, and occupied a city on its western frontier.[38] Romanus was impelled quite as much by strategic as by religious motives. During the second half of the ninth century, Khazar Judaism had begun to spread among the Alans, a group of tribes in the Caucasian foothills, and, when Christian missions had repaired some of the damage, the Khazars had not only defeated the Alans in war but had reconciled them to alliance by a dynastic marriage.[39] This was reason enough for Romanus to seek Russian friendship. Whatever the reason, the intervention of the Khazars on behalf of Byzantine Jews did not succeed.

The second international repercussion also had a Khazar aspect but its main importance was for the relations between Byzantium and Muslim Spain. There was another intervention on behalf of Byzantine Jews, at the very end of Romanus' reign, which brought not only the persecution, but the whole Macedonian policy towards the Jews, finally to an end. The flight into Khazaria indicated that the persecution had been both general and severe. But, as in the time of Basil, its worst effects were felt in Byzantine Italy. While the attacks were short, two or three days —perhaps that was why Ahima'atz said nothing of them—their results were serious. At Bari, sacred books were burned. Warning reached Otranto in time to save the Scrolls of the Law. But the Rabbi Menahem there lay in prison. One of his disciples, the merchant Elijah, had been strangled; another, Samuel, had only escaped after torture. The rabbi Isaiah, 'a learned man the like of whom we have not seen', in despair, pierced his own throat with a knife. At Oria many of the community took flight.[40] These events were related by the Jews of Bari in a letter to Hasdai ibn Shaprut, chief minister at the court of the caliph 'Abd al Rahman III at Cordova. Hasdai was an extraordinary figure for any age. Physician, scientist and scholar, an ornament to the efflorescence of Spanish-Jewish culture, he was also possessed of great personal charm and enjoyed the complete confidence of his master, for whom he gained many diplomatic triumphs in the confused manoeuvring of the caliphate among the rising and mutually hostile Spanish Christian kingdoms. And yet, despite the variety and quantity of his responsibilities, he found time to be a God-

8

fearing Jew, interested and anxious for the welfare of the most distant communities. His correspondence with the king of the Khazars is a major, if continually disputed, source, as is the account of the embassy he sent there for further information, which did not get beyond Constantinople. It is for the problems of his connection with the Khazars that he is best known today. But his reaction to the news from Bari is clear enough. He was aware of what was happening; he had made enquiries, but the messenger with the reply—the same Samuel, understandably willing to leave Italy—had been ambushed by robbers and the despatches were lost. Now, after a delay of nine months, Ḥasdai knew the full extent of the disaster.[41] He immediately appealed to the Byzantine government, and the way he did it showed how familiar he was with the Byzantine situation.

Romanus had fallen, or was about to fall. The legitimate emperor, Constantine VII, at last in power, had not been idle during his period of waiting. He too, like every Macedonian, wanted to distinguish himself in the grand enterprise of the re-conquest of Muslim occupied territories and had long meditated an attack on Crete, whose raiders infested the Aegean and had necessitated the building of special fortifications to defend Athens.[42] For this campaign the neutrality, or the friendship of Muslim Spain was desirable. In the year 945, Byzantine ambassadors at Cordova had the friendliest of receptions. The gift of a Greek work on botany and medicine, afterwards translated by Ḥasdai into Arabic with the help of a Greek monk specially sent for this purpose, was particularly appreciated.[43] Ḥasdai knew of the preparations for this embassy, as a fragment of a letter of his to Constantine, filled with the compliments demanded by diplomatic protocol, undoubtedly implies.[44] But when Ḥasdai intervened on behalf of Byzantine Jewry he did not write to Constantine, to avoid the risk of addressing the wrong person if the palace revolution did not succeed after all. Instead he wrote to Helena, Constantine's wife and at the same time the daughter who could influence Romanus by an exceptional shrewdness and force of character.[45] And so Ḥasdai begged Helena to 'take pity on the remnant of the Jewish nation, by giving the Jews her royal protection'.[46] It is impossible to say whether it was as wife or as daughter that Helena explained how important Ḥasdai's favour was for Byzantine strategic interests, whether it was Romanus at the end of his reign, or Constantine at the beginning of his, who halted the really serious persecution almost as soon as it had been launched. We only know that the persecution stopped.

The original purpose of the Spanish-Byzantine negotiations came to nothing. In 949, Constantine sent an expedition to Crete but failed to drive out the Muslims. Perhaps it was because Ḥasdai was no longer important to Byzantium that his envoy to the Jewish Khazars, Itzḥāk ben Nathān, when he reached Constantinople early in the next decade was treated with due courtesy but was not allowed to proceed further.[47] Yet this courtesy was an indication that Ḥasdai's intervention in Byzantine affairs had nevertheless succeeded. The persecutions had not been resumed. And the Jews finally emerged from the uncertainties and perils that had beset them for the previous seventy years. The new situation of relative confidence in their surroundings had practical results, to be discussed in the next chapter, towards the end of the tenth and at the beginning of the eleventh century. However, there was an earlier sign. A mystical Hebrew text, usually called the *Vision of Daniel*, because of its opening with the appearance of the angel to Daniel, had some significant things to say about the emperors from Michael III to Constantine.[48] Michael was a blasphemer who 'made mock priests'. He 'brought low the congregation of God'. Basil's was a reign of conquest and riches. First he restored the people who had been brought low, but then he baptized them by force. Leo granted freedom to the 'worshippers of the Most High'. Romanus persecuted them, however 'by means of expulsion, not by destruction, but mercifully'. Of Constantine the *Vision* spoke in unreservedly glowing terms. The reason why the *Vision*, while in part confirming other sources, nevertheless so explicitly contradicted them is to be found in what it said about Basil and Michael. Its contrast of the conqueror who brought prosperity to Byzantium and the blasphemer was precisely the contrast made by Basil's biographer. According to him, Michael's murder was justified by his blasphemies, the worst of which had been a parade of nobles dressed as priests with a mock patriarch at their head.[49] And it was not Michael who began to drive the Muslims out of Asia Minor, but Basil.[50] In other words, the writer of the *Vision* was so impressed by the improvement of conditions under Constantine that he not only praised him but was influenced by his version of Macedonian history. That was why the *Vision* turned Basil's blandishments to the Jews into acts of positive benevolence, while Michael, in contrast, had to be their persecutor. But the *Vision* went further. In satisfaction at the turn of events, it even had a good word to say for Romanus, who was scarcely a favourite with Constantine. For the *Vision*, Romanus, with his political and military achievements, was no less a Macedonian than Basil. That was why the flight of Jews to Khazaria became 'merciful expulsion' instead of 'destruction'. The significance of this attitude appeared in the concluding section of the *Vision*, which spoke of the Last Days and of the coming of the Messiah. There was a complete contrast to the usual apocalyptic prophecies of the mutual destruction of Christian and Islāmic power. The final struggle was to be between Rome and Constantinople, between the old Rome, irredeemably sunk in corruption, and the new. The old Rome would perish, and it was from victorious Constantinople that the Messiah would judge the nations of the world. This whole-hearted partisanship of the Byzantine empire in its continuous struggle against western pretensions reflected a high degree of Jewish identification with Byzantine interests. It indicated that the persecution had had little effect on those close relations between Jews and non-Jews which we have frequently noted, relations which may even have been strengthened when that persecution had come to an end.[51]

Notes

1 Cf. H. Grégoire, 'Les sources de l'histoire des Pauliciens', *Bulletin de l'Académie Royale de Belgique*, 22 (1936), pp. 95–114; M. Loes, 'Le mouvement paulicien à Byzance', *Byzantinoslavica* 24 (1963), pp. 258–86; 25 (1964), pp. 52–68
2 *Vita Basilii XCV*= Theoph. Cont., pp. 341–2, on Bulgaria beginning in

XCVI, p. 342; Doelger, *Regesten*, 478 for complete list of sources, some of which will be referred to here (though his date is inexplicably wrong); trans. Starr, *Jews in the Byzantine Empire*, no. 69, no. 77

3   F. Cumont, 'La conversion de Juifs byzantins au ix-ième siècle', *Revue de l'Instruction Publique en Belgique*, 46 (1903), pp. 11–15

4   *Photii patriarchae epistolae II*.13 (= MPG vol. 102, col. 829A)

5   E.g. *Georgii Cedrenia Historiarum Compendium*, MPG, vol. 121, col. 1128C; *Joannis Zonarae Epitome Historiarum XVI.10*, ed. Dindorf, vol. 4, p. 35; *Symeonis Magister Annales de Basileo Macedone X*, ed. B. G. Niebuhr, CSHB (1838), p. 691

6   *Georgii Hamartoli Chronicon V.9*, ed. B. G. Niebuhr, CSHB (1838), p. 842

7   *Sefer Yuḥasīn* (The Book of Genealogies), ed. A. Neubauer, *Medieval Jewish Chronicles* (*Anecdota Oxeniensa*; Semitic series), vol. 2 (Oxford 1895), pp. 120–1; trans. Starr, *Jews in the Byzantine Empire*, no. 68

7a Cf. Runciman, *Byzantine Civilisation*, p. 257; G. Downey, *Constantinople in the Age of Justinian* (Oklahoma 1960), p. 113

8   *Sefer Yuḥasīn*, pp. 115–17; trans. Starr, *ibid.*, nos. 64, 65, 66; cf. *The World History of the Jewish People*, Second series, vol. 2 (ed. C. Roth) (Tel-Aviv 1966), pp. 104–6

9   *Sefer Yuḥasīn* p. 124

10 J. Schirman, *An Anthology of Hebrew Verse from Italy* III.1, (Berlin 1924), p. 4 (in Hebrew); trans. Starr, *ibid.*, no. 62

11 I. Sonne, 'Note sur une Keroba d'Amittai publiée par Davidson', REJ 98 (1934), p. 83

12 J. Marcus, 'Studies in the Chronicle of Aḥīma'atz', PAAJR, 5 (1933–4), pp. 88–90

13 A. Neubauer, 'The Early Settlement of the Jews in Italy', JQR (old series) 4 (1892), p. 614

14 Baron, vol. 3, p. 180; pp. 315–16 (note 7)

15 F. C. Conybeare, 'Ananias of Shirak: The Tract on Easter', BZ 6 (1897), p. 579

16 *Auxilii de ordinatibus a Formosa papa factis XXXIX*, ed. E. Duemmler, *Auxilius und Vulgarius* (Leipzig 1866), pp. 109–10; trans. Starr, *Jews in the Byzantine Empire*, no. 72

17 A. A. Vasiliev, *Byzantium and the Arabs* (867–959) (St Petersburg 1902), part 2, pp. 69–70 (in Russian), cf. Starr, *ibid.*, no. 61

18 *Sefer Yuḥasīn*, p. 118, trans. Starr, *ibid.*, no. 56; cf. M. Amari, *Storia dei Musulmani di Sicilia* (Cantania 1933), vol. 1, pp. 513–25. For the military and political situation, see Ostrogorsky, *Byzantine State*, p. 201, pp. 210–12

19 *Procheires nomos XXXIX*.31, 32; ed. J. and P. Zepes, *Jus graecoromanum* vol. 2 (Athens 1931), p. 219; trans E. H. Freshfield, *A Manual of Eastern Roman Law* (Cambridge 1928), p. 154; cf. Starr, *ibid.*, no. 60

20 *Epanagogē IX.13*, ed. Zepos, vol. 2, p. 255; trans. Starr, *ibid.*, no. 75

21 See Ostrogorsky, *Byzantine State*, pp. 212–14

22 *Nomocanon XIV titulorum XII.2, 3*; ed. J. B. Pitra, *Iuris Ecclesiastici Graecorum Historia et Monumenta*, vol. 2 (Rome 1868), p. 601, p. 604; mentioned but content not described by Starr, *ibid.*, in note to his no. 75, as above

23 *Sefer Yuḥasīn*, p. 117; trans. Starr, *ibid.*, no. 78

24 Novel 55, ed. Zepos, vol. 1, p. 125; ed. and trans. P. Noailles and A. Dain, *Les Nouvelles de Léon VI le Sage* (Paris 1944), pp. 208–11; cf. Starr, *ibid.*, nos. 70, 84

25 Novel 65, ed. Zepos, vol. 1, p. 136; ed. and trans. Noailles and Dain, pp. 238–9; cf.C.Th.XVI.7.3 (= Pharr, p. 466); C.I. 1.7.2. (= Krueger, p. 60)

26 Cf. N. A. Popov, *The Emperor Leo the Wise and his Reign* (in Russian), Moscow (1892), pp. 194–6

27 Cf. Baron, vol. 3, p. 316, note 8

28 On apostates see *Basilicorum libri LX* 54.22, 23; ed. D. Heimbach, vol. 5 (Leipzig 1850), p. 894; on the scriptures, see I.1.52; ed. H. J. Scheltema and N. Van der Wal, Groningen-Gravenhage, series A, vol. 1 (1955), pp. 12–14; cf. Starr, *ibid*, no. 83 for trans. of all sections, and references to Justinian's code. But his *Basilica* sections do not always correspond with Scheltema or Heimbach

29 Popov, pp. 204–14

30 *Sefer Yuḥasīn*, p. 117:

    ‏... ‏וּשְׁקְעָה הַשֶּׁמֶשׁ שְׁנַיִם עֶשְׂרִים וַחֲמֵשׁ ...

31 E. Duemmler, *Gesta Berangarii imperatoris*, Halle (1871), p. 158; cf. Doelger, *Regesten*, no. 624; Starr, *Jews in the Byzantine Empire*, no. 90

32 Mann, *Texts and Studies*, vol. 2 (1935), pp. 18–22; on the probable date of this source, cf. L. Nemoy, *Karaite Anthology*, Yale Judaica Series, no. 7, New Haven (1952), pp. 69–71; p. 231; pp. 233–4

33 For this complaint of the Jerusalem-born Arab geographer al-Mukaddasi (also for the source in note above), see N. Golb, 'A Convert to Judaism who fled to Egypt at the beginning of the Eleventh Century' (in Hebrew), *Sefunot* 8 (1964), pp. 95–6

34 Vasiliev, *Byzantium and the Arabs (867–959)*, part 2, p. 22, cf. S. Runciman, *The Emperor Romanus Lecapenus and his Reign* (Cambridge 1929 and 1963), p. 77

35 Runciman, *ibid.* p. 231

36 Ali al-Mas'ūdi, *Murūj al-dhahab*, ed. and trans. C. Barbier de Meynard and Pavet de Courteille, *Les Prairies d'Or* (Paris 1861), vol. 2, pp. 8–9; see D. M. Dunlop, *History of the Jewish Khazars* (Princeton 1954), p. 89

37 On the conversion and its effects, see Dunlop, pp. 144–8, and for a sketch of the whole Khazar question with references to the bibliography see Baron, vol. 3, pp. 196–206

38 S. Schechter, 'An Unknown Khazar Document', JQR new series 3 (1912–1913), p. 208 (text) p. 217 (translation)

39 J. Brutzkus, *The Letter of a Khazar Jew of the 10th century* (in Russian) (Berlin 1924), p. 17, p. 27

40 Mann, *Texts and Studies*, vol. 1 (1931), text, pp. 23–5, commentary, pp. 12–14; cf. Starr, *Jews in the Byzantine Empire*, no. 94

41 Mann, *ibid.*; cf. Starr, *ibid.*, no. 95. On Ḥasdai ibn Shaprūṭ and his background, see H. Graetz, *History of the Jews* (4th edn. trans. A. B. Rhine) (New York 1930), pp. 103–15

42 cf. Vasiliev, *Byzantium and the Arabs (867–959)*, part 1, p. 271; Hitti, p. 451

43 Doelger, *Regesten*, nos. 657 and 659; Vasiliev, *Byzantium and the Arabs (867–959)*, part 1, pp. 270–8

44 Mann, *Texts and Studies*, vol. 1, p. 23
45 Runciman, *Romanus Lecapenus*, p. 79
46 Mann, *ibid.*, text: pp. 21–2, commentary (and on text in note 44, above): pp. 10–12; cf. Starr, *Jews in the Byzantine Empire*, no. 99 and Baron, vol. 3, pp. 305–6 (note 40)
47 Text in A. Kahana, *Sources of Jewish History*, vol. 1 (Warsaw 1922), p. 38 (in Hebrew); cf. Starr, *op. cit.*, no. 97; Dunlop, p. 143
48 Text and commentary in Hebrew by L. Ginsberg, *Ginzei Schechter*, vol. 1 (New York 1928), pp. 313–23 and by Even-Shmuel (also in Hebrew), *op. cit.*, pp. 232–52; cf. two short extracts trans. Starr, *op. cit.*, nos. 71 and 79. See below, Appendix I
49 Theoph. Cont., pp. 244–5
50 For these and other Macedonian falsifications, see H. Grégoire, 'Études sur l'épopée byzantine', *Revue des Études Grecques* 46 (1933), pp. 37–8
51 For this analysis, see A. Sharf, 'The *Vision of Daniel* as a source for the history of Byzantine Jews' (in Hebrew) *Bar-Ilan Annual* 4–5 (1967) pp. 197–208 as against S. Krauss, 'Un nouveau texte pour l'histoire judéo-byzantine', REJ 87 (1929), pp. 1–27

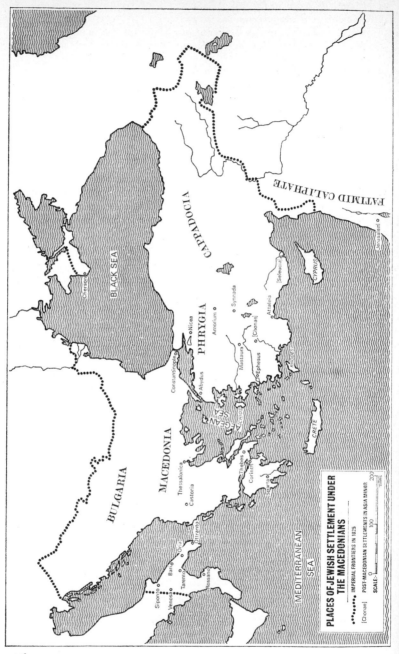

PLACES OF JEWISH SETTLEMENT UNDER THE MACEDONIANS

IMPERIAL FRONTIERS IN 1025

•••••• POST-MACEDONIAN SETTLEMENTS IN ASIA MINOR

[Chonae] POST-MACEDONIAN SETTLEMENTS IN ASIA MINOR

SCALE: 0 — 100 — 200 MILES

CHAPTER VI

The Eleventh-century Expansion

During the last years of the tenth century and the first years of the eleventh there was a noticeable migration of Jews to Byzantium from Muslim lands. It began for two reasons. The first was the changed military and political situation in the period of the great Macedonian victories. In 961, the island of Crete with its nest of Muslim raiders which had resisted Constantine VII fell to the general Nicephoras Phocas. During his reign as emperor (963–969), and under his successor John Tzimisces (969–976), more and more Muslim territory was reconquered in the east, including Antioch, Aleppo and most of the Syrian and Palestinian coast to Caesarea—perhaps even to Jaffa. Then John Tzimisces wrote triumphantly to Ashot III, the king of Armenia: 'All Phœnicia, Palestine and Syria has been freed from the tyranny of the Muslims and obeys the Romans (i.e. Byzantines). The great mountain of Lebanon recognizes our laws'.[1]

It was deliberate exaggeration to encourage an ally: the Byzantines had also driven the Muslims out of much of Armenia.[2] But it also reflected the mood of the time. To those who saw Byzantine troops where none had been seen for over three hundred years it seemed quite likely that John's claim would be easily substantiated. The balance of power had shifted, and there was good reason to expect an indefinite renewal of Byzantine rule throughout the eastern Mediterranean. This prospect was particularly welcome to the Jews. For the Byzantines might continue what they had begun with the capture of Crete and, when fully in control of the area, might get rid of all the raiders who infested it—something which no Muslim rulers, with their own conflicting interests, had ever seriously tried to do. And safe travel was always of primary importance. Jews had continually to cross and re-cross the Mediterranean. It was thus that distant communities kept in touch with the centres of learning in Egypt and in Palestine. Jewish trading ventures had also considerably developed. From the middle of the ninth century, the best-known organized group of Jewish merchants, the *Rādaniyā*, whose members were both skilled negotiators and accomplished linguists, used the port of Pelusium (near modern Port Said) for bringing the products of China to the markets of Constantinople, of France and of Spain.[3] Their base was within Muslim territory, but others traded, or voyaged on private affairs, out of Bari, out of Attaleia, out of Oria. And no traveller, no port was safe. In 925, for example, the most famous of the Amittai family, the physician Donnolo of whom we shall say more in Chapter VIII, only just escaped being carried into captivity in an Arab raid on Oria, while, in the same raid, 'ten learned and pious rabbis were slain'.[4] In 952, other members of the family were not so lucky when they were seized by raiders and 'sent across the sea'.[5] Not long after, four rabbis were seized and held to ransom while on a voyage between Bari and Alexandria.[6] At the beginning of the eleventh century there were instances of Jewish merchants suffering the same fate on voyages from Attaleia.[7] It was this unsatisfactory situation which the Byzantine ascendancy might alter. And so there were Jews in Syria and Palestine, witnesses of this ascendancy, Jews in Aleppo and in Caesarea who had suffered from the destruction caused by the contending armies, who instead of fleeing with the Muslims preferred to move north and west into Byzantium proper—attracted to the new source of peace and security, to the new source of power.[8]

The second reason for the beginning of the migration was also a question of security—the security given to Byzantine Jews by Constantine VII. It was not disturbed by his successors. The

Macedonian persecutions were never resumed: the ruling institution finally became reconciled to the impossibility of removing the Jewish anomaly by force. The improvement in conditions which had so impressed the author of the *Vision of Daniel* was maintained, and was well-marked enough to become known outside the frontiers of the empire; Elīsha bar Shināyā, head of the Nestorian Christians in Persia from 1008 to 1046, when expounding the superiority of his sect (with its own doctrine of the nature of Jesus) over both the Chalcedonites and the Monophysites, found it convenient to use the example of the privileges enjoyed by Byzantine Jews in one of his arguments:

> The Romans tolerate a large number of Jews in their state. They give them protection, allow them openly to adhere to their religion and to build their synagogues . . . the Jews in their cities may say 'I am a Jew'. He may belong to his religion and say his prayers. No one attacks him for this, prevents him from acting thus or puts obstacles in his way . . . Just as in Egypt women, children and other unfit persons are allowed to enter the priest's sanctuary, so the Jews may enter the churches of the Romans—while in Egypt they may even approach the altar.[9]

Of course, the Jews were not allowed to build synagogues or to enter churches in Byzantium, nor were the monophysite clergy of Egypt as lax in their ritual discipline as Elīsha alleged. But the exaggerations of his polemic, intended to prove the degenerate condition of his opponents, did not reduce the value of his evidence that the Byzantine state had explicitly renewed its official protection of Judaism. Indeed, Elīsha, an acute and meticulous observer, was careful to make a perpetually necessary distinction. He understood that in Byzantium official protection existed side by side with an equally explicit hostility. In another part of his exposition he referred just as plainly to that aspect: concerned to show that the mere power of the ruler could never prove the truth of the religion in his dominions, he pointed out how the indisputable power wielded by the Byzantine emperors had never convinced the Jews of the truth of Christianity, in spite of the fact that 'in that land, in the very centre of its power (i.e. in Constantinople) there were many Jews who endured humiliation and hatred'. It was because the exercise of such power could never prove the validity of a faith that the Jews continued to uphold their beliefs.[10] The essential ambivalence of the Byzantine Jewish situation had not changed: Elīsha was able, without contradicting himself, to strengthen his arguments by examples of how, at one and the same time, Byzantine Jews were both very well and very badly treated. Yet his vivid illustration of the legality of Judaism, in contrast to the bare mention of 'humiliation and hatred', left no doubt as to which aspect impressed him most: it was the fact that the period during which legality had been actively or potentially threatened had decisively come to an end. His assessment is all the more striking when it is remembered that it must have been made in the knowledge of how Jews were treated who lived, as he did, under Muslim rule and who were generally better off than those under the Christians.

There is evidence that there were Jews in Syria and Palestine who made the same assessment when the Byzantine reconquest had faced them with this sort of comparison. A Palestinian apocalyptic text of the period, also in the name of the prophet Daniel, expressed as favourable an attitude to Byzantium as had the author of the *Vision*. The final struggle between Islām and Christianity had begun—but it would be the victory of Christianity which would presage the last days and the coming of the Messiah.[11] As in the *Vision*, this was a complete departure from the usual prophecies which had always spoken of the mutual destruction of the two contenders. Nor were the victories of John Tzimisces alone responsible for this departure. The victories of the later Heracleians, the destruction of the Muslim besiegers of Constantinople by Leo III had had no such effect on Messianic expectations. Thus, those Jews who immigrated from Syria and Palestine to Byzantium towards the end of the tenth century were not only influenced by Byzantine ascendancy. Such an influence was certainly one of the reasons—apart from the apparently improved prospects of security in the eastern Mediterranean. For there were monophysites, too, who hurried north to Antioch anxious to make their peace with the new authorities.[12] But the Jewish immigrants were also inspired by the hope of new possibilities when they saw how the Macedonian emperors had changed their Jewish policies. And there even existed a sufficiently convincing proof of this change: in 940 there had been a riot at Ashkelon when Jews had joined with Muslims in attacks upon churches and other sacred Christian buildings. The full weight of the Romanus persecution had been felt in Byzantine Italy not long after. Although there was no connection between these events, it could scarcely have passed unnoticed that, when in 966 a similar outbreak took place in Jerusalem, there followed nothing which could give this impression of reprisals against Byzantine Jews.[13]

It was this hope of comparatively good conditions that encouraged more Jews from Muslim lands to settle in Byzantium during the second decade of the eleventh century. This time, there was also a need to find a place of refuge. The Egyptian caliph al-Ḥākīm (996–1021) was a religious fanatic—some said to the point of insanity. He began by plaguing the Jews with derogatory, if not especially damaging, restrictions of the sort customary in Byzantium: for example, much as the Quinisext Council had warned Christians, he told Muslims not to mingle with Jews at the public baths; as Benjamin of Tudela was to notice at Constantinople, he forbade the Jews to ride on horseback.[14] In 1013, he invited both Jews and Christians

'to go to Greek lands with their families, their goods, their chattels and all they possessed . . . in all tranquillity and security, as a sign of his goodness and benevolence to them, without compelling a single one of them to go, but giving them the freedom of choice'.[15]

Many Christians, although they were, of course, monophysites, immediately accepted this offer. The Jews were at first unwilling to take a similar risk.[16] However, they gradually discovered that the alternative was the withdrawal of the toleration they had so long enjoyed under the Muslims. Ḥākīm forgot his 'goodness and benevolence'. The power of the Egyptian caliphs at that time extended over Palestine and the Lebanon. Synagogues were destroyed in those parts not under Byzantine control, while in Lebanese Tripoli the whole Jewish quarter was burned down.[17]

Then it was that, between 1016 and 1019 (when Ḥākīm abandoned these proceedings as inexplicably as he had embarked upon them) there was a migration of Egyptian Jews to Byzantium.[18] This was not because there was nowhere else for them to go when suddenly faced with the necessity of flight. They had had warning enough, and Muslim Spain at least was always open to them. There had even been a hint that life in Byzantium might not be without its difficulties: at the height of the persecution, an appeal to the south Italian communities had had to be regretfully turned down for lack of funds.[19] Byzantium was a deliberate choice, based on the same kind of assessment that the Jews of Syria and Palestine had made, the same kind as that made by Elīsha of Nisibis.

These favourable assessments proved to be largely justified. The immigrants came at the beginning of a long period during which the Byzantine communities were able to develop undisturbed. Not only were there no further attempts at forced baptism, no further threats to legal status; there was also no deterioration of conditions because of the imposition of new disabilities or the stricter interpretation of old ones, in the way that there had been under Justinian. Collections of laws which derived from the work of Basil I and Leo VI were quite free from this tendency—in contrast to Justinian's legislation on the Jews which derived, as we saw, directly or indirectly from the usually milder legislation of Theodosius. The so-called 'Major Synopsis', which was compiled between 964 and 968 and which acquired great juridical authority, merely repeated with slight verbal changes all the privileges and prohibitions listed in the *Basilica*.[20] That this was no automatic repetition can be inferred from what was thought worthy of inclusion by the authors of smaller collections. The prohibitions most frequently repeated were those of owning Christian slaves, the punishments for those circumcising a Christian or for any kind of proselytizing activity.[21] These repetitions, which began at about the same time as the compilation of the 'Synopsis' and continued throughout the eleventh century, showed that the Jews had regained and kept a secure enough position to elicit this particular choice—a position that made it both possible and desirable to buy Christian slaves and to mix with Christians at the risk of irritating the government in its most sensitive spot by suspicions of spreading Jewish influence. Thus, the Jewish sections of the 'Synopsis' constituted a general recognition that, whatever damage the Macedonian persecutions had done, the Jews were again at once an integrated and an alien element of Byzantine society. There was even an indication that the degree of integration was greater than it had been for many years. An addition to the *Epanagogē* at the end of the tenth century and a revision of Basil's 'Handbook' compiled during the eleventh century, emphasized at length the impossibility of a Jew holding a civil or military appointment. Should a Jew, nevertheless, have succeeded in getting one through the exercise of political influence, he was to be fined thirty pounds in gold and 'suffer the fate of a *cohortalis*'.[22] Now, a *cohortalis* was the name given to the lowest grade of clerk employed by provincial governors. His wages were minimal, his status traditionally despicable. His duties were not only exceptionally burdensome but also universally unpopular: he had to report infringements of tax and customs regulations.[23] However, he was incontestably a government employee. This new formulation of one of the oldest of Jewish disabilities had, therefore, important implications. Certain government employment was again possible, as it had been in the time of Theodosius and Justinian, on condition that, in the spirit of Justinian's novel regarding the decurions, 'the pains and penalties outweighed the benefits'.[24] And there were Jews with powerful enough connections to use the opportunities of such employment to rise higher—this was why part of their punishment was reversion to their former rank. Nor, in this respect, was there discrimination against Jews. Promotion from the rank of *cohortalis*, and from various equivalents, was barred to all. In the Code of Theodosius it was even provided that those who somehow obtained it would not only be demoted, but would disqualify their children, if not otherwise ineligible as the Jews were, also from applying for appointment to the higher ranks.[25]

Apart from the evidence of the collections, there were specific enactments which suggested that there had been complete recovery after the persecutions. An imperial instruction to the guilds of Constantinople regulating manufacture and marketing, probably issued in its final form under Nicephoras Phocas, included a section prohibiting the supply of raw silk 'to Jews and merchants who might sell it outside the city'.[26] The significance of the prohibition in the present context was that Byzantine Jews, as distinct from the earlier, *Rādaniyā* Jews, were now handling this most expensive of products on a scale comparable to other exporters who might defy the government's monopoly. And this development was part of a general expansion in commercial activity. In 992, Venice was granted a trading privilege of the sort eventually ruinous to Byzantium: her ships were granted preferential treatment in Byzantine ports. A condition was that no non-Venetian merchants should be carried, and Jewish merchants were thought important enough to be specially mentioned in this category.[27] But not only were exporters and merchants prospering. There is evidence of the economic potentialities of the Jewish smallholder. While property never became a primary interest for them, Byzantine Jews, ever since the Jewish farmers of Antioch before the Arab conquest, had continued to hold land. For, in contrast to western custom, there was nothing in Byzantine law to prevent them. The Basilian persecution left a member of the Amittai family in undisturbed possession of land near Oria.[28] A legal manual on the tenure of real property prepared for the Emperor Basil II (976–1025) contained no anti-Jewish restrictions.[29] In 1033, a Jew of Taranto bought a plot of land with two vineyards 'for himself and his heirs in complete possession', adding to it a similar plot in 1039.[30]

In 1049, an imperial chrysobull showed that the value of such holdings was not to be despised. The taxes and rents payable by the Jews on the island of Chios, fifteen families in all, were granted to the local monastery, to which they 'who had been wholly free and subject to no one were henceforth to be subject'.[31] This formula had no special Jewish application. It had become a common one in Byzantine land law. The 'wholly free' were those smallholders whose commitments were solely to the imperial authorities. The 'subject' were those whose commitments had been transferred to private landlords, ecclesiastical or secular,

whose semi-feudal tenants they had thus become.[32] These transfers were the result of that decay of the Heracleian land settlement
against which the emperors had vainly fought. Transfers to
ecclesiastical landlords were thought to be the lesser of two evils
and were often deliberately made in order to forestall someone
politically dangerous from adding to his wealth. We do not know
if there was this risk in Chios, we do know, however, that in 1044
the same monastery had acquired lordship over twenty-four
Christian families.[33] The two chrysobulls were not identical. The
one transferring the Jews began with the derogatory preamble
normal in all Jewish legislation. It also used an unusual fiscal term
which has since been variously interpreted regarding the question
of a Jewish tax in Byzantium, to which we shall return in the
last chapter. In the present context the important fact is that,
for one reason or another, the transfer of both these Jewish and
these Christian smallholders to the monastery was considered to be
a gift worth making. In the event, the income from the Jewish
smallholders turned out to be good enough for the monks to
ensure that the transfer was confirmed twice—in 1062 and in 1079
—and for the authorities to add to the first confirmation a stricter
definition of what precisely had been granted:

> Whereas according to the above-mentioned (i.e. the 1049)
> chrysobull fifteen Jewish families were assigned to the said
> monastery, by the present all the Jews on the island are estimated
> at that number. They are obliged to reside in the premises belong-
> ing to the monastery, near their appointed overlord, on penalty
> of triple the amount of the rent and of the tax. Further, the island
> shall be inaccessible to Jews from outside, while all children born
> into the families of the local Jews shall also belong to the mon-
> astery.[34]

It may be that the eventual effect of these provisions was to change
for the worse the status of Jews in a number of Mediterranean
communities by setting a precedent for restrictions on freedom
of movement.[35] But their original purpose was to ensure that
the monastery benefited no more or no less than was its due.
They confirmed what was quite usual in the eleventh century:
that tenants became the virtual property of the estate to which

they had been transferred by grants of this kind.[36] On the other hand, this transfer as all such transfers was limited. New Jewish settlers were forbidden, so as to avoid the possibility of the monastery adding them to those whose rents and taxes it was already collecting, thus depriving the imperial treasury of potentially substantial payments.

In fact, Byzantine Jews enjoyed the same freedom of movement that all citizens had both within the empire and, when circumstances allowed, beyond its frontiers. Thus Rabbi Hananel ben Paltiel, one of the Amittais, had only to get the permission of the Muslim authorities to leave North Africa for a journey through Byzantine Italy in search of family belongings saved from the disasters that had struck Oria in a previous generation. When it was argued that, according to a Talmudic ruling, he who saved articles from fire, flood or an invading army thereby became their owner, Hananel went to Constantinople and returned with an imperial document which 'by way of compromise' got him the return of some old clothes and a copy of the Pentateuch.[37] About the year 1000, the only difficulty facing a Jew of Kiev on a journey across Byzantium to Jerusalem was lack of money, or letters of introduction which might supply it. He was helped on his way by the leaders of the community at Thessalonica.[38] As a Jewish pilgrim in Jerusalem he was soon to be one of many. In 1047, a high administrative official from the Persian province of Khurasān, on a journey through Syria and Palestine, noticed how 'from all the lands of the Greeks the Christians and Jews come unto Jerusalem in great numbers, in order to make their visitation of the church and synagogue that is there'.[39] But it was not only journeys made with the blessing of the authorities that were possible. The aftermath of a riot that broke out at Constantinople in 1042 showed how, for some time past, the Jews participated in that drift to the capital which the authorities, as we noted in connection with population statistics, were energetically but vainly trying to check. The rioters had included 'many aliens— Armenians, Arabs and Jews . . . and the king commanded that there should not remain in the city anyone who had entered it during the last thirty years . . . then there went out close on a hundred thousand souls'.[40] The Jewish newcomers, whatever their proportion and however exaggerated the total figure, were probably the result of the waves of immigration from Syria and Egypt, the prey of that universal attraction Constantinople exercised on them as on all the rest that wished to settle there.

The riot pointed to another aspect of integration. Its cause had been the suspicion that the emperor Constantine IX (1042–1055), who was not of imperial descent, had tried to make sure of his throne by murdering two Macedonian princesses, the last representatives of the dynasty—which by then commanded great popular support. It was only when the two were produced to the people and were seen to be unharmed that the riot was quietened, and it was only by marrying one of them that Constantine was able finally to legitimize his position. It was, therefore, in furtherance of a popular demand that Jews had joined with non-Jews— exactly as they had at Antioch in the fifth and in the sixth century, at Constantinople in the sixth and in the seventh. To the role of the Jews within the urban population of those days there may, in the eleventh century, have been an even closer parallel. Although for hundreds of years the factions of the hippodrome had been no more than fulfilling functions of court ceremonial, the confusions and uncertainties attending the decline of the Macedonians temporarily revived their old political importance. But there was this new development: their most active and turbulent members were now coming from across the Golden Horn, from the suburbs of Pera and Galata where, since the time of Constantine VII, they had been organized in branches which were described as containing mixed racial elements.[41] And now it was in those suburbs that Jews had begun to settle: Pera towards the end of the eleventh century was to become the principal Jewish quarter. In the context of the factions there was no mention of Jews, but it may be supposed that they did not ignore an activity which had once so noticeably been theirs. In any event, two years before the riot in defence of the Macedonian princesses, there had been a clear enough example of Jew and non-Jew uniting in the struggle of another urban organization. When a short but dangerous revolt broke out in the Balkans and spread to Greece it was the urban guilds which remained predominantly loyal and which, as was noted in the first chapter, fought side by side with the imperial troops against the rebels. At Thebes and at Thessalonica it was the guilds of the silk workers that led the way.[42] And it was these guilds which, by then, had a substantial Jewish membership. Jewish workers in silk had existed at least a hundred years earlier,[43] while, as we have seen, they were to reach a high degree of skill, and be recognized for it, by the time of Benjamin of Tudela.

The return of relative security before the law, the return of a relatively strong economic position, and, most of all, the return of that peculiar relationship between Jews and non-Jews which marked off Byzantine Jews from those living under western Christian regimes, were the salient characteristics of the eleventh century—the eleventh-century expansion. In the first place it was a physical expansion: the new conditions, or their possibility, had encouraged immigration. But this expansion was not limited to the Jews of Constantinople, of whose increase in numbers the expulsions after the riot of 1042 had been a sign. The immigrants had not only been drawn to the capital. Their effect was discernible on the provincial communities of Greece and Asia Minor which, as distinct from those of Byzantine Italy, only began to establish themselves—so far as the Byzantine period is concerned—during the eleventh century. The earliest Byzantine reference to the Jews of Thessalonica was by the biographer of its patron saint Demetrius who more than once at the beginning of the seventh century miraculously saved it from the onslaught of the Slav tribes. On one of those occasions, 'the accursed children of the Hebrews' watched with 'the holy baptized' from the ramparts as the Slavs were routed.[44] Stripped of its hagiography, the story suggests the continuity of Jewish settlement at Thessalonica from pre-Byzantine periods. While this continuity, for all we know to the contrary, remained unbroken, the next definite reference was only at the beginning of the eleventh century when, as we have seen, the Jews of Thessalonica helped the traveller from Kiev on his way to Jerusalem. The singling out of the silk guilds for the part they played in 1040 was the first indication that the community was growing in size and importance. As for Thebes, the reference to the silk guilds there was the first in the Byzantine period from which the existence of a Jewish community might be supposed.

In Asia Minor, the risky voyages from Attaleia provided the first evidence of an established community there. Between 1020 and 1030 there were several instances of travellers, merchants and others being captured by Arab raiders and taken to North Africa. The Jews of Alexandria heard of ten such from whom 'much money was taken'. The captives were usually allowed to send news of their fate so that ransom could be demanded. The size of the ransoms for those from Attaleia confirmed that their financial standing was thought to be quite high. Seven merchants cost the Jews of Alexandria $233\frac{1}{3}$ dinars. A woman, a 'handsome and intelligent' young man and a boy, together cost twenty-four.[45] An Egyptian dinar was equivalent to a Byzantine gold piece, the bezant, or, as by then it was commonly called, the *nomisma*. At the beginning of the tenth century, a merchant from Asia Minor was considered to be rich if his total wealth could be reckoned at a thousand nomismata.[46] This reckoning remained applicable until the reign of Constantine IX (1042–55), for he it was who first began to lower the gold content of the coinage.[47] There is similar evidence that a community of comparable financial standing had come to be established at Mastaura, a little town on a tributary of the river Meander in western Asia Minor. A ransom of one hundred dinars was demanded for three Jews captured on a voyage from there. This evidence is supported by a marriage contract, to be mentioned in another context, of the year 1022, which estimated the bride's possessions at over thirty-five gold pieces. The traditional 'bride-price', the biblical *mohar*, was given in dinars, possibly because the bridegroom's family was itself of immigrant origin.[48]

The eleventh-century expansion was not only physical. It did not only consist of increased numbers, increased prosperity, of new or renewed Jewish settlement in areas of the empire seldom previously mentioned in this connection. The immigrants also brought with them a new element. They included a high proportion of Karaites, a sect which had sprung up over three hundred years before in the Mesopotamian centres of Jewish learning, but which eventually found most of its members in Egypt and in Palestine.[49] The Karaites claimed to be guided strictly by the scriptures, rejecting the whole of the 'Oral Law', that is the rabbinic interpretations embodied in the Talmud and its commentaries as accepted by the orthodox. There is no need to enter into the development and intricacies of Karaite doctrine—a subject quite outside our scope—in order to appreciate that long before the eleventh century there had developed Karaite interpretations which were fiercely defended against the ruling of the rabbis. It was this controversy, already endemic in Egypt and Palestine, that the immigrants brought with them to Byzantium. It is not certain when the first Karaites arrived. The earliest definite mention of them is in the tale of the seven ransomed merchants from Attaleia—three of them were Karaites. Clearly, then, they had been settled for some while. By the middle of the century, the effects had become considerable. Between 1060 and 1070, a dispute broke out in the community of Thessalonica over a particularly sensitive point—the dates of the festival calendar. The Karaites, it was alleged, had 'desecrated the divine festivals' by incorrectly celebrating the New Year and, not content with that, had complained to the authorities about the conduct of the orthodox. Whatever the truth of the accusation, the latter were fined 'one thousand hyperperian dinars'.[50] And, according to the tendency of many an extraordinary levy, this fine turned into an annual charge on the Jews of Thessalonica. It was remembered by them as the punishment they had to suffer for having permitted a heresy.[51] The disputes continued. By the time of Benjamin of Tudela a wall was separating the Karaites from the orthodox at Pera, built to prevent unnecessary clashes. Both these events illustrated the seriousness of the Karaite controversy, serious enough to disrupt communal life and to draw unwelcome official attention. The Thessalonica fine also suggested a high estimate of financial capabilities. For it was even heavier than it seemed. During the second half of the century, devaluation of the coinage had rapidly proceeded and standards of living had had to adjust themselves to this. But the term 'hyperperian' meant 'purified by fire'—hyper-pure, as it were.[52] In other words, payment had to be made in pre-devaluation coinage, a provision which was to become a common one in general taxation practice under Alexius I when it could add anything up to thirty per cent over the nominal sum.[53]

However, the coming of the Karaites had another and, in the long run, a far more important result. They brought an intellectual stimulus. It was only with them that, outside Byzantine Italy, definite references began to be made to the achievements of Byzantine Jewish learning. Of course, the immigration as such laid the basis, strengthening and renewing the links between the communities of Greece and of Asia Minor with the scholars of Alexandria and Jerusalem. The first non-Italian reference had no Karaite connection. At the beginning of the eleventh century, 'a learned Jew of Thessalonica with the aid of another sufficiently expert in the Law' made an impression in a Christian-Jewish debate.[54] But the first non-Italian Byzantine Jewish scholars whose names became known were themselves Karaites who drew their knowledge from traditional Karaite centres. About the year 1050, Tobiah ben Moses, born in Constantinople but educated in Jerusalem, became known for his Hebrew translations of Karaite works written in Arabic and for some liturgical poetry. And he became the virtual founder of the indigenous Karaite movement. He wrote a lengthy commentary on the Book of Leviticus which constituted a full-scale rebuttal of orthodoxy, his *Otsar Nehmad*, or 'Desirable Treasure'.[55] It was not surprising that the substance of the new learning continued as it began—largely polemical. Thus, towards the end of the century, the Karaite Jacob ben Simon translated a disquisition on the question which was as bitterly disputed as the festival calendar—the prohibited degrees of marriage. This was the *Sefer ha-ʿArayot*, or 'The Book of Incest', the work of the great Jerusalem Karaite Abū 'l-Farāj Furkān (Yeshuʿa ben Yehudā).[56] About the same time, Jacob ben Reuben produced a popular compilation of basic Karaite commentaries and rulings for the benefit of his Byzantine fellow sectarians which, appropriately enough, was called *Sefer ha-ʿOsher*, or 'The Book of Riches'.[57] It was attacks such as these that brought into prominence the first orthodox scholar of note who was not of Italian origin. From the end of the century, Rabbi Tobiah ben Eliezer of Castoria, again a community of which before then very little was heard, devoted much of his labours to refuting the Karaites. His outstanding achievement, of far more than merely Byzantine Jewish significance, was his midrashic scriptural commentary *Leḳaḥ Ṭov*, or 'A Goodly Doctrine'.[58]

It is against this background of relative security, numerical expansion, increased prosperity and the spread of learning to new areas, that some striking examples illustrative of Jewish influence, and of the non-Italian element within it in particular, have now to be considered. Towards the year 1066, Andreas, the archbishop of Bari, became very interested in Judaism. The upshot was that

> abandoning his land, his priesthood and his dignities, he went to the city of Constantinople and there circumcised his flesh. There-upon sorrows and evils afflicted him, and he arose and fled for his life from the uncircumcised, who were looking for him to kill him. . . . But the wicked saw what he had done, and they too entered into the Covenant of the Living God.[59]

The adventures of Andreas, extraordinary though they sound, were in the main real enough. They were related by another, better known convert to Judaism, the Norman proselyte Johannes or 'Obadiā, whom they profoundly impressed when he heard of them as a child, encouraging him later to take the step he did, and the accuracy of whose recollections of his subsequent life in Syria and Palestine has not been questioned. His reliability in this and in other details of his own story makes it initially probable that his account of the conversion of Andreas was also reliable. It is supported by what is otherwise known about him and about the politics of his day. He became archbishop in 1063, when Bari was the focus of the last stage in the Byzantine-Norman struggle for mastery of south Italy. Until Bari fell to the Normans in 1071, the chief protagonists there were various pro-Byzantine and pro-Norman ecclesiastical factions whose manoeuvrings were complicated by an obscure papal intrigue. Andreas was a prudent, pious and humble man, 'the angelic archbishop' they called him. He was a lover of the arts—he designed an elegant pulpit for the cathedral.

He was least suited to the situation at Bari and he fell a victim to it: his journey to Constantinople (apart from the religious doubts that had begun to trouble him) was to escape from it into a virtually self-imposed exile.[60] However, it was not till 1072 that another archbishop was presented to his see, and the appointment was not confirmed for several years more. The delay was partly due to continued intrigues, partly to the change of régime, but mostly because nobody wanted to believe that Andreas had actually decided to abandon Christianity together with his office.[61] Yet the situation at Bari was certainly one reason for his decision. His sensitive nature made him disgusted with ecclesiastical meddling in politics and impelled him to look for a purer path to God. At the same time there were reasons why this disgust should have been accompanied by a sympathetic interest in Judaism. There were recent instances of Jews falling innocent victims to political aims or religious fanaticism. At Bari itself, in 1051, the Jewish quarter had been burnt down to placate the citizens after the crushing of a revolt.[62] In the very year of his appointment to the archbishopric, an expedition against the Muslims of Spain had turned aside to persecute the Jews there and in the south of France fiercely enough to produce a letter of condemnation from the pope Alexander II.[63] In 1065, the Lombard duke of Benevento tried to force baptism on his Jewish subjects in anticipation, as he thought, of the wishes of his Norman masters.[64]

And these events could explain the most significant aspect of the story of Andreas: the completion of his conversion at Constantinople instead of in the shelter of one of the neighbouring Italian Jewish communities, of which Benevento was one, to be found both in Norman and in Lombard territory. His assessment must have been similar to that of the immigrants at the beginning of the century. Italy was passing out of Byzantine hands, and conditions for Byzantine Jews were likely to be easier than for Jews under western rulers. How accurate was his assessment? On the one hand, conditions in south Italy were not as bad as they seemed. The incident at Bari was an isolated one. Aḥīma'atz even left it out of his chronicle. And, in the event, the duke of Benevento was wrong: in south Italy, at least, the Normans turned out to be not illiberal in their treatment of their Jewish subjects.[65] On the other hand, however good the conditions in Byzantium the apostate from Christianity was still subject to the death penalty decreed by Leo VI. The apostasy of Andreas caused an exceptionally great scandal, infuriating, as was to be expected, both the ecclesiastical and the secular authorities. That was why he had to flee from those 'who were looking for him to kill him'—to spend the remainder of his days in Egypt where, obviously, life was safer for a Christian convert to Judaism. Nevertheless, in the most important respect, Andreas had been right. The truth of the information that his conversion was followed by others was supported by subsequent events. Towards the end of the century there were more conversions. Another ex-cleric, of whose identity nothing else is known except that he was certainly neither Andreas nor 'Obadiā, was learned enough in exegesis to present the patriarch with fourteen tractates showing the superiority of Jewish over Christian doctrine.[66] And the Byzantine rabbinate was bitterly attacked by a Jew who thought that unnecessary obstacles were being placed in the way of intending converts.[67]

Finally, Jewish influence and the relation between Jews and non-Jews was illustrated by events on the eve of the First Crusade. The approach of a vast host, whose composition and purpose was unknown except that it was on its way to Jerusalem, engendered a messianic excitement among the Jews throughout the lands of the eastern Mediterranean comparable to that at the beginning of the eighth century. Some of its results in Byzantium were described in a letter, whose provenance as well as whose destination are unknown but whose contents merited circulating to the heads of the communities in Egypt and in Palestine. All the congregations of Byzantium 'have been stirred', the writer declared, 'and have repented before God with fasting and almsgiving'. Some small congregations at Constantinople and across the Bosphorus were stirred enough to announce that the Messiah had indeed come, to be forthwith declared heretical by the rabbis—just as the followers of Severus had been. And for the same reason. The movement attracted Christians and Jews in common. When those Crusaders who were taking the land route had crossed the imperial frontier into Greece, both Christians and Jews began to spread reports of 'signs and great miracles'. The strongest effect was at Thessalonica,

> where the Christians have always hated the Jews most intensely . . . For had the signs and great miracles not taken place, and had the king not heard of it, not one of the Jews would have escaped. At the present time, they dwell in great security, free of the poll-tax and other levies. They sit garbed in prayer-shawls and do no work. We do not know what they are expecting and we are in constant dread lest it become known to the Gentiles (i.e. where the writer lived) and they kill us. And now, the governor himself and the archbishop say, 'Oh Jews, why remain in Saloniki? Sell your homes and property—the emperor protects them and no man may harm them. You have not yet set out, despite the fact that we have definitely learned that your Messiah has appeared'.[68]

Thus, on this occasion, a popular movement of Jews and Christians was powerful enough to force recognition of an unusual kind from the authorities. For the emperor, that is, Alexius I, did more than release the Jews from certain taxes (the nature of which we must again leave to a later discussion). Michael II had done something similar in circumstances suggesting close relations between Christians and Jews. Alexius also granted a holiday from work to those whose chief employment was in the silk industry— the prestige and profit of which were a primary government interest. And Alexius was as concerned for the right exercise of the Byzantine emperor's spiritual functions as Michael had been unconcerned. He was an ardent defender of Christian orthodoxy. By his special instructions, a vast collection of possible deviations from it was assembled for the guidance of his subjects. He fought a relentless struggle against various dissident sects, causing the leader of one of them to be burned alive—the only instance of such a punishment in the whole history of Byzantium. To his contemporaries, at least, he became known as 'the thirteenth apostle'.[69] While nothing is specifically otherwise known about his treatment of his Jewish subjects, it may be supposed that his attitude was not exceptionally sympathetic when they had encouraged Christians to participate in a movement which was unmistakably heretical. And so, the blessing he gave to the messianists was all the more remarkable.

Yet, as always, this instance of Jewish influence, of the peculiar status of Byzantine Jewry, had its ambivalent side. Co-operation of Christians on a common issue did not mean friendship with Jews. The Christians of Thessalonica had temporarily ceased hating their Jewish fellow citizens 'most intensely' because of an adventitious circumstance—just as in 1040 the rebel threat to Thessalonica put Christians with Jews in the ranks of the militia of the silk guilds. Alexius' protection of the Jewish messianists was equally ambivalent. His invitation to them to leave Thessalonica and meet their messiah, if not exactly an order of expulsion, was a plain hint that the religious turmoil, with its possibilities of disorder, must end. Naturally enough, it was its Jewish leaders who must suffer by having to abandon their homes, however well these might be looked after in their absence, just as it had been the Jewish participants who had had so often to suffer in the aftermath of many previous urban disorders. During the eleventh century, as in other periods, this ambivalence was always present. Byzantine Jews could never escape the consequences of their anomalous position within a Christian state. And these consequences had been even more clearly illustrated by a far less extraordinary event at the beginning of the century. An epidemic broke out in Sparta, only ceasing, so it was asserted, when the Jews had been expelled.[70] Here was one of the most common accusations, repeated on innumerable occasions in the history of western European anti-semitism, to show that the Jew was the inveterate enemy of society. Even in a period of relative security, of economic and cultural expansion, the consequences of this belief were always a possibility in Byzantium too. 'The Lord God of Israel has been gracious unto me and has saved me from great tribulations,' wrote a Jew sometime between 1060 and 1075 after he had escaped from a Byzantine prison to the freedom of Muslim-ruled Jerusalem.[71] Nevertheless, for all that, there was a real difference between Byzantium and the west. The Jews of Sparta had found Christians there, working in the same trades, fervent enough defenders to call down the wrath of the monk who was engineering their expulsion. The burning of the Jewish quarter of Bari had a parallel when the future emperor Nicephorus III captured Constantinople in 1076. Then, too, the Jewish quarter was severely damaged but the difference was this: both Jewish and Christian property suffered, and both suffered accidentally as the inevitable result of prolonged street battles.[72] But the strongest contrast between eastern and western christendom was provided by the Crusaders. Their march through Germany was marked by the pillage and slaughter of the Jewish communities in their path. They tried to bring their behaviour with them. They attacked a small Jewish settlement on their march through Greece.[73] But they were unable to infect Byzantium. The religious excitement which attended their coming had, as we have seen, quite the contrary result. Byzantine Jewry did not suffer as German Jewry had done. Its achievements during the century of expansion were untouched. Its anomalous position, with all its advantages and disadvantages remained, for the moment, unaffected.

Notes

1   *The Chronicle of Matthew of Edessa*, ed. and trans. E. Dulaurier, *Receuil des Historiens des Croisades, Documents Arméniens*, vol. 1 (Paris 1858), p. 19
2   Cf. N. Adontz, 'La lettre de Tzimiscès au roi Ashot (Ašot)', BYZ 9 (1934), pp. 371–7
3   Ibn Khurdadhbā, *Kitāb al-masālik wa'l mamālik* (The Book of Roads and Kingdoms), ed. and trans. M. J. de Goeje, *Bibliotheca geographiae arabicae VI* (Leyden 1889), p. 153 (text), p. 115 (trans); cf. Starr, *Jews in the Byzantine Empire*, no. 45. The etymology of *Rādaniyā* has been much disputed; e.g. the Rhone (Starr, *ibid.*), the Persian *rāhadān*= 'knowing the way' (Dunlop, *op. cit.*, p. 138, note 69). But the simplest derivation would be from the Arabic ردن *radan*= 'silk cloth'
4   *Sefer hakhmoni le-rav Shabbetai Donnolo*, ed. D. Castelli, *Il commente di Sabbetai Donnolo sul libro della creazione* (Florence 1880), (text) pp. 3–4; Starr, *op. cit.* 87
5   *Sefer Yuḥasīn*, p. 125; cf. Starr, *op. cit.*, nos. 103, 104
6   Mann, *Texts and Studies*, vol. 1, p. 86; cf. Starr, *op. cit.*, no. 111
7   A. Cowley, 'Bodleian Geniza Fragments (IV)', JQR old series 19 (1906), pp. 251–4 (cf. Starr, *op. cit.*, no. 132); Mann, *Jews in Egypt*, vol. 2, p. 87 (cf. Starr, *op. cit.*, no. 128); for a similar incident, cf. Starr, *op. cit.*, no. 130
8   Cf. Ankori, *op. cit.*, pp. 103–4
9   Elīsha bar Shināyā, *al-burhān 'alā saḥīḥ al-imān* (The Proof for the Truth of Faith), trans. L. Horst, *Des Metropoliten Elias von Nisibis Buch vom Beweis*

der *Wahrheit des Glaubens* (Colmar 1886), p. 42, p. 103; cf. Starr, *op. cit.*, extract from Arabic text (only portion ever printed from Vatican Codex Arabicus 180), p. 246, trans., no. 131; on Elīsha, see E. Kerim-Delly, *Dictionnaire de Spiritualité*, vol. 25, cols. 573–4

10 Horst, p. 117; Starr, *ibid.*

11 Ankori, *op. cit.*, pp. 94–5

12 Yahya ibn Saʿīd al-Antakyā, *al-kitāb alladhī sannaʿahu*, ed. and trans. J. Kratchkovsky and A. A. Vasiliev, *Histoire de Yahya ibn Saʿid d'Antioche*, PO 23, p. 506; cf. Michael the Syrian, XIII.4–5 (= Chabot, vol. 3, pp. 130–132)

13 For both riots, see Yahya ibn Saʿīd PO 18, p. 719; pp. 799–802

14 H. F. Wuestenfeld, *Geschichte der Fatimid Chalifen nach arabishcen Quellen*, *Abhandlungen der koeniglichen Gesellschaft der Wissenschaften zu Goettingen* 27 (1881), p. 114

15 Yahya ibn Saʿīd, PO 23, p. 519

16 *Ibid.*, p. 511

17 Mann, *Jews in Egypt*, text: vol. 2, p. 71; p. 73; commentary: vol. 1, pp. 72–3

18 Wuestenfeld, *ibid.*; cf. Mann, op. cit., vol. 1, p. 32; Ankori, *op. cit.*, pp. 166–168

19 Mann, *op. cit.*, text: vol. 2, pp. 73–4; commentary: vol. 1, p. 73

20 *Synopsis Basilicorum*, alphabetical section 'I', ed. Zepos, vol. 5, pp. 317–19; on its date and authority, cf. Zepos, *ibid.*, p. 10

21 See e.g. *Epitomē legum XLV*.43, 44; ed. Zepos, vol. 4, p. 576, p. 579 (middle of tenth century); *Michaelis Atteliatis ponema legis XXXIII*.148, 235, 238; ed. Zepos, vol. 7, p. 477, p. 485 (about the year 1073–4); *Ecloga ad prochiron mutata*, *XXXVI*.15, 16; ed. Zepos, vol. 6, p. 298 (compiled from middle of tenth to middle of twelfth century); cf. *ibid.*, *XXXVI*.2; ed. Zepos, vol. 6, p. 296

22 *Epanagogē aucta LII*.24; *LIII*.7; ed. Zepos, vol. 6, p. 202, p. 214; *Ecloga ad prochuron mutata XXXVI*.13; ed. Zepos, vol. 6, p. 297

23 Pharr, p. 573, p. 589

24 Novel 45 (= Schoell and Kroll, pp. 277–9); cf. C.Th.XVI.8.16 (= Pharr, p. 469, 594)

25 C.Th.VIII.3.30 (= Pharr, p. 194)

26 *Eparchicon biblion VI*.16; ed. and trans. J. Nicole, *Le livre du préfet* (Bordeaux 1893), p. 33 (= Zepos, vol. 2, p. 379); Starr, *Jews in the Byzantine Empire*, no. 108

27 Doelger, *Regesten*, no. 781; Starr, *ibid.* (wrongly dated), no. 117

28 *Sefer Yuḥasīn*, p. 124; cf. Starr, *ibid.*, no. 81

29 For this work, see E. H. Freshfield, *A Provincial Manual of Later Roman Law* (Cambridge 1931)

30 F. Trinchera, *Syllabus graecarum membranarum* (Naples 1865), pp. 29–31; 36–8; cf. Starr, *ibid.*, nos. 137 and 138

31 Doelger, *Regesten*, no. 892; text in G. Zolotas, Ἱστορία τῆς χίου vol. 2 (Athens 1924), pp. 282–4; trans. P. Argenti, 'The Jewish Community in Chios during the Eleventh Century', *Polychronion: Festschrift Franz Doelger* (Heidelberg 1966), pp. 40–1 (note 4); cf. Starr, *op. cit.*, no. 143

32 cf. H. J. Scheltema, 'Byzantine Law', CMH, vol. 4, pt. 2, (1967), pp. 75–6

33 Doelger, *Regesten*, no. 862; Zolotas, pp. 266–70
34 Text in B. K. Stephanides, οἱ κώδικες τῆς Ἀδριανουπόλεως BZ 14 (1905), pp. 593–4; trans. Argenti, pp. 42–3 (note 14); cf. Starr, no. 147; for 1079 see Argenti, pp. 43–4
35 cf. Argenti, pp. 49–50
36 On all this development see G. Ostrogorsky, *Pour histoire de la féodalité byzantine* (Corpus Bruxellensis Historiae Byzantinae: Subsidia I) (Brussels 1954)
37 Sefer Yuḥasin, p. 127; Starr, *Jews in the Byzantine Empire*, no. 116
38 Mann, *Jews in Egypt*, vol. 2, p. 192 (text); vol. 1, p. 165 (trans); cf. Starr, *ibid.*, no. 119
39 Abū Mu'in Nāṣir, *Sefer nameh*, trans. G. Le Strange, *Nāṣir-Khosrau: Diary of a Journey through Syria and Palestine in 1047 A.D.*, Palestine Pilgrims Text Society no. 4 (London 1888), p. 23; cf. Starr, *ibid.*, no. 142
40 E. A Wallis Budge, *The Chronology of Gregory Abū al-Farūj called Bar-Hebraeus* (Oxford 1932), vol. 1, p. 203; cf. Starr, *ibid.*, no. 140
41 *Constantini porphyrogeniti De ceremoniis aulae byzantinae* I.17; cf. R. Guilland, Études sur l'hippodrome de Byzance', *Byzantinoslavica* 23 (1962), pp. 208–10
42 Cf. W. Miller, *Essays on the Latin Orient* (Cambridge 1921), p. 48; E. Frances, 'L'État et les métiers à Byzance', *Byzantinoslavica* 23 (1962), pp. 231–49
43 J. Starr, 'The Epitaph of a Dyer in Corinth', BNJ 12 (1936), p. 42; cf. *Jews in the Byzantine Empire*, no. 85
44 *S. Demetrii miracula*, MPG vol. 116, col. 1332B; cf. I. S. Emmanuel, *Histoire des Israélites de Salonique* (Paris 1936), p. 36
45 Mann, *Jews in Egypt*, vol. 2, pp. 87–8 (text); vol. 1, pp. 90–1 (translation); Cowley, *ibid.*; Starr, *Jews in the Byzantine Empire*, nos. 128, 129, 132
46 R. S. Lopez, 'The Dollar of the Middle Ages', *Journal of Economic History* 11 (1951), p. 215
47 P. Grierson, 'The Debasement of the Bezant in the Eleventh Century', BZ 47 (1954), pp. 382–4
48 T. Reinach, 'Un contrat de mariage du temps de Basile le Bulgaroctone' *Mélanges Schlumberger*, vol. 1 (Paris 1924), pp. 118–32. For the location of Mastaura, see W. M. Ramsay, *Historical Geography of Asia Minor* (London 1890), map at p. 104. On the *mohar* see Chapter VIII
49 For an introduction to the Karaites see Baron, vol. 5, pp. 209–85; 388–416
50 Mann, *Texts and Studies*, vol. 1, pp. 48–51; cf. Ankori, pp. 332–4—more convincing than Starr, *Jews in the Byzantine Empire*, no. 125 in his location and dating
51 Ankori, p. 331
52 Lopez, *ibid.*, p. 212
53 Ostrogorsky, *History of the Byzantine State*, pp. 327–8. See below, pp. 191–2.
54 *Vita Ioannis atque Euthymii XXIX–XXX* = P. Peeters, 'Histoire Monastique Géorgienne', *Analecta Bollandiana* 36/37 (1917–19), pp. 38–9
55 For a detailed analysis, see Ankori, pp. 418–33
56 Mann, *Texts and Studies*, vol. 2, pp. 34–9

57 Ankori, pp. 196–8
58 Ankori, pp. 261–80; cf. M. Molho, *Histoire des Israélites de Castoria* (Salonica 1938), pp. 11–14
59 A. Scheiber, 'Fragment from the Chronicle of 'Obadyah, the Norman Proselyte: From the Kaufmann Geniza', *Acta Orientalia* 4 (1954), p. 276; Hebrew text; English commentary, pp. 271–5; latter reprinted in JJS 5 (1954), pp. 32–5 followed by an English translation of text by J. L. Teicher (pp. 36–7)
60 Cf. Francesco Nitti di Vitto, *La Ripresa Gregoriana di Bari* (Trani 1942), pp. 79–104
61 B. Blumenkranz, 'La conversion au judaïsme d'André, Archevêque de Bari', JJS 14 (1963), pp. 33–6
62 J. Gay, *L'Italie méridionale et l'empire byzantin* (Paris 1904), pp. 485–6
63 B. Blumenkranz, *Juifs et Chrétiens dans le monde occidental 430–1096* (Paris 1960), pp. 383–4
64 P. Jaffe and W. Wattenbach, *Regesta pontificum romanorum* (Leipzig 1885), vol. 1, no. 4581, cf. C. Roth, 'The Lombard Lordships', *The World History of the Jewish People*, second series, vol. 2 (Tel-Aviv 1966), p. 111
65 Roth, *ibid.*, pp. 111–12
66 S. Assaf, *Texts and Studies in Jewish History* (Jerusalem 1946), pp. 143–4 (in Hebrew) cf. N. Golb, 'Notes on European Christians and Judaism in the Eleventh Century', JJS 16 (1965), p. 73; S. D. Goitein, 'Obadya, a Norman Proselyte', *ibid.* 4 (1953), pp. 76–7
67 Assaf, *op. cit.*, pp. 144–6
68 Hebrew text edited with commentary by A. Neubauer, 'Egyptian Fragments II (B)', JQR (old series), 9 (1896–97), pp. 26–9; for better edition (with commentary in Hebrew); cf. J. Mann, 'Messianic Movements in the Days of the First Crusade', *Ha-Tekufã* 23 (1925), pp. 243–61; English translation of text by Starr, *Jews in the Byzantine Empire*, no. 153; cf. also A. Sharf, 'An Unknown Messiah of 1096 and the Emperor Alexius' JJS, 7 (1956), pp. 59–70
69 *Annae Comnenae Alexiad XIV*.8.8., ed. and trans. B. Leib, *Anne Comnène, Alexiade* (Paris 1937 and 1967), vol. 3, p. 181; cf. F. Chalandon, *Essai sur le règne d'Alexis I-er Comnène* (Paris 1900), pp. 310–20
70 *Niconi metanoitis vita*, MPG vol. 113, cols. 979C–981D; cf. Starr, *op. cit.*, no. 115
71 J. Starr, 'On Nahrai b. Nissim of Fustāt', *Zion* 1 (1936), p. 443 (in Hebrew); cf. Mann, *Jews in Egypt*, vol. 2, p. 248; Starr, *Jews in the Byzantine Empire*, no. 146
72 *Michaelis Attaliatis historia*, ed. I. Bekker, CSHB (Bonn 1853), p. 252; cf. Starr, *Jews in the Byzantine Empire*, no. 150
73 L. Brehier, *Histoire anonyme de la première croisade* (Paris 1924), p. xiv, pp. 22–3

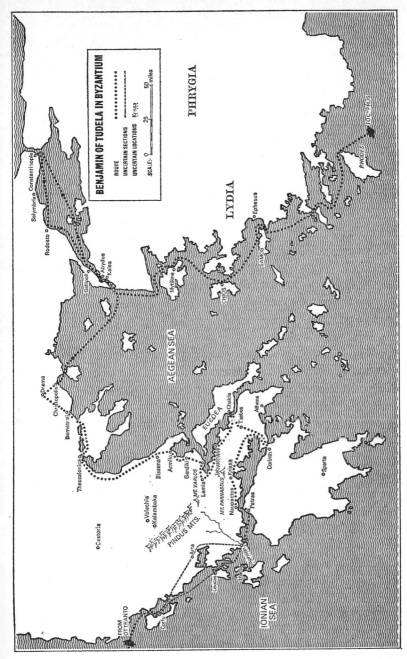

BENJAMIN OF TUDELA IN BYZANTIUM

ROUTE ....
UNCERTAIN SECTIONS ----------
UNCERTAIN LOCATIONS Kissa

SCALE: 0   25   50 miles

PHRYGIA

LYDIA

Constantinople
Selymbria
Rodosto
Abydus
Gallipoli   Kales

Drama
Chrissopolis
Bemetra
Thessalonica
Castoria
Valachia
Kalambaka
Bissena
Armilo
Gardiki?
MT. VARCOS
PINDUS MTS.
MT. PARNASSUS
Naupactos
Arta
Lamia
Gabula?Synon
Krissa
Thebes
Chalcis
Athens
Corinth
Patras
Sparta

Myttlene

CHIOS
SAMOS

Ephesus

EUBOEA

AEGEAN SEA

Leucas
Ithaca
Corfu
Kephalonia
FROM
OTRANTO

IONIAN
SEA

PHOCEA
TOCXPHUS

CHAPTER VII

The World of
Benjamin of Tudela

The story of Byzantine Jewry within the limits here set for it paradoxically had to begin with a reference to one of its closing episodes: the visit to Byzantium in 1168 by Benjamin of Tudela— because he was the only one to have stated specifically how many Jews lived there, and because he was the principal authority for the work in which urban Jews were chiefly engaged. But Benjamin's information was more important in its own contemporary context. From Tudela, on the banks of the Ebro in the Spanish Christian state of Navarre, Benjamin travelled through parts of southern France and Italy to Greece, and through Greece to Constantinople. He visited the islands of Chios, Samos, Rhodes and Cyprus (then under Byzantine rule). He then went on to Syria, Palestine, 'Irāk and Persia, returning home via Egypt. Everywhere he went, he frequently noted not only the size of the Jewish communities, but also many details both of Jewish and of non-Jewish relevance. For Byzantium, these details are valuable not only by themselves but also because, just then, Byzantine society as a whole was undergoing a crucial change.

Byzantium was profoundly and irreversibly influenced by the incursion of the Crusaders into her territories. The state that they set up in Syria and Palestine after their capture of Jerusalem created an entirely new problem. Firstly, it destroyed the delicate balance between Muslim and Christian principalities in Asia

Minor which had given relative security on the eastern frontier of the empire. Secondly, its existence suggested the possibility of more conquests to the land-hungry leaders—whether at the expense of the Muslims or of the Byzantines. By the middle of the twelfth century there was already open talk of a direct attack on Constantinople. Thirdly, this state, the so-called 'Latin Kingdom', was as western as the crusaders who had made it; its rulers continued to come from the west, and it looked to the west for support against its enemies—whether Byzantine or Muslim. The Second and Third Crusades were the response of the west to such a call for help—in 1147 after the fall of Edessa, and in 1191 after the fall of Jerusalem. Intended, as they were, to stop this successful Muslim counter-attack, in Byzantine eyes they were just as much invasions of imperial territory as the First Crusade had been. This view was supported by the fact that the Norman invasions of Greece in 1147 and in 1185 were the deliberate acts of anti-Byzantine coalitions inspired by those same Crusaders.

Byzantium could not fight the whole west. And so, throughout the twelfth century, Byzantine foreign policy either concentrated on searching for western allies of its own or tried means of fomenting trouble in the rear of the enemy—as was done more than once in Norman Italy and Sicily. To finance this policy, the economic concessions to Venice and to other Italian trading cities forced upon Alexius I had to be continued and expanded. From all these western involvements, whether a particular emperor was inclined to favour them or no, there was no escape: they culminated in the disaster of 1204. This turn to the west decisively influenced the internal life of the empire. There were years when western customs were carefully copied and western advisers welcomed. This was especially striking in the reign of Manuel I (1143–80) who relied on a German alliance and was enthusiastically pro-western. In 1182 there was a reaction when hatred of everything foreign led to a massacre of western residents in Constantinople. The following year power fell into the hands of the bitterly anti-western Andronicus I. Both these extremes were new phenomena, both constituted dangers of a new kind for the stability of Byzantine society. More dangerous than either was the fact that, on the whole, western ideas prevailed and typified the period. For they encouraged an already existing tendency in a fundamental Byzantine institution: land ownership and the relation of the great landowners to the state. The Byzantine type of feudalism which had succeeded the old land settlement (an example were the grants on the island of Chios) gradually gave way, under western pressures, to something approaching the full western system—with disintegrating effects on finance, administration and imperial authority. Andronicus surpassed the massacre of the foreigners by a massacre among the ranks of this new feudal nobility. But their deaths made no difference. The turn to the west continued the process which had baffled the emperors of the eleventh century and virtually completed the liquidation of the original Byzantine social structure. It is in relation to these developments that the story of the Jews in twelfth century Byzantium has to be considered. It was this changed Byzantium which was visited by Benjamin of Tudela. Benjamin's account of his travels has been published in various forms at least twenty-eight times. However, the light the Byzantine passages throw on the Jews in this new situation is so interesting, and the particulars they give are so much fuller than anything else we possess (indeed for other periods too—only Aḥīmaʿatz is at all comparable) that they are worth repeating at some length.[1]

Here is what Benjamin says about Thebes, Thessalonica and Constantinople:

> Thebes, a large city with about two thousand Jews. They are the best in the land of Greece at making garments of silk and of purple cloth. There are among them great scholars in Mishna and Talmud, and others great in their generation. Their leaders are: the Chief Rabbi, R. Kuṭi, his brother R. Moses, R. Ḥiyyā, R. Elijah Tiruṭoṭ and R. Yokṭan. There are none like them in all the land of Greece, except for the city of Constantinople.
> Salonica, which King Seleucus built—one of the four Greek kings left to rule after King Alexander—is a very large city with
> 10 about five hundred Jews. R. Samuel has been appointed over them by command of the king. With him are his sons, who are scholars, his son-in-law R. Shabbetai, R. Elijah and R. Michael. The Jews suffer oppression there. They work in the silk industry.
> Constantinople is the capital of all the lands of Yavan which is

called Greece. And there is the throne of King Manuel, the emperor. He has twelve kings under him, each one with his own palace in Constantinople. They possess castles and cities and they rule over the whole land. At their head is the Royal Eparch. The second is the Great Domestic, the third the Dominus, the fourth the Great Ducas, the fifth the Great Economus, while the rest have similar titles. The city of Constantinople is eighteen miles in circumference, half towards the sea and half towards the land. It lies between two arms of the sea: one which flows from the Sea of Russia, one from Spain.[2] All kinds of merchants come from Babylon and Shin'ar, from Persia and Medea, from all the kingdoms of Egypt, from the land of Canaan, from the kingdom of Russia, from Hungary, from the land of the Petchenegs, from Khazaria, from Lombardy and from Spain. It is a tumultuous city; men come to trade there from all countries by land and by sea. There is none like it in all the world except for Baghdad, the great city which is Ishmael's.[3]

In Constantinople is the church of St Sophia, and in it the Pope of the Greeks, for they do not obey the Pope of Rome. This church has as many altars as there are days in the year. Its riches are vast and immeasurable; year by year tribute is brought to it from two islands, from the castles and towns that are on them. Wealth such as this is not to be found in any church in the world. Inside it there are pillars and lamps, of gold and silver, more than a man can count. Near the wall of the palace there is a place for the king's amusement called the Hippodrome. Every year, on the day of the birth of Jesus, the king holds there a great spectacle. Every sort of person appears before the king and queen, performing with magic and without magic. And they bring on lions, tigers, bears and wild asses, causing them to engage in combat one with another, and just as many varieties of birds. In no other land can one see a similar entertainment. Now, this King Manuel has built a great palace for his royal residence on the sea-shore, in addition to the palaces built by his forefathers and has called it Blachernae. He has covered the pillars and walls with gold and silver, and has depicted on them both the battles of the past which took place before his day, and those in which he himself participated. He has made a throne of gold and precious stones, and a golden crown hanging on a golden chain exactly over where he sits. In the crown there are jewels of inestimable price. And, at night, candles are unnecessary—for one can see everything by the light which these jewels shine forth.

Constantinople has countless buildings. Year by year tribute is brought to it from all the land of Greece, whereby castles are

filled with garments of silk, purple and gold. Such buildings, such
60 riches can be seen nowhere else in Greece. They say that the city's
daily income, what with the rent from shops and markets and
what with the customs levied on merchants coming by sea and by
land, reaches twenty thousand gold pieces.[4] The Greeks who live
there have a wealth of gold and jewels. They walk about dressed
in silk, with patterns of gold sewn or embroidered on their
garments. They ride their horses like princes. Now the land is very
abundant in good fruits, in bread, in meat and in wine, so that
no other can be compared to it in richness. It has men learned in
all the books of the Greeks. Its inhabitants, each and everyone, eat
70 and drink beneath their vine and their fig tree. But to fight their
wars against Mas'ūd, king of the Turks, they hire men from all
the nations they call 'strangers', for they have no stomach for
fighting and are weak as women in war.

The Jews are not amongst them, within the city, for they have
transferred them behind an arm of the sea: an arm of the Sea of
Russia surrounds them on one side so that they cannot leave
except by sea in order to trade with the inhabitants of the city.[5]
There are about two thousand Rabbanite Jews, and about five
hundred Karaites in one part divided by a fence from Rabbanites.
80 The Rabbanites include scholars. Their leaders are: the Chief
Rabbi R. Abṭalion, R. 'Obadiā, R. Aaron,[6] R. Joseph[7] and the
head of the community. R. Eliaḵim. Amongst the Jews there are
craftsmen in silk, merchants and many rich men. No Jew is
allowed to ride a horse, except for R. Solomon the Egyptian who
is the King's doctor. Through him, the Jews find much relief in
their oppression—for they live under heavy oppression. Most of
the hatred towards them comes because of the tanners, the workers
in leather, who pour out their dirty water outside the doors of
their houses and thus defile the Jewish quarter. For this the Greeks
90 hate the Jews, whether good or bad, and hold them under a
heavy yoke. They strike them in the streets and give them hard
employment. Yet the Jews are rich, kind and charitable. They
observe the commandments of Scripture and cheerfully bear the
yoke of their oppression. The name of the place where the Jews
live is Pera.

Apart from these three cities, Benjamin, on his journey through
Byzantium, visited twenty-three other places where he found
Jews living. Again, some details are worth recalling.[8] He entered
Byzantine territory from the island of Corfu where he found
'one Jew', that is one Jewish family. From Corfu, he crossed

either to the island of Leucas or to the Greek mainland at Arta, at one of which places he found a hundred families.[9] Then, from either Leucas or Arta, he went south, via a place he called Aphilon, probably at the mouth of the river Achelous near Ithaca, where there were thirty families. He crossed the Gulf of Corinth and visited Patras, its western port, where there were fifty families. Following the Gulf he re-crossed it to Kifto (Naupactos), with a hundred families, and turned north to Krissa, probably lying between the Gulf and the foothills of Mount Parnassus.[10] It is tempting to identify it with the modern village of Khrisa (spelt until recently 'Krisa'), five miles north of today's ferry at Itca (where Benjamin may well have crossed). But we know of no authority for this identification. There he found two hundred families, living, as he put it, 'alone', who sowed and reaped lands which were their own possession. He returned to the Gulf, visited Corinth itself where he found three hundred families, and then resumed his journey northward. After his visit to Thebes, he crossed to the island of Euboea where, at Egripo (Chalcis), he found two hundred families. He then came back to the mainland and went via Jabustrissa 'a city upon the sea coast', now unidentifiable, with a hundred families, to Rabenika, then a port facing the northern tip of Euboea, where there were also a hundred. Next he turned inland to 'Sinon Potamo'—Zeitun 'of the river'—(modern Lamia) in Thessaly, at the eastern foothills of Mount Varlos, the southernmost tip of the Pindus range. It had fifty Jewish families enjoying an unusual privilege: the people lived in perpetual fear of the Wallachians, whose robber bands no reprisals by government troops could discourage. But the Jews did not fear them so much, since they were only likely to be robbed—not murdered. The reason was, according to Benjamin, that these Wallachians were lukewarm Christians with Jewish inclinations. They called Jews their brothers and gave themselves Jewish names.

From Lamia Benjamin travelled north-east to Gardiki, 'mostly in ruins, with a few Greeks and Jews'. It was probably on the Gulf of Volos. He then came to Armilo (Halmyros, near modern Volos but not to be confused with modern Almiros forty miles to the south and not on the coast) where he found a community of four hundred, and many merchants from Venice, Pisa and Genoa. Close to Halmyros, he passed through the inland town of Bissena (Vissena or Bezena) with a hundred families, on his way to Thessalonica.[11] From Thessalonica he followed the northern coast of the Aegean to Demetrizi (near Amphipolis) where he found fifty families.[12] He then turned inland to Drama where he found a hundred and forty. Now, Drama stood on the main road from Thessalonica to Constantinople—the great Via Egnatia. But Benjamin did not continue along it. Instead, he came back to the coast, to Christopolis (modern Kavalla), which had twenty families. Then he took ship to Abydus, near the entrance of the Dardanelles on the eastern shore, and to Constantinople. The remainder of his journey within the empire was also by ship. First he sailed through the Sea of Marmora, touching at Rhaedestus (Rodosto) where there was a community of four hundred and at Gallipoli where there were two hundred. Then he sailed across to the eastern shore of the strait once more, to Kales (Chanak-Kale or Chanak-Kalessi) about three miles south of Abydus, where he found fifty families. Lastly he visited the islands in the Aegean and in the Mediterranean. At Mytilene he found ten dispersed communities whose numbers he did not note, on Chios he found four hundred families, on Samos three hundred and on Rhodes four hundred. On Cyprus, again without any numbers he noted the existence of Rabbanites, Karaites and others he called 'Epikorsi', that is heretics, 'whom Jews everywhere have excommunicated, since they profane the Sabbath eve keeping the Sabbath on the eve of Sunday—which is the going out of the Sabbath'. And he reported that other unnamed islands had many Jewish communities.

Such was Benjamin's story of his travels in Byzantium. His statistical picture of Byzantine Jews (apart from the fact that he did not visit Byzantine Asia Minor and so did not report on the communities there) was incomplete. He did not mention Castoria. At Thessalonica, he may have omitted to include a Karaite community.[13] He certainly did omit the Jews living in two villages near by—to whom we shall return in a later context. On his voyage from Constantinople to Rodosto he missed Selymbria (also on the northern coast) where, as we shall see in the next chapter, there was some evidence of Jewish life. And he gave no figures for Mytilene or for Cyprus. Nevertheless, the scope of his information, the very wealth of the details he did give, makes the question of his reliability exceptionally important. And precisely for that reason it is an exceptionally difficult question, since so little of the information is capable of being tested by other sources. Under those circumstances, it is justifiable to begin by noticing the high reputation for reliability that Benjamin has always enjoyed. The original reference to it perhaps need not be taken too seriously. Those to whom he related his story on his return, so the opening words of the story itself go, said that he was a man of intelligence and understanding, a man of truth, for what they had examined they had found to be 'correct, relevant and consistent'.[14] However, the first outside comment, by R. Samuel Zarza in 1368, was equally respectful.[15] Essentially, Zarza has been echoed until our own day by writers both on Jewish and on non-Jewish subjects.[16] The flat rejection in 1734 of most of what Benjamin related by Barratier, a young theological student (whom Gibbon, with his usual felicity, called 'that marvellous child, who has added his crude store of learning'), has, so far as we know, been only repeated once—in 1941, by the Italian orientalist Di Tucci.[17] Now, while it is not possible to test this high reputation of Benjamin's by what he related of Byzantine Jews, it is possible to do so by what he related of Byzantine institutions and of Constantinople. Here it is amply supported.

For example, Benjamin correctly named the titles of five senior administrative officials including one, the Dominus, which had actually been created by the emperor Manuel.[18] And whether there were really twelve such each with a palace to himself or no, it is worth recalling Gibbon's statement that the emperors of the twelfth century owned many houses in Constantinople twelve of which they had allotted to their principal ministers.[19] Much of Benjamin's description of Constantinople, of its buildings and of what was in them, of its inhabitants and what they did, was equally authentic: visitors had always been impressed by the pillars and lamps of St Sophia.[20] But it is the detail of 'as many altars as there are days in the year' which is peculiarly striking. It has always puzzled commentators, but it was, in fact, confirmed by Antony, Archbishop of Novgorod, who came to Constantinople not long after Benjamin and who saw in St Sophia what he called 'three hundred and sixty-five holy precincts'.[21] In the Hippodrome, special spectacles, including a variety of animals, had been customary between Christmas and Twelfth Night ever since Constantine VII. But it was under Manuel, very fond of such entertainments, (and then under Andronicus), that there were instances of their being held on Christmas Day itself.[22] And magic was very popular in Constantinople. So popular indeed, that a master of the art, a certain Michael Sicidites, was blinded by Manuel's orders when he went too far and amused a sea-shore audience by causing the crew of a cargo ferry to smash with their oars some valuable jars of oil in the belief that they were beating a sea monster.[23] The Palace of Blachernae stood at the north-west corner of the city, overlooking the Golden Horn. Dating back to the fifth century, it was entirely rebuilt by Michael in 1150 on a magnificent scale, with many golden mosaics and wall paintings celebrating his diplomatic and military triumphs.[24] And Benjamin's description of the other riches of Constantinople, of the splendidly dressed people, of the precious materials he saw lavishly used everywhere, was accurate enough. Where fancy intruded, as with the city's daily income or the artificial light generated by Manuel's crown, it was only to impress his audience yet more by a society which had so deeply impressed him. For the economic difficulties of the empire had not affected the life of the capital. Benjamin correctly stressed that merchandise flowed to it from all the countries he mentioned, that is from most of the known world. This did not mean, however, that it was Byzantine merchants and, thus, the state, which profited on the scale they had in the days of Byzantine greatness. The wealth he saw was real and, no more than any tourist, would he have noticed the other reality: the horrible condition of the poor, the filthy streets, the prevalent epidemics.[25]

Of course, Benjamin made mistakes. However, in Byzantine

matters they were rarely gross ones. Thus, for example, he was wrong in calling the eparch 'royal' and placing him first of his administrative officials. In that list, the highest was the Great Domestic.[26] But, a hundred years earlier, the eparch had indeed held first rank in the table of civil appointments with a status of 'imperial dignity, lacking only the purple'.[27] His importance had since much decreased, but it is probable that Benjamin's informants were still under the spell of a vanished glory. Thessalonica was not founded by Seleucus. But it was founded (about B.C. 316) by one of his allies, Cassander, who, together with the others, Ptolemy and Lysimachus, could reasonably be called 'the four kings left to rule after King Alexander'.[28] In our context the point is that such mistakes, however harshly judged, were based on second-hand information. Of all that he actually saw, Benjamin was a good and conscientious observer.

If, then, his report on the Jews was likely to be accurate, it still remains to be asked what his special interest was in making it. There have been several suggestions about the purpose of his journey. Perhaps, like other Jews of the middle ages, he simply liked travelling. Perhaps, he had some commercial plan in mind. Perhaps his careful survey of Jewish and non-Jewish life (not only in Byzantium but everywhere he went) indicated an interest in the possibilities of refuge for Jews suffering persecution in western Europe.[29] Perhaps he was looking for signs of deliverance from that persecution—for signs of the coming of the Messiah.[30] Or, his may have, in the first place, been just the traditional pilgrimage to the land of Israel.[31] All these suggestions must remain speculative, since none of them has any explicit support in the text. However, if his motives must remain unknown, the text does contain two pieces of information suggesting a particular attitude. The first is that he came from Tudela, from a part of Spain reconquered for Christianity from the Muslims. At that stage of the reconquest, conditions for the Jews were favourable. Refugees from that Muslim persecution which had driven Maimonides to North Africa found a ready welcome in the new Christian territories where they were installed in the towns evacuated by the Muslims. Conditions were particularly favourable in Tudela under Sancho VI (1150–94) who granted the Jews many privileges, establishing long-lasting precedents for the freedom and security of Spanish Jewry.[32] Coming from such a background, Benjamin was likely to notice conditions less good than those to which he was accustomed. Secondly, it is equally apparent that Benjamin heartily admired Byzantium. Throughout the whole of his account, his solitary criticism was a repetition of the age-old western allegation of Byzantine cowardice: 'strangers' had to be hired to fight the subjects of King Mas'ūd, that is Mas'ūd ibn Kilij Arslan, the former ruler of Seljuk-held Asia Minor, whose sudden attack on Byzantine fortresses in 1151, after an unsuccessful attempt to turn him against the Crusader princes, had nearly wrecked Manuel's policies.[33] No more than other westerners did Benjamin understand that the break up of the old military system, already before Alexius, had made the use of mercenaries inevitable. Yet, with this exception, Benjamin's pro-Byzantinism is startling. One cannot help comparing his admiration to the extremely negative reactions of a western visitor exactly two hundred years earlier: to the dislike and disgust evinced by Liutprand, Bishop of Cremona, for what he saw at the court of Nicephorus II.[34] It is in the light of all these considerations that Benjamin's report has to be assessed.

The first conclusion to be drawn from it is the flourishing of many communities in provincial Greece and on the islands. Benjamin's figures, however interpreted, show that the Jews of Constantinople constituted less than 30 per cent of his total. Obviously, if the figures were known of the communities which, as we noted, he did not visit, and of those which he did but for which he gave no figures, this contrast would become very much stronger. The size of particular communities was remarkable. The Jewish population of Thebes was comparable to that of Constantinople. The figure of five hundred for Thessalonica, which Benjamin rightly called 'a very large city', was comparable to those given for Corinth, Halmyros, Rodosto, Chios, Samos and Rhodes. The communities Benjamin saw were well established. The great majority of them had recognized leaders whose names he was able to record. And their organization was good enough to enable him to visit those of whose existence, still less of whose location, he could hardly have had any more than the vaguest idea. In his day, Byzantium was an unknown land. Times had changed since Ḥasdai ibn Shaprūṭ had had an envoy at Constantinople halted on the way to Khazaria, when the persecution of the Jews of Bari was known to him, when he had successfully intervened with the emperor on their behalf. The Spanish Jewish scholar, Abraham ibn Daud, whose *Sefer ha-Kabbalā* (The Book of Tradition), written in 1160–61, included a survey of contemporary Jewry, had only the sketchiest of references to Byzantium. There was a slight possibility that he had heard of the community at Naupactus.[35] His only explicit assertion, however, was that there were Jews to be found 'on all the islands of the Greek Sea, from the land of Venice and Genoa as far as Constantinople and Byzantium'.[36] This assertion was not only topographically unhelpful to an intending traveller but also a piece of unreliable hearsay, for it was based on an unusually inaccurate Arab geographer who had made Genoa and the heel of Italy into two of these 'Greek islands'.[37] Thus, Benjamin's zig-zag route in the region of the Gulf, as his detours to Chalcis and to Drama, suggest arrangements for passing him on from one community to the next. At the same time, these arrangements were far from perfect. Benjamin did not visit all the communities he might have done. The reason is that communications were poor. His decision to travel the last stage to Constantinople, and the first from it, by sea suggested a deterioration in the excellent Byzantine road system. This was the difficulty that the communities had to overcome in order that an honoured visitor from a distant land should see as much as possible.

The provincial communities which Benjamin saw in Greece were thus likely to have been quite prosperous. The Jewish silk-workers of Thebes and of Thessalonica profited from the importance of silk in the Byzantine economy, an importance which increased when commercial competition and growing financial difficulties made the export of silk worthy of particular attention. This was the reason why at Thessalonica the government was concerned that the headship of the community should be an official appointment—'by command of the king', as Benjamin put it.[38] And we have seen earlier that not only at Thebes and at Thessalonica but at Corinth too there were Jewish silk workers— Jewish dyers of silk garments.[39] Then, Thessalonica, Corinth and most of the other communities also profited from the Mediterranean trade: most of them were on the islands, on the Gulf or in coastal towns. The fact that this trade was passing out of Byzantine hands, as Benjamin himself implied in regard to Halmyros, did not mean a decrease in its volume. The Mediterranean area remained prosperous, even if Byzantium did not, and those supplying its trade with its many ancillary services were not affected by the change. The prosperity of the communities on the mainland was especially striking. They had had to recover after a destructive period. The second wave of crusaders had robbed and destroyed far and wide on their march through Thessalonica and northern Greece.[40] Immediately after, the Normans had captured Corfu, Cephalonia (another island south of it), and had then overrun much of the country from Arta to Corinth—territories which had then to undergo the miseries of reconquest. In both these disasters for Byzantium, the Jews had been specifically involved.

The Second Crusade had been accompanied, as had the First, by an outburst of anti-semitic violence in Europe. The Cistercian monk, Radulph, had called upon the participants to kill the Jews in all the cities and hamlets on the route as enemies of the Christian faith.[41] This time, we cannot be sure that Byzantium was not affected. We do not know if the Jews of Thessalonica itself suffered. But Jewish life in the area as a whole probably did. A highly detailed account, written towards the middle of the century, of the Fair of St Demetrius in Thessalonica, in a list of people and nations attracted from near and far to that famous occasion for trade, failed to mention the Jews.[42] The work of which this account formed a part was a satire on Byzantine society.[43] It is difficult to imagine that it would have readily forgone a dig at the Jews. As for the Normans, they captured both Corinth and Thebes. They made prisoners of the best silk workers they could find and took them back to Sicily, by this means establishing a successful silk industry at Palermo. They also took Jews and non-Jews, presumably skilled in other crafts, from Corfu, from Cephalonia, and from unnamed places on the mainland.[44] The treaty that Manuel eventually made with the Normans in 1159 did not ask for their return.[45] This was the reason why Benjamin found only 'one Jew' on Corfu, and why there was no need to go to Cephalonia. Yet the recovery as a whole, especially that of Thebes, seems to have been complete. Places which had been entirely or partly depopulated of their Jews were quickly enough, and adequately enough, resettled to be as well established as they were when Benjamin saw them twenty years later.

The rehabilitation of the communities which had suffered from Crusaders or from Normans was a striking enough pheno-menon. But Benjamin's report also showed that it was part of a more fundamental demographic development. Firstly, there was a tendency to settle in the smaller centres of population. His list of communities on the mainland of Greece, with the exception of Thebes, Corinth and Thessalonica, consisted of places never previously mentioned in a Jewish context, and all of them smaller than those three cities. The most that can be assumed is that some in the south were included among the unnamed places from which the Normans seized their skilled craftsmen—that there were already communities there by 1147. A negative argument is notoriously unsatisfactory. Yet it is difficult to believe that of these nineteen smaller places none would have earned a mention if there had been something there much earlier. The same may be said regarding the islands. Mytilene and Samos are fairly large, and their communities had had no previous mention. But the islands with the 'many communities', no matter which they were, are insignificant spots in the Aegean or the Mediterranean compared to those on which communities had existed previously: Chios, Rhodes and Cyprus. Secondly, the number of the communities, their size and the relation of the total figure they made up to the figure for Constantinople, indicated a general tendency to settle in the provinces. The outstanding example was the figure for Chios. It will be remembered that in 1049 there were fifteen families on the island. Benjamin's figure of four hundred could not have been reached by a natural increase, irrespective of whether it stood for families or for individuals. In the former instance, it would have meant an increase of more than twenty six times the original population. In the latter, with the normally accepted estimate of five to a family, an increase of nearly six times—also extremely unlikely. It is possible that four hundred was merely a mistake—Benjamin's own, or a copyist's.[46] But no doubt has been cast on his other figures, however disputed their interpretation, and there is no reason to doubt them here. The increase in the Jewish population of Chios was, as in innumerable instances in Jewish history, the result of an influx of new settlers.

There is another conclusion to be drawn from this increase. It took place in direct defiance of the order contained, as will be remembered, in the confirmation to the rescript of 1049, that, for fiscal reasons, no Jews were henceforth allowed to settle in Chios or to leave it. Was such defiance possible? There is reason to suppose that it was. In 1153, Manuel enumerated the sources of income at the disposal of St Sophia. These included the taxes on 'the Jews of Strobilos, wherever these Jews may be found'.[47] In other words, some of those Jews too had ignored a previous fiscal instruction. The parallel to Chios may have been closer. Nothing else is known of the Jews of Strobilos, and its location is doubtful. It may have been on the south-west coast of Asia Minor, roughly opposite Rhodes.[48] But, in 1079, the monastery of St John the Baptist on an island named Strobilos in the Aegean had been granted fiscal autonomy in the same way as had the monastery in Chios.[49] Although in that context no Jews were mentioned perhaps it was that arrangement which had broken down. The Jews could not be brought back. If they could be identified, their taxes would not be forgiven them. But they would have to be devoted to some other holy object.[50] For this reason, their taxes were reassigned to St Sophia. Possibly, this new arrangement applied to the whole population of Strobilos. Benjamin spoke of two islands which paid their taxes to St Sophia.[51] The chance of evading such arrangements involved the possibility of evading a semi-feudal status which, as we discussed in the last chapter, was their basis. The Jews of Krissa provided evidence of this possibility, although in an opposite sense. The semi-feudal status was not enforced in the first place. Benjamin's report that they lived 'alone' working the land, which was their own possession, meant that in the sense of Byzantine land law they had remained 'wholly free and subject to no one'—just as originally had been the status of the fifteen Jewish families on Chios.

Possibilities such as these were as much an encouragement to provincial expansion as economic opportunity. There was another factor: in the whole of Benjamin's report on the provinces, there was nothing about the Jews being officially or unofficially ill-treated (though, with his background he would have been on the look out for this) with the exception of his comment that in Thessalonica they were 'oppressed'. But this comment, without any particularisation, stood in strong contrast to the details he gave of what the Jews of Constantinople had to undergo—a point of great importance, to which we shall return. So far as Thessalonica was concerned, the lack of particularization suggested that oppression there was not a serious matter. Quite probably, it chiefly expressed itself in the supervision the government imposed on workers in the silk industry, a supervision which might have been stricter for the Jews than for others—because of suspicions of their reliability lingering on from the time when messianic excitement had produced the ferment which had infected their Christian fellow-citizens. That the Jews of Thessalonica enjoyed favourable conditions was attested by the great theologian and scholar Eustathius, its archbishop from 1175 to about 1194.[52] Previous to his appointment, he had had a long career at Constantinople both as a teacher and an administrator. He was a favourite of the emperor and of the patriarch Michael III, until whose death in 1180 he would often return to Constantinople to officiate at some special function.[53] At Thessalonica, for unknown reasons, he passed through a long period of unpopularity. His flock, he complained, 'had prepared a bitter brew for him and wished him dead, accusing him, among other things, of senile decay'.[54] Such was the archbishop who, shortly after his appointment, wrote to his friend the patriarch asking his advice on a delicate problem. Jews who, to his evident surprise, had never been confined to one quarter of the city, had bought or rented houses from Christians, some of them with holy pictures still on their walls. This was what worried Eustathius. But the matter had actually been brought to his attention not for that reason at all, but because of a number of disputes over rents and prices.[55] It might be thought immediate intervention with the authorities in favour of the Christian land-lords was not only the obvious step to take but one which would also have strengthened his own shaky position. Yet Eustathius did not take it. And this was not because he was tolerant in a way which would have made him a truly extraordinary exception to the usual Byzantine ecclesiastical attitude.[56] One of his Lenten sermons was very revealing both on this point and on the whole Jewish situation in Thessalonica, explaining why it was that Eustathius had hesitated. In this sermon, he rebuked his flock for their lack of fellow feeling, of charity to one another, of Christian brotherliness, in sad contrast to the tolerance they extended to the Jews. 'Why else,' he asked, 'have the Jewish people come to this city other than to benefit from it?—They to whom it has been permitted to practise their religion as they wish, and to share in all things necessary in a generous manner?'[57] No doubt, there was exaggeration here inspired by the 'bitter brew' which was his own portion. But there was sufficient truth in his opinion of the citizens' tolerance towards Jews to make him seek the support of Constantinople before intervening against those who had been the subject of a complaint by Christians and who, besides, in his eyes, were potential desecrators. This experienced and highly educated public servant was clearly faced with a situation quite new to him and with which he was unable to deal.

Not long after, Eustathius again bore witness to a measure of good relations between Jew and Christian. In 1185, the Normans once more invaded Greece and after a long siege captured Thessalonica. As we have seen, this was exactly the kind of event when accusations of Jewish treachery were most likely to be made. We mentioned in the first chapter that some of the stoutest defenders of Thessalonica were the militia of the guilds. These, of course, included the silk guilds with their Jewish members. Eustathius, in his account of the siege, the best and fullest that

148

exists, never suggested any sort of Jewish unreliability, unmistakably implying that the Jews participated in the defence no less than the Christians. He complained, indeed, of the meagre quantities of food available when food could still be brought in, while Jews and Armenians living in two nearby villages 'were sufficiently supplied, and somewhat more than sufficiently'. But it was the Armenians whom he went on to attack most bitterly, calling them inveterate scoundrels and blaming them for the shortage. He had no word of reproach for the Jews.[58] While none of this foregoing evidence of Eustathius is conclusive, it does support the probability that the oppression in Thessalonica spoken of by Benjamin was not serious enough to prevent relations between the Jews and the world around them from being noticeably, even unusually favourable.

In Benjamin's report on the Byzantine provinces and islands there were two instances which were comparable to the evidence of Eustathius on the Jews of Thessalonica. The first concerns the Wallachians of Lamia who according to Benjamin had acquired Jewish inclinations. This was quite possible. As we have noted in regard to eighth- and ninth-century Phrygia, such a syncretism proceeded from some antecedent readiness to be influenced by Judaism. Now the Wallachians, the ancestors of present day Rumanians, had been a collection of nomad tribes, of no fixed cultural or religious allegiance, who in their wanderings through the Balkans had acquired a smattering of Christanity. In Benjamin's day, great quantities of them had spread into Greece. Thessaly, on the edge of which province was Lamia, came to be known as Great Wallachia. The Wallachians who remained in the north became the allies of the Bulgarians, fighting side by side with them to throw off Byzantine rule. They became a fully Christian people and were recognized as such by the papacy.[59] The position was very different in Thessaly. The Byzantines, unlike the Bulgarians, held the Wallachians in deep contempt, calling them 'Greek cripples' if they tried to assimilate to their surroundings.[60] So they remained an alien and problematic element. Until comparatively modern times, the robbers who fell upon a traveller on some lonely path of the Pindus were called Wallachians.[61]

Thus the Wallachians of Thessaly, rejected by the local Christians, could easily be attracted by an apparently similar monotheistic faith whose precepts for 'strangers within the gate' were simpler to grasp than complex Christian dogma, even if they did not necessarily alter the way in which these Wallachians continued to make their living. But then the corollary was also true as in Phrygia; the ability to gain half-converts of this kind meant a degree of integration and stability for the Jews.

The second instance were the heretical Jews of Cyprus whom Benjamin rightly distinguished from the Karaites. They were followers of the ninth-century Jewish sectarian Mishawayh (or Meswi), a native of 'Ukbara in the neighbourhood of Baghdad, who originally differed from the orthodox over the liturgical calendar. For him the day ran from sunrise to sunrise (and not sunset to sunset as is the Jewish custom), the Day of Atonement always fell on the Sabbath and the first day of Passover on a Thursday.[62] But the injunction to observe the Sabbath itself on Sunday was a late Mishawite doctrine, the result of a Christianizing tendency. By the middle of the eleventh century this tendency had become marked enough for the Byzantine Karaites to make it the main subject of their anti-Mishawite polemic: Mishawite assimilation to Christian customs was the burden of the accusation against them by Tobias ben Moses in a section of his commentary 'Otzar Neḥmad.[63] His accusation was mistakenly levelled at the whole sect from its beginnings, because he was judging by the only example known to him—by the example of Mishawites in Byzantium. These were the Mishawites on Cyprus, where they had settled during the Jewish immigration from Muslim lands in the period of the great Byzantine victories, and after Cyprus had been reconquered in 965 by the emperor Nicephorus II.[64] It was there that their boycott by Karaites and Rabbanites alike had driven them, in a Christian milieu, to drift further and further from Judaism.[65] And that drift may have initially been encouraged by official Byzantium taking a certain benevolent interest in them precisely because of their calendrical expertise. At the beginning of the eleventh century, a dispute about the correct method for computing the date of Easter had involved the whole

Christian East. Byzantium was particularly concerned because Syria, with Antioch but lately in Byzantine hands, was hesitating between two conflicting versions.[66] The theologians of Constantinople got Basil II to settle the dispute, and avoid the disorders that such disputes always threatened, by the advice he received from a Moses of Cyprus who, according to them, was 'a great scholar of the Hebrews, having since his childhood acquired a vast learning in the science of the calendar'.[67]

There is some reason to believe that this Moses was a leading Mishawite.[68] Possibly helped by this initial advantage, their relations with the Christians became good enough to cause that syncretism to flourish of which later Tobias complained, and which Benjamin still later recorded. In any case, the very existence for many years of Rabbanites, Karaites, Mishawites and Christians all on one island was itself some indication of stable and secure relations between Christians and Jews. These, then, were some of the ways in which the towns of Greece and the islands visited by Benjamin had favourable conditions for Jewish settlement.

Of Jews in Asia Minor between the First and the Fourth Crusade, unfortunately very little is known. A single reference to Attaleia—reconquered from the Seljuks by the Emperor John II Comnenus (1118–1143)—is to a dispute over property between a converted Jew and his family. Its interest lies in the light it throws on the legal status of Jews in that period rather than on local conditions, and we shall return to it later in that context. The only other references are to Strobilos (if it was in Asia Minor) and to two other communities not mentioned till then: at Seleucia and at Chonae. However, these two provide an interesting footnote, as it were, to the information given by Benjamin. Seleucia was on the coast of the Mediterranean, about seventy miles west of Tarsus, reconquered by John II when he had reconquered Attaleia. Always important in imperial strategy, it was now practically a frontier town. In 1137, not long after it had come back into Byzantine hands, it had a well-established and prosperous community, a proportion of which were recent immigrants from Egypt. From Seleucia, a doctor, who was also a composer of liturgical poetry, wrote to other members of his family at Fusṭāṭ (Old Cairo) that he was very satisfied with his new surroundings, and suggested that they join him. He gave news of other emigrants, including one who had been a professional beggar in Acre (then also under Egyptian rule). It seemed that even for him emigration to Byzantium had proved beneficial. The doctor's relations with the authorities were excellent: John II had just crowned what promised to be a brilliant campaign by advancing from Tarsus into Syria and threatening Aleppo. Next year he was to capture Antioch from the Crusader Prince Raymond of Poitiers. 'I have asked our commanders,' wrote the doctor, expecting John's complete success in Syria, 'to take along any medical books for me, from Aleppo or from Damascus, which might fall into our hands'.[69] It is not beyond conjecture that relations such as these could only have been the result of Jewish aid to the Byzantines at the fall of Seleucia. However that may be, the conditions enjoyed there by the Jews after that event equalled, if they did not surpass, those described in the provinces visited by Benjamin.

The Jews of Chonae had not been so fortunate. Their community, of which also nothing is known before the twelfth century, had by 1150 been expelled by Nicetas, the Archbishop of Chonae, and its members had dispersed to a number of unknown towns. They were craftsmen, dyers of cloth and workers in leather. Before their expulsion, their relations with the Christians had been sufficiently good, and their work—although Nicetas stressed his disgust at its nature—so valued by them that they offered it for the embellishment of the local churches. It was this offer which particularly angered the archbishop.[70] And at Chonae, no Christian fellow craftsmen protested against the expulsion, as they had at Sparta. There may have been a reason for their bad luck. Chonae, in south-east Phrygia close to the Aegean coast, was set on a rocky hill guarding a junction of roads which led east and south-east into Seljuḳ territory.[71] The latter was the route a party of Crusaders took in 1147 on their way from Phrygian Laodicea to Attaleia.[72] Now Phrygia, as we have seen, was an old area of Jewish settlement. This circumstance could have inflamed their anti-semitism, this time, unlike in 1096, with effects on the local inhabitants in spite of their previous good relations, bringing disastrous consequences to the Jews of Chonae. Their fate, though incomparably less cruel than that suffered by western communities in the path of the Crusaders, was unusually so for Byzantium, where there had been no persecutions for two hundred years. It was in ominous contrast to the generally favourable situation we have been describing. Whether the Crusaders were responsible or no, Chonae, in any event, suggested western ideas—the ominous signs of a new age.

Seleucia showed that Byzantium was still thought of as a desirable place to live in: the immigration from Egypt was continuing; it did not need to be confined to Seleucia, and could well have helped to bring some of the communities visited by Benjamin to their remarkable size. But such new settlers, for example in Corinth where dyers worked, could just as well have come from Chonae: side by side with the attractions of economic opportunity and good conditions, Chonae showed the insecurity of Jewish life in twelfth-century Byzantium. It was to this insecurity that Maimonides later alluded when he warned a member of the rabbinical court in Alexandria, a certain Pinḥas ben Meshullam, who had previously spent some years in Byzantium, to think twice before returning there—for he would now be leaving security for a place where life had been spoilt by arbitrary orders.[73]

That this insecurity was serious enough, that it was not an aspect merely of that Byzantine ambiguity towards Jews we have often stressed, but a symptom of something worse, appeared in what Benjamin had to say about the Jews in Constantinople.[74] His description of their condition contrasted sharply with the rest of his Byzantine story. First of all, the Jews were confined to a particular quarter, to Pera—on the other side of the Golden Horn. It is true that they had not been expelled from the city. As we said in the first chapter, Alexius I only gave administrative expression to a process which had begun before his day when he allotted a landing-stage for the Jews just as he did for the Venetians. But, when Benjamin saw them, the Jews had lived in Pera for nearly a hundred years. The situation had become permanent and irreversible. It had nothing in common with Jewish life in Thessalonica and much with western arrangements. Then, it is with Benjamin's bare mention of oppression in Thessalonica that we must contrast the way in which he stressed the oppression suffered in Constantinople. It was a 'heavy oppression', a 'heavy yoke'. The striking of Jews in the streets may have been an exaggerated generalization from single incidents seen or heard about. It must not be forgotten that, coming from the tolerance of Tudela, Benjamin would have been exceptionally shocked by incidents of this kind. On the other hand, his obvious admiration for Constantinople and all its inhabitants would have prevented a generalization which was completely unfounded. To the heavy oppression and, specifically, to the 'hard employment' which it included, there was another witness. Rabbi Petaḥiā of Ratisbon, who visited the Middle East about ten years later, reported that the 'Jews of Greece' were grievously oppressed and were compelled to do servile work.[75] It is usually supposed that Petaḥiā passed through Byzantium on his return journey.[76] But it is doubtful if he saw anything except Constantinople, for his only other comment (in the same passage) was that there were so many communities of Byzantine Jews that the Land of Israel would not contain them—a comment which in its vagueness recalled the communities said by Abraham ibn Daud to dwell on 'all the islands of the Greek sea'. It is highly probable that Petaḥiā's more definite comment was limited to Constantinople. And we may believe, therefore, that it supported Benjamin's implication of worse treatment there than elsewhere in Byzantium.

What was the reason? Benjamin himself gave one: disgust at the Jewish leather workers, the tanners—the disgust that Nicetas expressed at Chonae. It was certainly an occupation that invariably made itself unpleasantly felt. But it was not a new one for Jews either in Christian or in Muslim lands. Centuries before, rabbinic law had made special provisions for it, among them a right of divorce for wives of tanners if they found the smell unbearable.[77] Even if it was a new occupation for the Jews of Constantinople, if it was an example, that is, of their servile work, their hard employment, it would be the result of the oppression rather than its cause. In any event, the reason must be sought elsewhere. For hatred showed itself towards all classes of Jews. To Benjamin's own patent surprise, it included the most respectable of them. There is other evidence of this attitude, indifferently despising Jews good or bad. It is vividly illustrated by a curious passage in a poem dedicated to Manuel's sister-in-law from the pen of the poet (and philologist) Johannes Tzetzes. The subject was a pedigree of gods and heroes modelled on Homer and Hesiod, but Johannes found it relevant to conclude by showing the cosmopolitan character of Constantinople—and his own linguistic abilities—with an explanation (in transliteration and translation) of how to greet in their own language the following people: Alans (a south Russian tribe), Russians (i.e. from Smolensk), Turks, Persians, Arabs, Latin speakers—and Jews. In all except the last the formula was simply an enquiry after the stranger's health. But to Jews, the correct greeting was: 'Oh sheepish bleater from Bethphage, oh honourable Beelzebub, oh Hebrew with heart of stone, the Lord has come and hurled lightnings at your head.'[78] Bethphage was the village near Jerusalem where Jesus was said to have chosen the ass by riding on which he would fulfil the messianic prophecy.[79] This 'greeting' of Johannes was not only insulting but conversionist in intent. It was the context that was especially unusual here: Johannes was not addressing himself to an emperor embarked on a policy of forced conversion, nor was he an ecclesiastic. However even an ecclesiastic could be impressed by the capital's attitude to Jews. Antony of Novgorod, whose visit to St Sophia we mentioned earlier in this chapter, thought it worth recording how an inexplicable blazing up of three candles before the great golden cross caused the congregation to cry a miracle, a sign of God's mercy, which would straightway lead all 'the accursed Jews' to baptism.[80]

These feelings did not merely express themselves in words—or blows. They influenced Byzantine legislation, again within the context of Constantinople. A general compilation of laws, belonging to the end of the twelfth or to the beginning of the thirteenth century, the *Liber Iuridicus Alphabeticus* or *Synopsis Minor*, exactly repeated the regulations with which we are familiar in the *Basilica*, in its associated legislation or in its commentaries. But in 1148, Manuel had, in Constantinople, introduced two innovations. Firstly, he abolished a custom that had arisen of certain cases involving Jews being settled by a minor official responsible for the peace of the Jewish quarter and re-affirmed that all were to be judged by the ordinary courts, a principle laid down as we know, in the Theodosian Code.[81] This innovation was part of a number of legal reforms introduced by Manuel, all intended to strengthen the central government against various sectional interests. For example he stopped a loophole in criminal law from which the church was deriving material benefit.[82] In regard to the Jews, his intention was to reinforce imperial authority over them —just as the fence between Rabbanites and Karaites was to ensure order. It was not to improve their status.[83] That such was very far from being his intention was clear enough from his second innovation introduced that same year. It had long been the custom to vary the formula for the oath required from a litigant according to his religious or national status, without any necessarily derogatory implications.[84] And for the Jews, too, the first recorded formula of this sort, the first oath *more judaico*, was harmless enough. It appeared as an addendum to the tenth-century imperial instruction on manufacture and marketing quoted in the last chapter. It required the Jew to gird himself with a bramble in memory of the Burning Bush and to swear to the truth of his testimony 'in the name of the Blessed Lord, the God of our fathers, who made the heavens and earth and led us on dry land across the Red Sea'.[85]

In 1148, a Jew of Attaleia went over to Christianity together with his brothers and turned his house into a monastery. The community managed to get hold of the furniture, and a suit for its return was brought before Manuel in Constantinople, after failing to be settled locally.[86] It was then that there first appeared an insulting variation of the oath *more judaico*. The Jewish party to the suit was ordered to follow a humiliating procedure meant to show the evil and magically dangerous character of his religion, a procedure which culminated in his having to spit on his circumcision.[87] It is true that this version did not become the sole possible one. Manuel himself, after objections from the defendant, allowed him to be sworn according to the earlier, milder alternative. But the existence of the other was now a fact, recalling the humiliating procedures normal in western Europe, which had begun in the time of Charlemagne.[88]

This contempt, then, this hatred had affinities with the West. In a city which had experienced plenty of anti-semitic violence, as all Byzantine cities had, but violence which had been generally preceded or followed by Jews and Christians combining in some popular riot against the authorities, this new, sustained contempt and hatred could not be explained by the stink of the tanneries. Benjamin himself gave a clue to its real nature when he spoke of the privileged position of Solomon the Egyptian, the king's doctor, privileged, according to one version of the text, specifically because of his medical knowledge.[89] For his position symbolized something quite different from that of his colleague in Seleucia with his interest in Byzantine victories, and quite different from everything hitherto said of the relations between Christians and Jews in Byzantium. It symbolized the classic Western situation: the favoured Jew as the sole defence of the community unable to rely on its social or economic links with the non-Jewish world around it. The treatment of the Jews in Constantinople was coming under the influence of Western ideas—the ideas to which Byzantium as a whole was being exposed. But this treatment was largely limited to Constantinople. For it was there, with a pro-Western emperor and a pro-Western nobility, that these ideas were strongest. At the same time, the change through which Byzantium was passing had weakened imperial power, weakened its effectiveness outside the capital. That is why, on occasions, Jews in the provinces could ignore it, or could be ignored by it. Therein lay the real attraction of provincial settlement. That was why the Jews of Constantinople constituted a comparatively small proportion of Byzantine Jews. Such was the world of Benjamin of Tudela.

1 The translation is our own, based on Adler's text (see Ch. I, note 3, above). Benjamin was also edited and translated by A. Asher, *The Itinerary of R. Benjamin of Tudela*, 2 vols. (London 1840), who listed twenty-two other editions or translations (see vol. 2, pp. 1–25). For versions since Adler, see F. Uspensky, 'Benjamin of Tudela's Notes on his Journey', *Annaly* 3 (1923), pp. 9–11 (in Russian, on Constantinople only); E. N. Adler, *Jewish Travellers* (London 1930), pp. 64–91 (condensed version of whole account); Starr, *Jews in the Byzantine Empire*, no. 182 (Byzantine Jewish references only); A. Ya'ari, *Palestinian Journeys by Jewish Travellers* (Tel-Aviv 1946), pp. 31–47 (text and commentary on Palestine only, in Hebrew; relevant here for introductory remarks on Benjamin himself, see note 31, below)

2 I.e. the Golden Horn, 'flowing' from the Bosphorus and thus from the Black Sea—the 'sea of Russia', and the Sea of Marmora, 'flowing' from the Dardanelles, and thus from the Mediterranean—for Benjamin, not unnaturally, from Spain

3 Babylon, Shin'ar, Canaan and Ishmael have, of course, their traditional meanings; 'the kingdoms of Egypt' is a historical reminiscence of the Fāṭimid empire, as is 'Khazaria' of territories which, since about 1016, had been under Russian rule. 'The kingdom of Russia' was the precursor of the Moscow principality then centred around Smolensk. The Petchenegs occupied territory to the north-east of the Danube

4 Adler reads המס . . . בכל שנה ושנה (= yearly income)—but this would hardly call for comment. The MS variants כל יום ויום or כל יום rejected by him (see Adler, text, p. 15 and note 39), i.e. daily income or income each day fit the context better; cf. Uspensky, p. 11

5 Adler reads זרוע יד רומי (= ? arm of the Roman hand) which is meaningless, and translates 'Sea of Marmora' which is geographically incorrect since the Sea of Marmora does not divide the old city from Pera. Uspensky *ibid.*, has 'inlet of the sea' (also from Adler's text). Starr has 'bounded by the strait of . . .' omitting the name. The MS variant זרוע ים רוסיא is at least explicable as the Golden Horn, as in note 2, above; cf. Adler, text, p. 16, note 22

6 To R. Aaron is given the cognomen בכור שורי (= 'the firstling of his bullock'), mistakenly transposed in the MSS from its place after R. Joseph where the reference is to the blessing of Moses on Joseph: 'His glory is like the firstling of his bullock'—Deut. XXXIII.17

7 To R. Joseph is given the cognomen שיר גירו (meant for R. Aaron), transliterated by Starr 'sir-giro' and by Adler 'shir-guru' (*sic*) but explained by neither. The MS variant סרגינו = sargino or sargeno (Adler, text, p. 16, note 33), which is Asher's reading (vol. 1, p. 23), suggests the late Greek σαργάνη = a basket—i.e. of sound learning; cf. the epithet 'a cemented cistern' bestowed upon the Talmudist Eliezer ben Hyrcanus (*Pirke Avot*, II.11)

8 Text in Adler, pp. 11–14; 17–18; trans. pp. 10–11; 14–15

9   For this problem of identification, never satisfactorily solved, see Starr, *Jews in the Byzantine Empire*, p. 233; A. Andréadès, 'Sur Benjamin de Tudèle', BZ 30 (1930), pp. 457–61; M. A. Dendias, 'Leucas or Arta?', *Ipeirotica Khronica* 6 (1931), pp. 23–8 (in Greek)

10 For this localization, see Asher, vol. 2, p. 36, note 64; A. Bon, *Le Péloponnèse byzantin* (Paris 1951), p. 87

11 For location of Bissena, see T. L. Tafel, *Thessalonica ejusque agro* (Berlin 1839), p. 496

12 On the location of Demetrizi, see Asher, vol. 2, p. 42, note 51; Tafel, *op. cit.*, p. 497

13 Ankori, *Karaites in Byzantium*, p. 149

14 Text in Adler, p. 2; trans. pp. 1–2; cf. Asher, vol. 1, introduction, p. xi

15 L. Zunz in Asher, vol. 2, pp. 251–2

16 On sources attesting to Benjamin's general reliability, see Baron, vol. 6, pp. 222–4; 435–6 (notes 88, 89)

17 Gibbon, *The Decline and Fall of the Roman Empire*, ch. 53= ed. J. B. Bury, vol. 6 (London 1902), p. 74, note 29; R. Di Tucci, 'Benjamino di Tudela e il suo viaggio', *Bollettino della R. Soc. Geogr. Italia* 7 (1941), pp. 496–517; cf. comment by S. G. Mercato in BZ 42 (1943–49), p. 337

18 Our translation, lines 18–20; cf. W. Ensslin, 'The Government and Administration of the Byzantine Empire', CMH IV.2, p. 23

19 Gibbon, *ibid.*, = ed. Bury, vol. 6, p. 75; our translation, lines 16–17

20 Cf. e.g. G. Downey, *Constantinople in the Age of Justinian* (Oklahoma 1960), pp. 109–112

21 Our translation, lines 33–4. Asher, vol. 2, pp. 46–7 (note 97), suggested emending במות = altars to בבות = gates, to which one tradition gave that number; cf. Tafel, p. 509. Alder (trans. p. 12) took במות as 'churches', altering the sense of the whole passage. For Antony, see *The Book of the Pilgrims*, ed. K. M. Loparev, *Pravoslavnyi Palestinskii Sbornik* No. 51, vol. 17, part 3 (St Petersburg 1899), p. 1, note 1; p. 42 (in Russian)

22 Our translation, lines 40–6; cf. R. Guilland, 'Études sur l'Hippodrome de Byzance', *Byzantinoslavica* 27 (1966), pp. 26–36

23 *Nicetae Choniatae De Manuelo Comneno* IV.7= MPG vol. 139, cols. 489D, 492B

24 Our translation lines 48–54; cf. A. Grabar, *L'Empereur dans l'art byzantin* (Paris 1936), pp. 40–2; p. 84

25 R. H. Jenkins, 'Social Life in the Byzantine Empire', CMH IV.2, pp. 86–91

26 Ostrogorsky, *The Byzantine State*, p. 327

27 *Michaelis Pselli Chronographia* X.3; ed. and trans. E. Renauld, *Michel Psellos, Chronographie* (Paris 1926 and 1967), vol. 1, p. 30; cf. Ensslin, pp. 23–4

28 Our translation, lines 8–9; cf. W. W. Tarn, 'The Heritage of Alexander', *Cambridge Ancient History*, vol. 3 (1953), pp. 482–483

29 Adler, introduction, pp. xii–xiii; cf. Asher, vol. 2, introduction, pp. ix–x; Uspensky, pp. 19–20

30 Asher, vol. 1, pp. 14–15 (the idea of an English editor in 1740)

31 Ya'ari, pp. 32–3

32 Cf. Y. Baer, *A History of the Jews in Christian Spain* (Philadelphia 1966), I.52–3

33 Our translation, lines 70–4; cf. Runciman, *A History of the Crusades*, vol. 2 (Cambridge 1952), p. 330

34 See F. A. Wright, *The Works of Liutprand of Cremona* (London 1930), pp. 240–3; 256–7; 268

35 Abraham ibn Daud, *The Book of Tradition*, ed. and trans. Gerson D. Cohen (London 1969), p. 143, note 33

36 *Ibid.*, text, p. 68; trans. p. 93

37 *Ibid.*, p. 93: note to lines 33–4

38 Our translation, lines 10–11

39 See above, Ch. VI, note 43

40 Runciman, *Crusades*, vol. 2, pp. 260–1

41 *Ottonis Frisigensis episcopi gesta Frederici imperatoris* I.37–9 = MGH SS XX (1867), p. 372

42 *Timarion, sive de calamitatibus ejus VI*; ed. M. Hase, 'Des Trois Pièces Satyriques,' *Notices et Extraits des Manuscrits de la Bibliothèque Nationale*, vol. 9, pt. 2 (Paris 1813), p. 173; on the Fair, see Runciman, *Byzantine Civilization*, p. 205

43 Cf. H. F. Tozer, 'Byzantine Satire', *Journal of Hellenic Studies* 2 (1881), pp. 231–46.

44 *Annales Cavenses*, MGH SS III (1839), p. 192; *Gesta Frederici* I.33 = MGH p. 370; cf. F. Chalandon, *La Domination normande en Italie et en Sicile*, vol. 2 (Paris 1907) and (New York 1960), pp. 136–7

45 Bon, p. 82

46 Cf. Ankori, *Karaites in Byzantium*, pp. 158–9 (note 77); Andréadès, BZ 30, pp. 461–2

47 Doelger, *Regesten*, no. 1390; Starr, *Jews in the Byzantine Empire*, no. 181

48 Krauss, REJ 87, p. 24, note 3

49 Doelger, *Regesten*, no. 1045

50 Cf. Starr, *ibid.*, p. 15; *idem*, *Romania* (Paris 1949), p. 112

51 Our translation, lines 35–6

52 On Eustathius, see R. Browning, 'The Patriarchal School at Constantinople in the XIIth Century', BYZ 32 (1962), pp. 186–93; A. P. Kazhdan, 'Eustathius of Thessalonica: A Byzantine Pamphleteer of the XIIth Century', *Vizantiiskii Vremenik* 27 (1967), pp. 87–93 (in Russian)

53 Kazhdan, pp. 94–7

54 Kazhdan, p. 101

55 *Eustathii metropolitae Thessalonicensis epistola XXII*, ed. T. L. Tafel, *Eustathii metropolitae Thessalonicensis opuscula* (Frankfurt 1832), pp. 339–40 (= MPG vol. 136, cols. 1299); trans. Starr, *Jews in the Byzantine Empire*, no. 184

56 There is nothing whatever to support Emmanuel, pp. 38–9, in his belief that Eustathius wanted 'justice à tous et, en particulière, aux Israélites'

57 *Opuscula*, p. 66. Emmanuel, p. 40, actually thought that the sermon was a plea for tolerance towards Jews

58 Opuscula, p. 293. *Eustathii de Thessalonica urbe a Latinis capta CXV, CXVI* = MPG vol. 136, cols 112–13; for CXV (the shortage, but not the attack on the Armenians) cf. Starr, *Jews in the Byzantine Empire*, no. 189. Nothing

supports the assertion by W. Miller, presumably derived from these passages, that 'there were traitors in the city and neighbourhood—Jews and Armenians', *Essays on the Latin Orient* (Cambridge 1921), p. 276

59 See Ostrogorsky, *Byzantine State*, pp. 358–9 (note 4)
60 M. Halevy, 'On the History of Rumanian Jewry in the Middle Ages', *Mizraḥ u-Ma'arāv* 3 (1929), p. 279 (in Hebrew)
61 Asher, vol. 2, p. 38, note 73. The present day village of Valachia, near Kalambaka at the foot of the central Pindus range, perhaps perpetuates their name
62 Ankori, *Karaites in Byzantium*, p. 377; Baron, vol. 5, pp. 195–6
63 S. Poznanski, 'Mesvi al-Okbari; Chef d'une secte juive au dixième siècle', REJ 34 (1897), pp. 179–70
64 Ankori, pp. 386–7 (note 86); Ostrogorsky, *Byzantine State*, p. 257
65 Ankori, p. 415
66 Yaḥyā ibn Sa'īd, PO vol. 23, pp. 481–6
67 Doelger, *Regesten*, no. 798; Starr, *Jews in the Byzantine Empire*, no. 127
68 See Betzalel (Cecil) Roth, 'On the History of the Jews in Cyprus', *Sefer Zikaron le-Yitzhak Ben-Tzvi* (Jerusalem 1954), pp. 287–8 (in Hebrew)
69 S. D. Goitein, 'Historical Evidence from the Pen of a Doctor and Liturgical Poet in Byzantium', *Tarbitz* 27 (1958), pp. 528–35 (in Hebrew); *idem*, 'A Letter from Seleucia (Cilicia)', *Speculum* 39 (1964), pp. 298–303. For John's campaign, see Runciman, *Crusades*, vol. 2, pp. 210–18
70 S. P. Lampros, Μιχαὴλ Ἀκομινάτου τοῦ χωνιάτου τὰ σωζόμενα (Athens 1879–80), vol. 1, p. 53; vol. 2, pp. 439–40; cf. Starr, *Jews in the Byzantine Empire*, no. 176
71 Ramsay, *Historical Geography* (London 1890), pp. 80–1; p. 343
72 Runciman, *Crusades*, vol. 2, pp. 267, 270
73 S. Assaf, 'Egyptian Jews in the time of Maimonides', *Moznaim* 3 (1935), p. 429 (in Hebrew); cf. Starr, *op. cit.*, no. 194 (his translation of בנייסות מקומות משובשות by 'places upset by troops' is inadequate, even if ours is too free)
74 Our translation, lines 74–95
75 *Sibuv ha-Rav Rabbi Petaḥiā*, ed. and trans. A. Benisch, *The Travels of Rabbi Petahiah of Ratisbon* (London 1856), text, p. 18, trans., p. 19; ed. and trans. L. Gruenhut, *Die Rundreise des R. Petachjah aus Regensburg* (Jerusalem-Frankfurt 1904–5), text, p. 10, trans., p. 13
76 Ya'ari, p. 50
77 Baron, vol. 4, pp. 165–7
78 See G. Moravcsik, 'Barbarische Sprachreste in der Theogonie des Johannes Tzetzes', BNJ 7 (1930), pp. 353–7; Vryonis, DOP 17, pp. 291–2 (note 9)
79 *Matthew*, XXI.1–5
80 Loparev, pp. 13–15; p. 77; part quoted by Starr, *Jews in the Byzantine Empire*, no. 192. His 'and Moslems' after 'accursed Jews' (in text, 'and Hagarenes') was a later interpolation; cf. Loparev, pp. 47–8 and introduction, pp. xv–xx
81 Doelger, *Regesten*, no. 1536
82 Doelger, *Regesten*, no. 1467; cf. also no. 1465

83 For the contrary view, see A. Andréadès, 'The Jews in the Byzantine Empire', *Economic History* 3 (1934–37), p. 15, note 5
84 Cf. E. Patlagean, 'Contribution juridique à l'histoire des Juifs dans la Mediterranée médiévale: les formules grecques de serment', REJ 124 (1965) pp. 146–7
85 Zepos, vol. 1, p. 375; MPG vol. 133, col. 717C; Patlagean, pp. 139–40
86 Patlagean, pp. 144–5
87 Zepos, vol. 1, p. 373; MPG vol. 133, col. 716(C–D) Patlagean, pp. 138–9
88 See Parkes, p. 222
89 הרופא מצרי מפני רפואתו (Adler, text, p. 16, note 38)

CHAPTER VIII

The Life of the Community

Such, then, was the story of Byzantine Jews from Justinian to the Fourth Crusade, such the peculiar relation between them and their surroundings which, in one way or another, persisted from the beginning to the end of that period. It was this relation which, on the one hand, was constantly reflected in Byzantine Jewish legislation with its reiterated privileges balanced by its reiterated restrictions while, on the other, it was as clearly reflected in everyday life, with its basic hostility to the Jews balanced by its moments of joint Jewish-Christian struggle against the authorities, or by instances of Christian inclination to Jewish practices. It was this relation which remained essentially unaffected both by outbursts of anti-semitic violence, whether ecclesiastical or secular, and by the four deliberate attempts by the authorities at forcible conversion. And it was this relation which, during the period of imperial decline, the period of western ascendancy, began to deteriorate—though, even then, it by no means disappeared: much of provincial Jewry continued to benefit from it, and Greece and Asia Minor actually saw the rise of new communities. In short, for close on seven hundred years, Byzantine Jews enjoyed much better conditions than those in western Europe. True, there were comparable conditions in the Spanish provinces newly conquered from the Muslims. But there, as elsewhere under their rule, the Muslims had encouraged an urban economy very similar to the Byzantine one which for the Jews had had similar results. It is the peculiarities of these conditions under Christian rule which give Byzantine Jewish history its primary interest, and it is chiefly these pecularities which have so far been examined. It must now be asked what effects they had on the internal life of the community, on its customs, on its level of Jewish learning. These topics are particularly important in an account of Byzantine Jewry. For, while favourable conditions in general were likely to favour the growth of a well organized community with strong communal institutions, examples of which were seen by Benjamin of Tudela, the absence of rigid social or economic barriers between Jews and Christians was equally likely to cause a weakening of the communal bond, an apathy towards Judaism, a progressive assimilation to the dominant culture. It is in the light of these opposing tendencies that the internal life of the Byzantine community must be approached, it is by an estimate of their relative strength that the place of Jews in Byzantium can finally be assessed. Unfortunately, it is precisely on the internal life of the community that information is disappointingly inadequate. References in the sources are often fragmentary, making generalizations more risky than those which have been suggested for the relations of the community with the external world.

The main exception, as there has been occasion to notice before, is the comparatively lavish information available on the communities of Byzantine Italy, especially in respect of Jewish learning. In one instance, it was only thus that the memory of a community was preserved at all. The only reference during our period to Jews at Siponto, then a town some sixty miles north-west along the coast from Bari, is that in the eleventh century it was the home of the Talmudist R. Anan ben Marinus Ha-Cohen.[1] However, the great centres for Talmudic study in Byzantine Italy were at places already familiar to us—at Oria, at Bari and at Otranto. At Oria, by the middle of the ninth century, there were well established Talmudic colleges. R. Amittai and his two sons, R. Shefatiyā and R. Ḥananel taught in them and expounded in public the precepts of the Oral Law. Their work was much advanced, according to Aḥīma'atz, by the arrival of a certain Abu

Aaron ben Samuel, a Talmudist from Baghdad, a mysterious figure of whom more will be said later. Aaron arrived before the death of Amittai, that is before 860, quickly making his mark not only as a teacher, but also as a member of the rabbinical court, the quality of whose decisions 'recalled the days of the Sanhedrin'. Thus, one that he found guilty of incest he condemned to death by burning, another to death by stoning for sodomy, a third to death by decapitation for murder and a fourth to death by strangulation for adultery, pronouncing those sentences 'before the assembled congregation'. The first three sentences were duly carried out; the fourth condemned man, named Theophilus (the only one of the four whom Aḥīma‘atz named), was saved by the imperial governor when he hinted that he might turn Christian. In the event, he remained faithful to Judaism. His change of mind caused him to be sent to prison where he was mercilessly beaten and his feet cut off. After these tortures, and after a year in prison, Theophilus still refused conversion. His steadfastness expiated the sin of which Aaron had found him guilty, and, by God's mercy, he was allowed, while still in prison, to arrange for his daughter's marriage. Then, on the morning after the Day of Atonement, his prospective son-in-law could not find him in his cell 'alive or dead, for God had taken him into his care'.[2]

Has this story of Aaron and Theophilus historical value? It is true that the Talmud had all but abolished the possibility of a rabbinical court passing a sentence of death. However, the phrase 'before the assembled congregation' might indicate that Aaron used another procedure, for which there was some precedent, whereby a death sentence became the common decision of the community.[3] It is also true that, whatever the procedure, no rabbinical court, no community, was ever given in Byzantine legislation the right to pass sentences of death, much less to carry them out. Accordingly, it has been suggested that Aḥīma‘atz appropriated the whole incident from some Spanish or Sicilian community where, under the Muslims, this amount of self-government was legally possible.[4] But this is unnecessary; this question of legality is irrelevant. Aaron and the Talmudists of Oria stirred the people to take vengeance on transgressors of the

Law, with small attention to the law of the land. In Byzantine eyes, it was a simple lynching from which one prospective victim was luckily saved. And it was probably preoccupation with Arab raids on Italy that allowed the whole affair, for the time being, to go unpunished. It could hardly have been unknown to Basil I in his dealings with Oria some fifteen years later. Lastly, there is the objection that it is particularly these points that Aḥimaʿatz stresses that sound so contrived. The four transgressions attracted the four types of execution prescribed in the Talmud, so that each could conveniently be mentioned.[5] The sufferings and salvation of Theophilus are more edifying than convincing. However, just as with the semi-legendary air that Aḥimaʿatz gave to his story of the Basilian persecution, these objections need cast no doubt on the essential facts in his information. The influence of the Talmudists had been strong enough for the community to judge four of their number guilty of acts meriting death, and to carry out its judgment on three of them. It was the fame of these events which inspired Aḥimaʿatz two hundred years later to add those details which, in his eyes, produced a suitable story with a satisfying moral conclusion.[6]

Talmudic studies continued at Oria during the first half of the tenth century, though in conditions of increasing difficulty because of the Arab raids in one of which the 'ten learned and pious rabbis died'.[7] Finally, the persecution of Romanus virtually destroyed the community.[8] At least one of the rabbis of Oria then fled to Bari and helped Talmudic studies there, whose organized establishment is not mentioned before that period. The first reference is in the letter from the Jews of Bari to Ḥasdai ibn Shaprūṭ describing the results of the persecution. The letter spoke of a Talmudic college and named five of its teachers.[9] And it was probably teachers from that college who disputed with Ḥananel ben Paltiel his claim to family belongings.[10] But the Talmudists of Bari acquired a more than local reputation. Their opinion, at the end of the tenth century, on a question involving property rights in the marriage settlement, was preserved by the French Talmudist Abraham ben David of Posquières (1120–98), and by his great contemporary Eliezer ben Nathan of Mayence (died

1171). The opinion had thirteen signatures: seven were of the members of the court that had given it, while six confirmed its correctness and the authenticity of the actual document.[11] The existence of a reputation outside Byzantium found its most vivid expression in Abraham ibn Daud's story of the incident which we mentioned to illustrate the danger of Mediterranean voyages in the second half of the tenth century: the capture of four rabbis on a voyage from Bari by an Arab captain who held them to ransom.[12] The four were on their way to take part in the so-called *Kallā* conference, organized twice every year (in early spring and early autumn) at the academies of Surā and Pumbeditā, for Talmudic study and to raise money for their upkeep.[13] Ibn Daud told what happened to three of the captives. One, R. Shemaria, was ransomed in Egypt and became head of the academy at Fusṭāṭ (Old Cairo). Another, R. Ḥushiel, was ransomed by the Jews of Kairawān, at that time the most important Faṭimid city after Cairo and Alexandria, where he also became the head of the academy. He may have particularly advanced scholarship there by initiating studies in the Palestinian Talmud, previously unknown to the Jews of North Africa.[14] The third, R. Moses, together with his young son Ḥanok, was ransomed by the Jews of Cordova. His learning made so deep an impression that he, too, became the leading scholar there, attracting students both from Spain and from North Africa. But his success led to greater consequences than that of R. Shemaria at Fusṭāṭ or of R. Ḥushiel at Kairawān. Those questions on problems of the interpretation of the Law which had hitherto been addressed to the rabbis of Surā and of Pumbeditā, were now addressed to R. Moses of Cordova and to his son Ḥanok after him. When Ḥanok died, 'the communities of east and west did not resume the sending of gifts to the Academies inasmuch as these scholars (i.e. Moses and Ḥanok) raised many disciples and the knowledge of the Talmud spread throughout the world'.[15] In other words, according to ibn Daud, the coming of R. Moses and his son was the immediate cause of the decline of the Gaonate.

Now ibn Daud, just as Aḥima'atz, embellished his story with details meant to be convincing but which detract from its credibility. Thus, the wisdom of R. Moses was dramatically recognized when 'in rags and a stranger' he corrected the then leading scholar of Cordova on a difficult point of interpretation. R. Ḥanok had to defeat a complicated plot against him reminiscent of the *Thousand and One Nights* before he triumphantly succeeded to his father's place. Many other details, particularly the chronology, showed signs of having been copied from a mixture of literary traditions for their symbolic significance or for their edifying value.[16] However, as with Aḥima'atz, these embellishments do not destroy the kernel of historical truth: the three rabbis whom Ibn Daud named were invited to the *Kallā* conference and, in one way or another, reached positions of consequence in Egypt, North Africa and Spain, whatever the exact circumstances of these events.[17] This alone was evidence of the level of Talmudic studies at Bari. But Ibn Daud's story implied something more. There is no doubt that at that time the Spanish rabbinate grew in importance at the expense of Surā and Pumbeditā. There were many causes, among them the general rise in influence of Spanish Jewry under the leadership of Ḥasdai ibn Shaprūṭ, which Ibn Daud preferred to gloss over for reasons of his own, and did so by putting everything down to the credit of the personal excellence of R. Moses and his providential arrival at Cordova.[18] However, this very explanation, to be at all acceptable, had to depend on the high reputation which Talmudic studies at Bari had acquired outside Byzantium, and which they were known to possess in his own day. Bari's reputation was shared by Otranto. The only specific information we have is that the exceptionally learned R. Isaiah perished in the persecution of Romanus.[19] Yet Otranto, together with Bari, must have supplied what had been lost with the decay of Oria, and must have succeeded to its place. For R. Jacob ben Meir of Troyes (1100–1171), the grandson of Rashi, called Rabbenu Tam, the outstanding rabbinical authority of his day, in his commentary on the mystical work *Sefer ha-Yashar* ('The Book of the Upright'), adapted the words of the prophet and declared: 'For out of Bari shall go forth the Law and the word of the Lord from Otranto'.[20]

The Jewish scholars of Byzantine Italy, did in fact, together with their achievements in Talmudic studies, pay considerable attention to mystical literature. They studied the *Hekhalot*, books about the (divine) palaces or worlds, which had originated in *midrashim* on Genesis and which had crystallized during the period of the Gaonate into doctrines concerning the direct vision of God, the angels and other celestial beings. An important part of them were writings called the *Merkabah*, or *Ma'aseh Merkabah*, interpretations of Ezekiel's vision of the divine throne-chariot.[21] It was said that these studies could be used by the adept to produce not always permissible miraculous results. Abū Aaron may have been forced to leave Baghdad on suspicion of having done so.[22] Subsequently, however, he was credited with repairing the results of such misuse by others. On his way through Italy he was said to have turned back into human form a boy who had been turned into an ass, and to have discovered that a young man leading the prayers was really dead, having been granted an artificial extension of life, by means of an insertion of the Divine Name into his right arm. When Aaron got to Oria he found that Shefatiyā and Hananel were already versed both in the *Hekhalot*, particularly the *Merkabah*, and in the *Sefer ha-Yashar*.[23] It may be supposed that it was by the application of this knowledge that Shefatiyā cured Basil's daughter, while another story of the dangers of its misuse showed its study was being pursued a hundred years later.[24] Of course, stories such as these made a big impression and were long remembered. Their value here is that they show how the Palestinian and Babylonian tradition in mystical literature was preserved in Byzantine Italy. In 982 Shabbetai Donnolo wrote a commentary on the *Sefer Yetzirā* (The Book of Creation). Although he had left Oria when the ten learned and pious rabbis died, he ought still to be counted to its credit since he was a member of the Amittai family. And it was in the introduction to this commentary that he described the Arab raid which caused the death of the rabbis. The *Sefer Yetzirā* was an example of another type of mysticism. It approached the divine not so much through the idea of a direct vision, but rather through calculations based on combinations of the letters in the Hebrew alphabet and on the ten primary numbers—supposed to correspond with ten finite embodiments of the infinite, that is with the humanly understandable attributes of God.[25] That such studies were sufficiently widespread in Italy can be inferred from the trouble taken by Donnolo to ensure the recognition of his authorship by stressing it, and the hard work it had given him, in a long rhymed section of his introduction, calling down divine punishment on any future copyist who dared to omit it.[26] The work of Shefatiyā, of Ḥananel and of Abū Aaron, of Donnolo and of his potential plagiarists had, as with the Talmud in Byzantine Italy, a more than local importance. Here too Byzantine Italy was the main channel through which traditional Jewish learning was transmitted to Europe. It was from Oria that the *Hekhalot* tradition reached R. Yehudā ben Samuel he-Ḥasid of Regensburg (died 1217), while his pupil, R. Eleazar ben Yehudā of Worms (1160–1238) used Donnolo's commentary. These two scholars were the founders of Kabbalā studies.[27]

Byzantine Italy also saw the beginnings of Jewish historiography. About the middle of the tenth century there appeared the so-called *Yosippon*, ostensibly a compilation of the writings of a Joseph ben Gorion, who was supposed to have lived at the time of the Jewish war against the Romans which ended with the fall of the Masada fortress in the year 73. The *Yosippon* was largely derived from the *Antiquities* of Josephus. Although its independent historical value was very small, it achieved a remarkable popularity, becoming the basis for most medieval Jewish historiography in France and Germany. It eventually made a big impression on Christian Hebraists who were inclined to place it above Josephus himself.[28] Long before that, it had aroused immediate interest outside Byzantium. The same Samuel who escaped from Otranto during the persecutions of Romanus, and who made his way to Spain, was bringing a copy with him at the request of ibn Shaprūṭ of which he was robbed at the start of his journey.[29] But the *Yosippon* eventually did reach Spain, and was extensively used by ibn Daud.[30] While the *Yosippon* was thus another example of the spread of Jewish learning from Byzantine Italy, a far more important work in its own right was, of course, the chronicle of Aḥima'atz itself which, although it was actually written, or completed, at Capua, in Lombard territory, can hardly be excluded from Byzantine-Jewish historiography. Its many fanciful peculiarities and its concern to praise the virtues of the Amittai family do not weaken, as has been repeatedly stressed here, its substratum of genuine information. It is the only connected story of the Byzantine communities in Italy that we possess and, after Benjamin of Tudela, it is probably the most valuable Jewish primary source to have survived for the history of Byzantine Jews as a whole. In the present context, the chronicle has a special significance. The preservation of material which enabled Aḥimaʿatz to reconstruct events over the previous two hundred years or more is in itself evidence of a persistent and living historiographical tradition.

Finally, in the ninth century, Byzantine Italy saw an efflorescence of liturgical poetry, a rebirth of ancient Palestinian styles and vocabulary. As with Talmudic studies, there was one instance when only in this way was the memory of a community preserved. The bare fact of Jews at Venosa from about that period is attested by a number of tomb inscriptions.[31] But its real importance was that it was the home of R. Silano, the liturgical poet whom we mentioned in connection with the Basilian persecution. On one occasion his poetic talent got him out of a difficult situation. Silano was a scholar as well as a poet. His reputation brought a rabbi from Jerusalem to pass some time at Venosa, where he expounded the Scriptures every Sabbath, while Silano added his interpretations. Silano had an unlucky sense of humour. One Sabbath, he somehow substituted a satirical comment of his own on a local quarrel for the prescribed midrashic passage, which it parodied—and the rabbi innocently read it out to the congregation. When he saw what he had done, he left Venosa in disgust and caused his colleagues in Jerusalem to pronounce a decree of excommunication against the man who had so wantonly insulted him. Then Silano adroitly adapted a penitential hymn to include a denunciation of the Karaites together with praises for the orthodox rabbinate. And the rabbis of Jerusalem were so impressed by his talent that, when the hymn was read to them by a member of the Amittai family on a visit during the Days of Penitence, they unanimously revoked the decree.[32] Apart from Silano, the finest examples of liturgical poetry were by Shefatyiā and by his son Amittai. Two examples of the latter's work, also referring to the Basilian persecution, have already been quoted.[33] As in other fields of Jewish learning, this efflorescence was not only important for its intrinsic worth but also for its influence outside Byzantium in later ages. To this day, passages from these three poets are said in the Concluding Service for the Day of Atonement according to the Ashkenazi rite.[34] And the poetry which they, with others, had revived inspired in its turn such poets as Solomon ben Yehudā of Rome, the poets belonging to the Kalonymos family of Lucca and the liturgists of France and Germany.[35]

In short, the achievements of the Byzantine Italian communities, in Talmudic and mystical studies, in historiography and in the composition of liturgical poetry, helped to revive or preserve traditional Jewish learning, transmitting it from its old centres to new centres north of the Alps and in Spain. This process was part and parcel of the general role of Byzantium. The historical and cultural link that these communities constituted between the old world and the new, between the world of the Talmud and the world of the French codifiers or the German mystics, was the Jewish side of what Byzantium as such was achieving: the preservation and transmission of the heritage of all the Mediterranean world, the cultures that had flourished under Greek or Roman rule and the Islāmic culture of its own day, for the benefit of the new culture which was gradually civilizing the barbarian West— with the partial exception of Spain which had had the great good fortune of an earlier link with Islām. This process of preservation and transmission, whether Jewish or non-Jewish, depended upon a prosperous urban economy and upon security in daily life, conditions which, outside Islām, Byzantium alone had been able to provide. Obviously, in the Jewish context, the prerequisite was specifically a secure life for the Jews. We have tried to show that, comparatively speaking, Byzantium did provide this too. And the way in which the Italian communities participated in the general Byzantine process of preservation and transmission reflected their specifically Byzantine conditions of existence.

A similar process was at work in other centres of Byzantine Jewry, particularly where it was most to be expected: in Constantinople and Thessalonica. But there it was on a somewhat limited scale in comparison to the south Italian centres. Firstly, it was virtually confined within the framework of the Rabbanite–Karaite dispute. The *Leḳaḥ Ṭov* of Tobiah ben Eliezer, who probably moved to Thessalonica from Castoria and made it his permanent home, was the only important exception. While it was influenced by the anti-Karaite polemic of Saʿadiā, the Gaon of Surā (882–942), and in turn influenced ibn Daud,[36] its general exegetic principles were eventually accepted by the rabbis of France and Germany.[37] The chief result was that the Karaites of Constantinople became the link between their Palestinian origins and their later European development. The learning brought by Tobiah ben Moses and by Jacob ben Simon from Jerusalem was eventually transmitted to the Karaites of the Crimea, of Lithuania and of Poland.[38] Secondly, in addition to this sectarian limitation, there is no evidence that the process of transmission took place against the background of that kind of revival which typified it in Byzantine Italy. The non-Italian references to Byzantine Jewish learning are relatively few. The author of the seventh century *Trophies of Damascus* told how the Jewish side in that dispute about the icons called for the assistance of scholars from the Byzantine province of Cappadocia.[39] In the middle of the ninth century there is an even vaguer reference to Byzantine Jewish scholars holding heretical opinions on Ezra the Scribe.[40] About the same time, there was also the possibility that the monk Cyril who, together with Methodius, brought Christianity to the Slavs and gave them their alphabet, was helped in the latter task by having received some Jewish learning at Cherson in the Crimea, then an outpost of the empire.[41] At the beginning of the eleventh century, occurred the only reference to Jewish learning at Thessalonica before the time of Tobiah ben Eliezer.[42] About the same time, the Gaon Hai ben Sherira (939–1038) spoke with respect of Greek rabbinical courts and mentioned students from Constantinople at Pumbedita.[43] The letter of a Byzantine-Jewish woman, a certain Maliḥā, written towards the middle of the twelfth century, exhibited the ornaments of a literary Hebrew style which indicated a reasonable level of general Hebrew for her to have learned this accomplishment.[44] For the bulk of our period, references to specific fields of learning are also sparse. Eleazar ben Kalir (early sixth century?), many of whose compositions are preserved in the Ashkenazi Festival Prayers, was the chief ornament of the Palestinian liturgical tradition, and so can be accounted to the credit of Byzantine Jewry under Justinian or Justin I. The tradition was continued under the Muslims by such poets as Yannai. But it was transmitted to the west through Italy; it had no followers elsewhere in Byzantium. So far as we know, only two non-Italian references exist: the passage said on New Year and on the Day of Atonement containing 'they shall build for Thee their altars, their idols overthrown, and their graven gods shall shame them, as they turn to Thee alone' may have been written in triumph at the reinstatement of iconoclasm by Leo V (813–820), a reinstatement which did not affect Italy.[45] The doctor of Seleucia who had such excellent relations with the authorities was also, apparently, a liturgical poet, but nothing is known of his compositions.[46] In regard to mysticism, Petaḥiā of Ratisbon, in the passage already quoted, believed that interest in the practical side persisted: 'They have among them young men', he said, 'versed in the names (i.e. the Divine Names of God), summoning up devils who serve them as their slaves'.[47] Finally, towards the end of our period, there lived three scholars, connected neither with Italy, nor with the Karaite controversy, whose reputation reached beyond the frontiers. They were R. Meyuḥas ben Eliyahū (it is not known from which community), who wrote commentaries on Genesis, Exodus, Chronicles and Job, R. Abraham Zuṭra of Thebes, who wrote on the *Sifra*, itself a commentary on a group of *midrashim*, and R. Hillel ben Eliakim of Selymbria (between Constantinople and Rodosto, which Benjamin of Tudela missed), who wrote both on the *Sifra* and the *Sifre* (commentaries on another group of *midrashim*).[48]

This impression of a contrast between the Jewish learning of

Byzantine Italy, particularly in its external influences, and the rest of Byzantium may, of course, be misleading. It may not reflect the reality but simply that one source survived rather than another. If the chronicle of Aḥimaʿatz had not been chanced upon some seventy years ago, little could have been said about Italy either. Yet it is difficult to believe that if a comparable efflorescence of learning had taken place at Constantinople or at Thessalonica, apart from Karaite polemics, and especially if it had influenced the rabbis of early medieval Europe, no trace of it should have remained. It cannot be accidental that Benjamin of Tudela was extremely brief on this subject. He did not name the 'great scholars in Mishnā and Talmud' of Thebes—not even R. Zuṭra. Regarding Thessalonica, he was content to give the bare information that the sons of the government rabbi 'were scholars'.[49] He spoke of the piety and wealth of the Jews of Constantinople, but not of their scholarship—with the possible exception of R. Aaron, if our interpretation of his nickname is correct.[50] What can be the explanation of this contrast with Byzantine Italy? Why did the large, prosperous, old-established communities of Constantinople and Thessalonica, and for that matter the other communities in Greece and Asia Minor which at least in the twelfth century were in a flourishing condition, contribute so little to Jewish learning? The answer must be conjectural for the sources shed little light on their internal life and institutions.

Part of the answer may lie in a decline of orthodoxy and of communal loyalties—as against that organizational efficiency of the community to which the journey of Benjamin of Tudela bore witness. There is some evidence of divergences from rabbinic Judaism. R. Isaiah ben Mali of Trani (near Bari), a copious Talmudist of the French school who wrote in the second half of the twelfth century, when south Italy had been outside the Byzantine orbit for a hundred years, complained that not a single Byzantine community understood the proper use of the ritual bath, customary for the post-menstrual purification and for the purification of the bride before marriage. This laxity may have been the result of Karaite influence since, according to R. Isaiah, it had come about because R. Hillel ben Eliakim had suggested that certain rules for the ritual bath were only rabbinic enactments.[51] R. Isaiah accused Byzantine Jews of other irregularities in connection with marriages. Betrothals could take place at an extremely early age, occasionally when the bride was only four years old. And, while it may have been decided beforehand that she would not leave her parents' house until an agreed time in the future, the fact that the 'Seven Benedictions' of the marriage ceremony were commonly recited at the betrothal made of it a proper marriage, possibly (though not certainly) legally binding—even without consummation.[52] Secondly, the marriage dowry always remained untouched in the custody of the wife or at her disposal, returning to her family in the event of her death, unless a specific condition to the contrary had been written into the marriage contract. Both these departures from custom can also be ascribed to Karaite influence. The Karaites were inclined to impose the obligation of fulfilling all the commandments of the Law (of which marriage is one) not at maturity, but as soon as the child could speak.[53] And, in regard to the marriage contract, they invariably favoured the wife's family.[54] Now, despite the frequently bad relations between Rabbanites and Karaites, even leading to the disorders which caused the government to intervene, to levy a heavy fine, and to build a wall between the two at Constantinople, there is some evidence of Karaite influence already in the early years of the Karaite immigration. The baptismal formula which we mentioned in connection with the Jews and the Montanists, and which was first extant not later than 1027, demanded that the Jewish convert to Christianity abjured his festivals according to a calendar, and with descriptions, more reminiscent of Karaite than of Rabbanite practice.[55] Tobiah ben Moses boasted of the Rabbanites who had become Karaites after seeing for themselves the errors of the Talmud.[56] This possibility of Karaite influence a hundred years later meant that the process had continued: it meant a weakening of communal loyalties among the Rabbanites, a weakening of the communal bond. R. Isaiah deplored two other Byzantine Jewish habits which suggest this conclusion. While one couple were so happy when their long-previously contracted marriage was consummated, that they asked for a second betrothal and marriage ceremony as a celebration, the custom of early betrothals and the peculiarities of the dowry system led to a large number of divorces. And then, either the father-in-law or the husband would often induce the government authorities to interfere and exercise compulsion on the unwilling party. There was one instance when an actual declaration of divorce was obtained in this way, instead of from the rabbinical court. But it was not only in the matter of divorce that Byzantine Jews might circumvent the Law, if it was an obstacle to them. Not one out of a thousand, complained R. Isaiah, bothered to consult the rabbis of his community over any dispute at all if he could conveniently come to a private arrangement.[57] How long had these tendencies to laxness existed? Again, a definite answer is impossible for lack of evidence. To the extent that Karaism was responsible, it is reasonable to suppose that they began to manifest themselves long before R. Isaiah's day, If so, they constituted an element which clearly differentiated the communities of Greece and Asia Minor from those of Byzantine Italy—since the latter were outside the sphere of Karaite influence. Thus, to the extent that these tendencies weakened the way of life and the communal basis necessary for the development of Jewish learning, they would not have affected the communities of Byzantine Italy.

A second element which differentiated the two areas was to be found in the social conditions with which we are familiar. In the great majority of instances, the events which illustrated the comparative absence of barriers between Jews and Christians, the readiness of Jews and Christians to riot together against the government, to work together in the guilds, to produce various combinations of Judaeo-Christian syncretism, occurred in Greece, in Asia Minor, in Syria before the Arab conquest—but not in Italy. Thus, whatever the reason, it can be concluded that the Jews of Oria, of Bari or of Otranto, while still freer in this respect than western Jewries proper, yet led a more isolated life than did the Jews of Constantinople or of Thessalonica. These circumstances constituted a greater encouragement for the development of Jewish learning in Byzantine Italy, particularly for the maintenance of links with the old centres of learning, than elsewhere in

Byzantium. These circumstances may be connected with a third differentiating element which, in turn, may have been a cause of the difference in levels of Jewish learning. That familiarity with Greek which, as we have noted, the Jews of Byzantium had had long before Justinian, seems to have declined in the Italian communities, both Byzantine and Lombard, by the end of the seventh or at the beginning of the eighth century, when tomb inscriptions, of which those at Venosa were later examples, began to appear only in Hebrew.[58] On the other hand, the comparatively free intercourse of Jews with Christians in Greece and Asia Minor produced a measure of cultural assimilation—or preserved it. There, Greek continued to be used liberally to supplement Hebrew for a variety of purposes. This was done either by transliterating the sound of actual Greek words into Hebrew, or by writing in Hebrew letters invented Greek equivalents of Hebrew usages. The *midrash* we quoted on the circus and throne of Solomon and another on passages from the Psalms perhaps of the ninth century, contained many examples of both methods.[59] The items of the dowry in the marriage contract of Mastaura, and in the ceremonial marriage gift which the bridegroom gave in addition to the *mohar*, appeared, in the main, as direct transliterations from the Greek. It should be noted that these methods must be distinguished from the use of Greek loan-words, of which Hebrew has a substantial number, at least from Talmudic times. These loan-words normally reached Hebrew through Aramaic, and are recognizable by the consequent changes their Greek form suffered in the process.[59a]. The baptismal formula of 1027 included evidence of the second method, though in a complicated way. In it, written, of course, in Greek, there appear two strange words which are actually re-transliterations of Hebraised Greek equivalents. The intending convert was exhorted to reject the teachings of the 'archiferekitai' and the 'archirebitai'. The first word was a combination of the Greek prefix meaning 'chief' followed by a transliteration of *pirka*—a passage in scripture—together with the suffix of the Greek plural. The whole word stood for *Reshei Pirkā*, the title originally given to the heads of Talmudic colleges but extended to mean the leaders of the community.[60] The middle component of the second word was a transliteration of 'rabbi', and its meaning was therefore 'chief rabbis'. That these were the forms of title actually used by Byzantine Jews is confirmed in a list, probably belonging to the twelfth century, where they appear with others, either similar constructions or real Greek words. The president of the synagogue was called the *archisynagogi*. The council was the *gerousia* (= council of elders). Its members were *archontes* (= magistrates). The *grammateos* (= secretary) was an official who combined the duties of compiler of the communal regulations, keeper of the communal archives, and of *sofer*—the professional copier of the Scrolls of the Law.[61] Finally, there is some evidence for the use of Greek proper names. The bride of Mastaura was called Eudokia. Their use gradually spread. Eventually a fair number were commonly given: some genuinely Greek, some derived in one way or another from Hebrew.[62]

In addition to these examples of Greek usages in personal or in institutional contexts, it also happened that, in exegetical texts, there were difficulties in understanding what was read without an explanation in transliterated Greek. Thus Tobiah ben Eliezer in his *Leḳaḥ Tov* not only used transliterated Greek by the two methods we have noted, but also was occasionally compelled to explain Hebrew words in this way, while Hillel ben Eliakim regularly did so for whole passages in his *Sifra* and *Sifre*, as well as for many single words.[63] And the gap of some fifty years between the two suggests the growing necessity for these explanations.

However, the possible extent of this intrusion of Greek at the expense of Hebrew, indicative though it was of a certain assimilation to the dominant culture, must not be exaggerated. Firstly, so far as is known, it did not extend to the service of the synagogue. The Byzantine Jewish order of prayers, the *Maḥzor Romania*, first printed at Constantinople in 1520 but derived from much earlier compilations and usages, has preserved no signs of such an intrusion. In fact, the only usage there which may reflect something specific in the history of Byzantine Jews is that, to the passage beginning 'And for slanderers let there be no hope' in the prayer of the Eighteen Benedictions, there was added 'and for heretics'.[64] This addition may have referred to the Karaites. Nor was Justinian's claim that the Hebrew of the scriptural readings could not be understood substantiated in our period. The earliest sign of the use of Greek there, was towards the very end of the twelfth century or at the beginning of the thirteenth, when the book of Jonah, the prescribed reading from the Prophets for the Afternoon Service on the Day of Atonement, began to be read in Greek at Corfu and, possibly, at Constantinople. As in our previous examples, the reading was from a Hebrew transliteration of a Greek text.[65] The suggestion has been made that rather later, perhaps in the fourteenth century, some communities in Greece began to apply the Greek term *paraskii megali* (= great preparation), *megali himera* (= great day) or *himera* to the Sabbath before Passover, in imitation of the Byzantine use of those terms for the last Saturday in Lent, and that this was the origin of the term *Shabbat ha-Gadol* (= Great Sabbath) which is the Sabbath before Passover.[66] It was later still, perhaps not before the Ottoman conquest, that the Book of Esther, the prescribed reading for the festival of Purim, was read at Constantinople in some sort of Greek version.[67] And it was only then, that is in the late fifteenth or early sixteenth century, that there were real difficulties in Hebrew. It was then that parts of the Pentateuch began to be reproduced in Hebrew and Greek explicitly for educational purposes—so that the Hebrew would be both understood and learnt from the Greek.[68] It may be also then that the use of Greek became so general as to introduce many Greek words and phrases into the ordinary spoken Hebrew of the Jews of Constantinople.[69]

Secondly, it is clear from all the foregoing, from the persistence of transliterations, that it was only spoken Greek which had become familiar—perhaps to the detriment of Hebrew. There are only two pieces of evidence that written Greek was familiar in our period, whether for ordinary communication or for scholarly purposes. Neither of them is impressive. There exists a tenth-century fragment of a Hebrew-Greek glossary of Mishnaic words. The Greek equivalents are written in a clumsy and unaccented script. For the sound PS, $\Pi\Sigma$ instead of Ψ is used. Out of 124 entries, 20 Greek equivalents are incorrect, 75 correct and the remainder indeterminable owing to the state of the manuscript.[70] Then, Yehudā ben Barzillai of Barcelona in his *Sefer ha-'Ittim* (chronology), written between 1090 and 1105, referred to a letter on the Khazars, which he regretted was lost, by 'a Jew of Constantinople in his own language'.[71] It is not surprising, therefore, that the evidence for a wider interest in Greek culture, as distinct from the language, is also very limited. In fact, it is confined to the Karaites. Tobiah ben Moses understood Greek philosophic terms, Yehudā Hadassi ('from Edessa'), in his encyclopaedia of Karaite doctrines, showed a more fundamental knowledge of Greek philosophic concepts and methodology.[72] This knowledge seems to have been acquired direct from its Greek sources and not, as might be expected, through the Arabic versions which might naturally have been familiar to the Karaites in their countries of origin.[73] That is, it was acquired in the same Greek speaking Byzantine milieu in which the Rabbanites lived. This is significant. For, whatever the Karaite influence in matters of custom and ritual, there was none discernible in the context of Greek philosophy. Nor is it surprising that, under these circumstances, the evidence for interest in non-Jewish learning generally, which a real assimilation to Greek culture might have encouraged, is no greater. It is virtually confined to medicine. Several examples of Jewish doctors have been given. The greatest in the field, as in so many others, was the versatile Shabbetai Donnolo, whose achievements were important not only among Jews but also for the whole development of western medical science. He was connected with the establishment of the first medical faculty, that at the university of Salerno, while his *Sefer ha-Yaḳar* (The Precious Book) was probably the first Hebrew medical textbook in the West.[74] Donnolo explicitly said that in order to acquire his medical knowledge he had had to study a variety of non-Jewish material.[75] And Donnolo was not only a doctor but also something of a physicist and an astronomer, while his best known contribution to Jewish scholarship, his commentary on the *Sefer Yetzirā*, illustrated, as did all his other work, some inspiration from non-

Jewish as well as from Jewish scholarship.[76] No wonder that the monk Nilus of Rossano, highly venerated for his holiness both by the Byzantine church and at Rome, accorded Donnolo a grudging respect, even a degree of friendship, as 'an extremely learned man'.[77] That Nilus was not over-fond of Jews is shown by his protracted and eventually successful pressure on the local authorities not to execute justice when an unoffending Jewish merchant was robbed and murdered.[78] But the very scope and quality of Donnolo's achievements emphasise by their exceptional character the paucity of interest in non-Jewish learning.

Thus, if the weakening of Judaism, whether because of Karaite influence or social conditions, if a certain familiarity with Greek and a decline of Hebrew were responsible for the low level of Jewish learning in Greece and Asia Minor, they did not lead to any true assimilation, however much this was to be expected. That something of the kind was expected, or feared, by the government in two specific respects was shown in the legislation throughout our period. Firstly, from the Code of Theodosius to the last redaction of the *Basilica* we quoted—the 'Minor Synopsis'— there appeared repeated prohibitions of marriages between Jews and Christians which, of course, could have taken place by concealment of the status of one of the partners.[79] But there is not the slightest hint anywhere in the sources (apart from the baseless rumours about Michael II's parentage) that a mixed marriage ever took place or was ever attempted. Secondly, it was believed that conversions to Christianity were a constant possibility. This belief must be distinguished both from the general doctrine of the church on this subject, and from the efforts of the four emperors who tried to convert the Jews by force: from the fourth century onwards, baptismal formulae, of which that of 1027 was an example, contained elaborate precautions to ensure that the conversion was genuine. Not included in the Codes, these formulae were nevertheless legal instruments. Their primary intention was undoubtedly to put into formal phraseology the doctrine which, as we discussed in Chapter II, insisted that conversion could not be from fear or from hope of gain. But the details of the declarations that the convert had to make in this connection bore a more than formal character. For example, he had to declare that his decision had not been taken because of 'any quarrel or dispute which I have had with people of my own religion'. Theophilus of Oria was a case in point. According to the formulae, he could not have been received as a convert.[80] However, there is no evidence that these formulae were ever applied in practice. The evidence for Jewish conversions to Christianity was of two kinds only; either the claims for the success of a decree of forced baptism, or the ritual conclusion to a Judaeo-Christian debate where the literary tradition, one might almost say, made it obligatory for the Jew to become an immediate convert through a combination of argument and miracle. There is no evidence of any real Christianizing tendencies. Throughout the whole of our period, so far as we know, the sole instances of a supposed converted Jew mentioned by name, was the tradition which made Cyril one—perhaps because of the Hebrew learning he may have acquired, and the story of Jacob 'the newly baptized' in the time of Phocas.[81]

Finally, apart from Solomon the Egyptian, the emperor Manuel's doctor, there is no instance of a Jew, converted or unconverted, occupying a position of confidence or authority. Not only was there no real assimilation, but the absence of barriers which we have repeatedly noted was strictly relative, and the opportunities that the empire offered were limited. This limitation is particularly striking in comparison with the opportunities for Jews in Muslim countries, whose economic and social conditions were comparable to those in Byzantium. Under the 'Abbasid Caliphs of Baghdad and the Fatimid Caliphs of Egypt, that is during the period roughly parallel to ours, the Jews held high professional positions. The Abbasid Caliph Mu'tadid (892–902) employed many in responsible offices of state.[82] Benjamin of Tudela expatiated on the honours accorded to the Exilarch, the head of the Babylonian communities.[83] So far as Jews converted to Islām were concerned, it is sufficient to recall the achievements of Ya'kūb ibn-Killis (died 991) who was the founder of the Fatimid administrative system and a famous patron of Muslim learning.[84] In short, while the opportunities for Byzantine Jews were far greater than for the Jews of early medieval Europe, they were far less than under Islām. This difference is crucial: the advantages of the Byzantine Jewish situation did not, and could not, permit the kind of assimilated life which was a commonplace in Muslim countries. Against that possibility there stood a permanent obstacle—the inveterate hostility of the Byzantine ruling institution, whether in its ecclesiastical or in its secular guise.

And yet, Byzantium was still a very different place from the West, despite the hostility, the contempt, the outbursts of violence. Two last examples may show how fundamental that difference was. When the Emperor Romanus IV returned, in 1072, from his captivity among the Seljuks after the battle of Manzikert he was barbarously executed on the orders of his supplanter, Michael VII. And, on these orders, a Jew performed the execution.[85] But no precedent for Byzantium was thereby created. Another instance did not occur until nearly two hundred years later, and that was on the orders of the Bulgarian emperor Asen II.[86] The deliberate and regular use of Jews as executioners, the forcing upon them of a universally hated and degrading employment, was a still later phenomenon in lands which had never had, or had long lost, any Byzantine influence.[87] It is even more illuminating to reflect on the eventual form taken by the story of the Jew and the icon which stood surety for his loan. It will be remembered that in its original Byzantine form it was by no means wholly hostile.[88] The story struck popular imagination and was repeated first in Slavonic, then in Latin translations. Gradually, it acquired more and more crudely anti-semitic characteristics, till, at last, it turned into one of the sources for the story of the *Merchant of Venice*. It created Shylock—the archetypal image of the Jewish moneylender, an image which has remained to plague humanity to this day.[89]

Notes

1   See H. J. Zimmels, 'Scholars and Scholarship in Byzantium and Italy', *The World History of the Jewish People*, second series, vol. 2 (Tel-Aviv 1966) p. 180, 182

2   *Sefer Yuḥasin*, pp. 112–14; 121–2

3   Juster, *Juifs dans l'empire romain*, vol. 2, pp. 158–9 (note 2) on Sanh. 82B

4 Cf. Baron, vol. 5, p. 316, note 69
5 For burning as the penalty for some forms of incest, see Sanh. 75A; for stoning as the penalty for sodomy, Sanh. 54B; for murder by 'slaying' (interpreted as decapitation) and for adultery by strangulation, Sanh. 52B
6 Cf. Starr, *Jews in the Byzantine Empire*, note to no. 52
7 See above, p. 108
8 See above, p. 99
9 See above, Ch. V, note 40
10 See above, p. 116
11 Starr, *ibid.*, no. 120
12 *Book of Tradition*, pp. 63–72 (trans.); pp. 46–53 (text); see above, p. 108
13 *Ibid.*, p. 64, note 13; and Gerson D. Cohen, 'The Story of the Four Captives' PAAJR 29 (1960–61), p. 58, note 9 for a fuller explanation of this term
14 Zimmels, *op. cit.*, p. 179
15 *Book of Tradition*, p. 71 (trans.); p. 53 (text)
16 Cf. Cohen's commentary, *The Book of Tradition*, pp. 200–5
17 Cohen, PAAJR 29, pp. 124–9
18 *Ibid.*, pp. 113–18
19 See above, p. 99
20 Cf. 'For out of Zion shall go forth the Law and the word of the Lord from Jerusalem' (Isaiah, XI.3); cf. I. A. Agus, *World History of the Jewish People*, p. 191
21 G. Scholem, *Major Trends in Jewish Mysticism* (New York 1941), pp. 40–75
22 See A. Neubauer, 'Abou Ahron, le Babylonien', REJ 23 (1891), pp. 231–2
23 *Sefer Yuḥasin*, pp. 112–13
24 *Ibid.* p. 125; see above, p. 88; cf. a similar story, *Sefer Yuḥasin*, pp. 119–20
25 Cf. Scholem, pp. 75–9; 213–22; on Donnolo cf. Starr, *Jews in the Byzantine Empire*, pp. 53–6
26 *Hakhmoni*, ed. Castelli, pp. 1–3; reprinted by J. Schirmann, *An Anthology of Hebrew Verse in Italy* (Berlin 1934), p. 15 (in Hebrew)
27 Cf. Scholem, pp. 82–4; 101–2
28 See Baron, vol. 6, pp. 189–95; 417–20
29 See above, p. 100
30 *Book of Tradition*, Introduction, pp. xxxiii–xli; cf. pp. 221–2
31 Starr, *Jews in the Byzantine Empire*, nos. 24, 26, 27, 29, 30, 31, 32, 33, 34, 35, 35A, 35B, 46, 46A
32 *Sefer Yuḥasin*, pp. 114–15
33 See above, pp. 87–8 and for a selection, Schirmann, pp. 2–11
34 For these passages, 'The sighs of those who praise Thee', by Silano, 'Lord, I remember and am sore amazed' by Amittai, and 'Israel is saved forever by the Lord', by Shefatiayā, see *The Service of the Synagogue, Day of Atonement Part 2*, 20th edn. (London 1955)—'The Routledge Maḥzor'—pp. 262–3, and for their authorship see Schirmann in *World History of the Jewish People*, pp. 251–2
35 For Solomon ben Yehudā, see Schirmann, *Anthology*, pp. 21–6; for the Kalonymos family, L. Zunz, *Literaturgeschichte der synagogalen Poesie* (Berlin 1899), pp. 108–9
36 *Book of Tradition*, p. 159

37 Zimmels, *op. cit.*, p. 186
38 Mann, *Texts and Studies*, vol. 2, pp. 287–91; 556 note 8; 580–3
39 PO vol. 15, p. 234; see above, p. 70
40 Starr, *Jews in the Byzantine Empire*, no. 48—the source is a Muslim essay on Christians: *Risāla firadd 'alā an-Naṣara*, ed. J. Finkel, Three Essays of Abu 'Othman 'Amr ibn Baḥr al-Jaḥīz (Cairo 1926), p. 35; trans. O. Rescher, *Excerpte und Uebersetzungen aus den Schriften des Philologen und Dogmatiken Gāḥiẓ aus Baçra* (Stuttgart 1931), p. 65
41 F. Dvornik, *Les légendes de Cyril et Méthode vues de Byzance* (Prague 1933), p. 359; cf. Baron, vol. 3, pp. 209–10; pp. 330–1 (note 47)
42 See above, Chapter VI, note 54
43 *Teshuvot ha-Geonim*, ed. A. Harkavy, *Zikron la-rishonim ve-gam la-aharonim* 4, part 1 (Berlin 1887), pp. 105–6 (no. 225)
44 Mann, *Jews in Egypt*, vol. 2, pp. 306–7 (text); vol. 1, pp. 241–2 (commentary)
45 Mann, *Texts and Studies*, vol. 1, pp. 234–5 (note 14); for text (trans. I. Zangwill), see the 'Routledge Maḥzor', New Year, pp. 151–2; Day of Atonement (part 2), pp. 154–5, On Kalir, see J. Marcus in *Ḥoreb* 1 (1934) pp. 21–31 (in Hebrew).
46 See above, pp. 151–2
47 See above, Chapter VII, note 75
48 For references to R. Meyuḥas, see Starr, *op. cit.*, no. 177; for R. Zuṭra and R. Hillel, see S. Schechter, 'Notes on Hebrew Mss in the University Library of Cambridge', JQR, old series, 4 (1891–92), pp. 94; 99
49 See above, p. 134 (lines 11–12)
50 See above, Chapter VII, note 7
51 Schechter, *ibid.*, pp. 99–100
52 S. Assaf, 'On the Family Life of Byzantine Jews', *Sefer ha-Yovel le-Professor Sh. Krois,* (Jerusalem 1936–37), pp. 169–70 (in Hebrew)
53 Nemoy, *Hebrew Union College Annual*, 7, p. 387
54 Assaf, *ibid.*, pp. 173–4
55 Ankori, *Karaites in Byzantium*, pp. 280–2; see above, Chapter IV, note 30; for the date, see Beneshevitch, pp. 218–23
56 See extract from *Otzar Neḥmad*, printed by P. F. Frankel, 'Ueber Ben Koreisch', MGWJ 30 (1881), p. 471; and cf. Ankori, *op. cit.*, p. 8, pp. 259–60
57 Assaf, *ibid.*, pp. 175–6
58 See Schirmann, *World History of the Jewish People*, p. 250
59 See J. Perles, 'Juedisch-byzantinische Beziehungen', BZ 2 (1893), pp. 572–3; cf. above, Chapter II, note 58
59a Cf. Reinach, *Mélanges Schlumberger*, pp. 128–30; on the *mohar* cf. *Jewish Encyclopaedia*, vol. 8, p. 337 on Gen XXXIV.12; XXII.16–17; Deut. XX,7; XXII.29; Hosea II. 19–20
60 Cf. Mann, *Jews in Egypt*, vol. 2, pp. 269–70
61 Galanté, p. 36; pp. 45–6
62 See S. Rosanes, *History of the Jews in Turkey*, vol. 1 (Tel-Aviv 1930), pp. 209–12 (in Hebrew)
63 Perles, BZ 2, p. 575; pp. 577–9
64 Rosanes, pp. 207–9

65 J. A. Romanos, 'Histoire de la communauté israélite de Corfu', REJ 23
    (1891), p. 64; this text differed frequently from the Septuagint, on its pro-
    venance see D. C. Hesserling, 'Le livre de Jonas', BZ 10 (1901), pp. 208–17
66 L. Zunz, *Die Ritus des synagogalen Gottesdienstes* (Berlin 1919), pp. 9–10
67 Galanté, p. 39
68 See L. Belleli, 'Deux versions peu connues du Pentateuque', REJ 22 (1891),
    p. 251
69 See list given by Rosanes, pp. 216–18
70 This Glossary is of words from the Tractates *Kilaim* and *Shvi'it* in the Jerusa-
    lem Talmud. It has been edited three times: by A. Papadopulos-Kerameos,
    'A Hebrew-Greek Glossary', *Festschrift zu Ehren des Dr A. Harkavy* (St
    Petersburg 1908), pp. 68–90 (in Greek); by F. Kukules, 'A Hebrew-Greek
    Glossary', BZ 19 (1910), pp. 422–9 (in Greek) (both with a photostat of
    the fragment), and by J. Starr, 'A Fragment of a Greek Mishnaic Glossary',
    PAAJR 6 (1934–35), pp. 353–67
71 See S. Assaf, 'R. Yehuda of Barcelona on the Epistle of Joseph, King of the
    Khazars', *Jeschurun* 11 (1924), Hebrew section, p. 115; cf. Mann, *Texts and
    Studies*, vol. 1, p. 8, note 1; whatever the standard of its Greek may have
    been, it was clearly a letter and not a 'work'—as Starr, PAAJR 6, p. 355
    rather misleadingly called it.
72 Perles, BZ 2, pp. 575–6
73 Ankori, *Karaites in Byzantium*, pp. 193–7
74 Cf. C. and D. Singer, 'The School of Salerno', *History* 10 (1925), pp. 242–6;
    for editions of *Sefer ha-Yakar*, see Starr, *Jews in the Byzantine Empire*, no.
    110, and for a short extract from it, Zimmels, *World History of the Jewish
    People*, pp. 299–300
75 *Sefer Hakhmoni*, ed. Castelli, pp. 4–5
76 I.e. *Sefer Hakhmoni*; see note 26 above and Chapter VI, note 4
77 *S.Nili Junioris vita VII.50* (= MPG 120, cols. 91–4)
78 *Ibid, V.35* (= MPG 120, col. 72 A–D); on Nilus, cf. G. Schlumberger, *La
    Epopée byzantine à la fin du dixième siècle*, vol. 1 (Paris 1896), pp. 463–86
79 C.Th.III.7.2; IX.7.5 (= Pharr, p. 70, p. 232); C.I. 1.9.6 (= Krueger, p. 61);
    Basilica, I.34; *Synopsis Basilicorum* (The 'major' synopsis), no. 2 (= Zepos,
    vol. 5, p. 317; *Liber Iuridicus Alphabeticus* (the 'minor' synposis), Zepos,
    vol. 6, p. 416
80 On the baptismal formulae, in addition to Beneshevitch, see Juster, *Les
    Juifs dans l'empire romain*, vol. 1, pp. 110–19; F. Cumont, 'Une formule
    grecque de renonciation au judaïsme', *Wiener Studien* 24 (1902), pp. 230–40
    and 'La conversion de Juifs byzantins au ix-ième siècle', *Revue de l'instruc-
    tion publique en Belgique* 46 (1904), pp. 8–15; V. Ermoni, 'Abjuration', *Diction-
    naire d'archéologie chretiènne et de liturgie*, vol. 1 (Paris 1924), cols. 98–103. The
    quotation is from the English translation of one of these formulae by Parkes,
    Conflict of the Church and the Synagogue, p. 398 (= MPG vol. 1, col. 1456)
81 F. Dvornik, *Légendes de Cyril et Méthode*, p. 133. For Jacob, see above,
    pp. 47–8
82 See Hitti, *History of the Arabs*, pp. 353–6; cf. Baron, vol. 3, pp. 152–4;
    303–4 (note 36); W. J. Fischel, *Jews in the Economic and Political Life of
    Medieval Islam* (London 1937), pp. 34–44

187

83 Adler, pp. 38–41 (text); 39–41 (trans.)
84 See Hitti, p. 627; cf. Baron, vol. 3, pp. 154–5; 304–5 (note 38)
85 Michael Atteliates, p. 178; cf. Starr, *Jews in the Byzantine Empire*, no. 149
86 See J. Mann, 'Une source d'histoire juive au xiii-ième siècle', REJ 82 (1926), p. 372
87 On the history of the Jews as executioners, see M. Lewin, 'Eine Notiz zur Geschichte der Juden im byzantinischen Reiche', MGWJ 19 (1870), pp. 119–22; Romanos, REJ 23, p. 65; C. Roth, *History of the Jews in Venice* (Philadelphia 1930), p. 296, p. 311; S. Assaf, 'Jewish Executioners', *Tarbitz* 5 (1934–35), pp. 224–6 (in Hebrew); Starr, *Romania*, pp. 28–9
88 See above, p. 551
89 Nelson and Starr, pp. 313–25

CHAPTER IX

The Jewish Tax

One final question must now be asked: did that hostility of the ruling institution which gave the Jews their legal but explicitly inferior status express itself in the most obvious way of all? Did Byzantine Jews pay a specific tax as Jews? The financial consequences of their legal disabilities from the Code of Theodosius onwards—the prohibition on owning slaves, the insistence on the service of the decurionate, made it inherently probable that they were also subject to some sort of discriminatory, fiscal burdens. But the evidence that exists for a special tax during our period is inconclusive and has been the theme of a prolonged controversy.[1] In order to form an opinion, it is first necessary to consider the system by which taxes were levied on the population as a whole.

Direct taxation was chiefly based on land tenure and derived from the system introduced by Diocletian. This was the *capitatio-iugatio*—a combination of land tax and poll tax. *Iugatio* stood for *iugum*—a unit of land assessed at a definite value, while *capitatio* stood for *caput*—a particular individual, the head of a family, supposed to be capable of cultivating this unit. The tax was paid in kind, from its produce. The *caput* and the *iugum* were not only fiscally inseparable but also legally: A man who left his land committed, in the first place, the offence of defaulting on his taxes and was subject to heavy penalties. The system was meant to put a stop to that drift from the countryside which was the great danger to the economy of the empire in the third century and earlier. Diocletian also collected, or tried to collect, some form of direct tax, in gold, from the urban population.[2] This system was modified as the economy, particularly in the eastern provinces, became healthier. The emperor Anastasius commuted the *capitatio-iugatio* to payments in gold. At the same time he abolished direct taxation in the cities, an act for which he was highly praised.[3] This act had a simple motive: Byzantium was beginning to benefit from that development of trade and manufacture to which we referred in Chapter I. Thus, indirect taxation was becoming more and more profitable. Municipal taxes on industrial and commercial premises, particularly heavy in Constantinople, together with duties both on exports and imports, brought in a growing yield which every sort of urban development, unhampered by direct taxation, was bound to increase. From the sixth century onwards this indirect taxation became a more and more important source of income for the imperial treasury. The only subsequent example of a direct tax on the urban population was the mysterious *aerikon*, the 'air tax', which had but a fleeting existence in the time of Justinian, and of which no proper explanation has ever been given.[4] For direct taxation, the next stage came with the completion of the Heracleian land settlement at the beginning of the eighth century. There was no longer any need, then, to prevent a decline of agriculture by a taxation system designed to bind the cultivator to his holding. However, it was hardly likely that a government would forgo a tax without something in return. The land tax continued to be paid by the small-holders of the themes. But the poll tax also did not disappear. It was merely separated from land tenure. It continued to be levied, at least in theory, on all heads of families not engaged in trade or industry.[5] Thus, it was levied on the 'free' peasants—those, as we discussed in Chapter VI in connection with the Chios grant, who were not the tenants of some lord—and on such tenants too, for whose payments their lord was responsible.[6] The *capitatio* had, in short, been separated from the *iugatio*.

At the beginning of the ninth century, this development was

marked by the introduction of a new term into the official nomenclature. When the emperor Nicephorus I abolished the tax exemption enjoyed for some time by the tenants of ecclesiastical landlords (that is by the landlords themselves since they had to pay it), the tax was called the *kapnikon*, the 'hearth tax'—that is, a tax explicitly on heads of families. It was then assessed at two *milesaria* per head annually. The *milesarion* was a silver coin nominally worth one twelfth of the gold bezant or nomisma.[7] It is unlikely that the *kapnikon* had a derogatory social significance, that it was the name given to the tax levied on tenants, as distinct from that levied on free peasants.[8] However, the *kapnikon* was not the only term applied. At some indeterminate point, the same tax began occasionally, though rarely, to be called the *kephaletion*, a literal Greek translation of *capitatio*. There is no reason to suppose that there was any distinction between the two. Since the tax was collected from heads of families and not from individuals, poll tax and hearth tax were identical in practice. Thus it was unlikely that the *kephaletion*, any more than the *kapnikon*, had a derogatory social significance.[9] During the tenth and eleventh centuries, this tax, under whatever name, and the actual land tax too, benefited the treasury less and less. The decay of the Heraclian land settlement caused the gross amounts of both taxes to decline. On the one hand, there were fewer free peasants from whom they could be collected, since their holdings were being swallowed up. On the other hand, the number grew of ecclesiastical and secular landlords who obtained the privilege of keeping their tenants' taxes for themselves or, at times when the ruling institution was especially weak, simply refused to hand them over. Secondly, the real worth of whatever actually was collected by the state became problematic. The emperors had tried to solve some of their financial difficulties, of which the decay of the land settlement was itself one cause, by devaluation of the coinage. The gold content of the bezant declined from $23\frac{1}{2}$ carats to $7\frac{1}{2}$ between the middle of the tenth and the last quarter of the eleventh century. The tax collectors tried to insist on payment in the old coins, but they were rarely successful.[10] In fact, their exactions encouraged more smallholders to abandon their land, further lowering the gross tax yield. The whole system of direct taxation gradually disintegrated, and the state came to depend wholly on its indirect urban taxes.[11] Benjamin of Tudela bore witness how diversified and how profitable these taxes eventually came to be, however exaggerated his estimate of the income they produced.[12] However the direct tax was not abandoned. It was collected as and when the opportunity offered and with no concessions. Often, there was fierce opposition. Between 1037 and 1040, the whole of the Balkans rose in a desperate revolt —that revolt which threatened Thessalonica.[13] Obviously, the state could not afford to forgo any possible source, and there is no reason to suppose that the situation changed for the better, except, perhaps, temporarily, during the reign of Alexius I, in the remainder of our period.

It is with this background in mind, that we must turn to the evidence for a special tax on the Jews. First of all, there is no doubt that, in the early Byzantine period, it existed. After the extinction of the Jewish patriarchate at the death of Gamaliel VI in the year 425, the regular yearly contributions that the Jews had been allowed to make towards its upkeep, and that of the Palestinian academies, since the middle of the second century, were gradually transferred to the imperial treasury. These contributions had been called the *aurum coronarium*, the donation in gold which, in the last years of the patriarchate had come to a considerable amount. In 429, the final step was taken. The *aurum coronarium* officially became a direct tax on the Jews. And it was to be collected as it always had been: by the leaders of the communities from their members, that is by a poll tax on each head of a family.[14] In a sense, this step was only the revival of an earlier practice, established by the emperor Vespasian who had similarly transferred the contributions to the Temple after its destruction.[15] It can hardly be doubted that the *aurum coronarium* was for the Jews an additional tax, for it is not to be supposed that they were thereby excused from the direct taxes on the urban population instituted by Diocletian. This discrimination continued. The instruction to collect the *aurum coronarium* was repeated by Justinian.[16] Thus the Jews, since the vast majority of them lived in the cities, continued to be burdened by that form of taxation from which the rest of the urban population had been exempted by Anastasius. There is even a slight possibility that the term *kephaletion* was already extant—in a Jewish context. It may be conjectured from the fragment of a receipt for tax paid by Jewish families of Hermoupolis in Egypt, perhaps in the first half of the sixth century.[17] However, after Justinian, the picture became far less clear. The only subsequent reference to the *aurum coronarium* was in that book of canon law, issued about the year 883, which we mentioned in connection with the Basilian persecution.[18] There were no references to any sort of Jewish tax in the *Ecloga*, in the appendix to it, in the *Basilica*, or in the various compilations based on the *Basilica*.[19] It is especially noteworthy that there was nothing in the *Peira*, a book of legal rulings based on the *Basilica* which included details of taxation practice, compiled between 1034 and 1056.[20] This absence of evidence in the legal sources, while no more conclusive than any negative argument can be, does indicate at the least that there was no organized collection of a Jewish tax for most of our period, that no permanent institution such as the *aurum coronarium* existed. It can, after all, be hardly accidental that Benjamin of Tudela, in the context of the oppressions that the Jews of Constantinople and of Thessalonica had to suffer, never hinted at it.[21]

At the same time, it cannot be denied that, apart from the specific reference to the *aurum coronarium*, there were a number of references after Justinian to some sort of taxes allegedly paid by Jews. The first two, mentioned earlier in other contexts, were very general. Michael II, among his other misdemeanours, was said to have 'declared the Jews released from taxes and free'.[22] But even if the basic untrustworthiness of accusations against Michael be discounted, this one need only mean that his pro-Jewish feelings moved him to forgive the Jews any kind of taxes that his other subjects had to pay.[23] The same argument is applicable to the second reference. It will be remembered that Basil I tried to convert the Jews by promising them, among other benefits, exemption from the burden of their former taxes.[24] 'Former' does have a slightly more definite implication, but far too slight to make

Basil's promise anything other than exemption from ordinary taxation. However, the possibility of a Jewish tax under Basil may conceivably be supported by the *Vision of Daniel* in its claim that Leo VI, when he halted his father's persecution, gave 'a release and freedom' (*hanaḥā ve-ḥerut*) to the Jews, on an analogy from the Book of Esther, where this same phrase meant a remission of Jewish taxes.[25] The next two references to be considered, on the other hand, are quite specific. One of the earliest of Arab geographers, ibn Khurdādhbih, the director of the post and intelligence service at al-Jibāl in Persia, in a book of itineraries which appeared about the year 846, wrote that in Cappadocia 'Jews and Magians pay 1 dinār per head, plus one dirhem per hearth, each year'.[26] Similar information was given in a Muslim philosophic work belonging to the first half of the eleventh century but based upon ninth century sources, according to which 'among them (the Byzantines) there are Jews and Magians from whom they collect the poll-tax, one dinār from each annually'.[27] The first of these passages has been accepted as definite evidence of a Jewish tax in Byzantium, perhaps even of its amount.[28] But the two together are not capable of supporting such a far-reaching conclusion, even if it be supposed that the second is more than an approximate copy of the first. One difficulty is that ibn Khurdādhbih spoke of two separate taxes on the Jews, for which there is no evidence at all. If his hearth tax was the Byzantine land tax as distinct from the poll tax, then such Jews as cultivated land paid it exactly as did everyone else. The second difficulty is that both passages mentioned the Magians, that is the Persians before their conversion to Islām, a highly unlikely element in ninth century Byzantium. Attempts to solve this difficulty have been strikingly unsuccessful. It has been suggested that the 'Magians' here were meant for the Athinganians or the Paulicians.[29] But their payment of any kind of tax would have implied recognition of a legal status for them which was inconceivable—no heretics in Byzantium ever obtained it.[30] In fact, these two passages should not be taken literally. Their information on Byzantine taxes was in terms of the Muslim system, where the privileges of the *jizyā* had, at an early date, been extended to in-

194

clude the conquered Persians.[31] Nevertheless, these passages have a limited value. Their reference to the poll tax and to the hearth tax, that is to the *kapnikon* and the *kephaletion*, although confusing, may indicate a knowledge of the fact that at one particular period, the middle of the ninth century, heads of Jewish families were paying a special tax. In other words, it may indicate that the paragraph on the *aurum coronarium* in the book of canon law of 883 expressed 'contemporary practice' rather than 'antiquarian reminiscence'.[32] But these passages can do no more: they cannot prove in general the existence of a Jewish tax in Byzantium.

Our next reference is no less inconclusive, though in a different way. It is the case of the fifteen Jewish families on the island of Chios whose taxes were granted to the monks of the local monastery in 1049.[33] The term used to describe the poll tax these families paid was *kephaletion*. Most of the discussion has been on the question whether here, at least, it had a derogatory meaning, perhaps one exclusive to those instances when it was Jews who paid the poll tax.[34] However, this question does not advance the present discussion. It is true that '*kephaletion*' did not occur in the chrysobull granting the same monastery lordship over twenty-four Christian families.[35] Thus, if the contention, made earlier in this chapter, that there was no real difference between the *kephaletion* and other names for the poll tax, be rejected, it might follow that its use to describe the poll tax paid by the Jewish families was in order to stress, in one way or another, their inferior status. And the preamble to their chrysobull, very similar to the preambles of the legislation in the Codes, made it clear that their status was thought of as inferior. But it would not follow that their poll tax, under whatever name and however derogatory, was an extra tax only payable by Jews. This conclusion could only be drawn if these families were proved not to have been smallholders, but to have been engaged in some trade or industry on the island. For then the general poll-tax, levied on free and feudal peasants alike, would not apply. But it is difficult to believe in a lordship granted over urban workers, of which this would be the solitary instance.[36] While the case of Chios possibly emphasized the inferior status of the Jews, it is doubtful if it added to the evidence of a poll tax levied specially on them. In the middle of the eleventh century there were two other inconclusive references. Tobiah ben Moses, in his *Sefer ha-ʿOsher*, used the word *gulgolet*, the Hebrew equivalent of *kephaletion—capitatio* to elucidate a passage in Nahum, and, again, a passage in Isaiah. It may be that he did so expecting his readers immediately to understand him because of an existing Byzantine institution which affected their lives as Jews. But it may equally well be that he was using *gulgolet* to translate *jizyā*, knowing that the Muslim tax would be perfectly familiar to the Byzantine Karaites of his day, since they had not long left their countries of origin.[37] Finally, we must mention the statement of a twelfth century chronicler that Leo III had forced his subjects in Byzantine Italy to pay new taxes including the poll tax (*kephaletion*) 'like the Jews'. The immediate inference might be that a Jewish poll tax existed in the chronicler's own day. However, it has been plausibly shown that the comparison to the Jews was merely the result of incorrectly copying an earlier source where Leo's exactions from the Italians had certainly been compared to Jewish taxes—but levied by Pharaoh.[38]

There is only one unambiguous reference, so far as we know, to the payment of a special Jewish tax in Byzantium during our period, after the mention of the *aurum coronarium* in the ninth century. It is in the description of the messianic excitement which seized Thessalonica in 1096. It will be remembered that, as a consequence the Jews were rendered 'free of the poll tax and other levies'.[39] First, what were these 'other levies'? The Hebrew word used for them was ʿ*onāshim*, the plural of ʿ*onesh*—literally, punishment but by then commonly meaning no more than an ordinary tax.[40] The suggestion has been made that, nevertheless, in this particular instance, ʿ*onāshim* had a punitive meaning. But this suggestion proceeded from the prior assumption that there were punitive, that is, discriminatory taxes levied on Byzantine Jews, and took this instance of ʿ*onāshim* as an example.[41] It has also been argued, because of the fact that in the first edition of the text the word was partially pointed ʿ*onashāim* עֲנָשִׁים, apparently the dual form instead of the plural, that the Jews had something extra to pay: a 'double tax', as it were.[42] But the photo-

196

copy provided by the second editor clearly showed the *ḳamatz* under the *nūn*, and not under the *shin*. Besides, even the pointing of the first edition would only be correct for the dual form in the pausal position—at the end of a phrase—for which there is no justification. The dual of ʿonesh in the place where it appears would have required a *pataḥ*.[43] There is little reason to suppose that these 'other levies' were discriminatory. It is more likely that they were only the various indirect taxes which all merchants and craftsmen had to pay. But the case of the poll tax here is very different. The Hebrew word used for it was, again, *gulgolet*. However, as distinct from all the other instances of references to a Jewish poll tax we have quoted, its context was quite unambiguous. For the Jews of Thessalonica, whether engaged in the silk trade (as was highly probable) or no, could not have been agriculturalists. They were employed in some trade or industry. And they were paying a direct tax which had been abolished by Anastasius for the general urban population, while it had been revived for the Jews alone in the transfer to the state of the *aurum coronarium*.

Yet, even if we may be reasonably sure that, on the eve of the First Crusade, the Jews of Thessalonica were paying a special tax, we still can make only a cautious generalization about Byzantium as a whole during our period. The payment of the tax in Thessalonica could not have been accidental. The other references, apart from those to the *aurum coronarium*, while individually inconclusive, undoubtedly make it difficult, when taken together and considered in the light of the tax at Thessalonica, to reject the possibility that, at certain times and in certain places, a Jewish tax was exacted. The fact that it was specifically a poll tax (under whatever name) which was often mentioned, is suggestive. The drying up of this particular source of taxation and the frantic efforts to collect it wherever possible, probably brought the state to revive from time to time the precedent of the *aurum coronarium* in order to collect the urban poll tax from the Jews, a normally prosperous element—and the one least able to defend itself against an exaction which, for their fellow citizens, had long fallen into desuetude. But the inconclusive character of most of our references, and the absence of any to an actual institution after the *aurum coronarium* itself, for collecting this tax, makes it probable that it was not heavy—and very sporadic: reasonably described as 'slight fiscal contributions'.[44] On the other hand, however slight, however haphazardly collected, the tax was a tax on Jews as Jews: it could not be anything but discriminatory. It was one aspect, if not a serious one, of the disabilities laid upon the Byzantine Jews, of the inveterate hostility and contempt of the ruling institution towards them, of their inferior, if legal status. To suppose any other meaning to the tax, once its existence is admitted (apart from its fiscal benefit) might, indeed, be to hold 'a truly naïve opinion'.[45]

However, for all that, the sporadic character of the Jewish tax, the fact that it was never formally embodied in Jewish legislation after Justinian, illustrates, perhaps more vividly than our other examples, the curious ambivalence of the Byzantine Jewish situation. The tax was discriminatory, but not quite in the sense of similar measures in the medieval west. It did not have their explicitly brutal character and intention. It was not a capricious exaction, by yielding to which the Jews were expected to buy a precarious and temporary safety from robbery or murder. It derived from legal precedents: from the *aurum coronarium*, from direct urban taxation. For in Byzantium, with its rule of law, with the power of its central authorities, with the official place given to the Jews in its society, there was no need for these Western barbarities. The Jewish tax is our last example of Byzantine-Jewish relations. It was part and parcel of them. Just as the participation of the Jews in the quarrels of the circus factions was the social expression of those relations, so what is known of the Jewish tax suggests that it was, no less, their fiscal expression. Thus, the predominant features of these relations can only be restated: Better off than in the West, worse off than under Islām, usually secure, occasionally threatened, potentially receptive to the culture around them but a very long way from assimilation, enjoying a legal but explicitly inferior status, the Jews in the Byzantium of our period constituted in various ways and in their various communities at once a link and a dividing line both between the East

and the West and between the classical and the medieval world—
just as, in a different way, did Byzantium itself. And this function
of theirs expressed the fascinating, the unique and the finally
unanalysable Byzantine-Jewish ambiguity.

Notes

1 The principal references are: A. Andréadès, 'Les Juifs et le fisc dans l'empire
   byzantin', *Mélanges Charles Diehl* (Paris 1930), vol. 1, pp. 7–29 (against the
   existence of a Jewish tax); F. Doelger, 'Die frage der Judensteuer in Byzanz'
   Vierteljahrschrift fuer Sozial- und Wirtschaftsgeschichte 26 (1933), pp. 1–24 (for
   it); Starr, *Jews in the Byzantine Empire*, pp. 11–18 agreed with Andréadès,
   but in *Romania*, pp. 111–13, partially came to agree with Doelger (see
   below, note 45). The arguments of these and subsequent discussions have
   been succinctly summarized by Argenti, pp. 54–60
2 See Ostrogorsky, *History*, pp. 37–8; Stein, vol. 1, p. 199
3 Malalas, p. 394; *Evagrii historia ecclesiastica*, ed. J. Bidez amd L. Paramentier,
   (London 1898), p. 144
4 See J. B. Bury, *A History of the Later Roman Empire*, vol. 2 (London 1923),
   pp. 350–1 (note 4)
5 G. Ostrogorsky, 'Das Steuersystem im byzantinischen Altertum und in
   Mittelalter', BYZ 6 (1931), pp. 229–31
6 Ostrogorsky, *History*, p. 121, note 2
7 *Theoph. Cont.*, p. 54
8 See Ostrogorsky, *History*, p. 167 note 2, as against F. Doelger, *Beitraege
   zur byzantinischen Finanzverwaltung besonders des 10 u. 11 Jahrhunderts*,
   Byzantinische Archiv 9 (Leipzig 1927), pp. 62–4
9 See H. G. Scheltema, 'Byzantine Law', CMII vol. 4, pt. 2, p. 73; as against
   Doelger, *Finanzverwaltung*, p. 50
10 Grierson, pp. 384–94
11 Doelger, *Finanzverwaltung*, pp. 48–60, p. 62; see W. Ashburner, 'A Byzan-
    tine Treatise on Taxation', *Journal of Hellenic Studies* 35 (1915), pp. 76–84
12 See above, pp. 136, 158 (note 4); and cf. A. Andréadès, 'Public Finances',
    Byzantium, pp. 80–1
13 Ostrogorsky, *History*, pp. 287–8; see above, pp. 10, 118, 126
14 First in C.Th. XVI.8.14 (=Pharr, p. 468); temporarily revoked in C.Th.
    XVI.8.17 (=Pharr, p. 469); finally decreed in C.Th.XVI.8.29 (=Pharr,
    p. 471); cf. *Ioanni Chrysostomi Orationes contra Gentiles XVI* (=MPG vol. 48,
    col. 835); Juster, *Les Juifs dans l'empire romain*, vol. 1, pp. 385–8, vol. 2,
    p. 287
15 Juster, *ibid.*, vol. 2, pp. 282–6
16 C.I. I.9.17 (=Krueger, p. 62)
17 Tscherikover, vol. 3, no. 506 (pp. 93–4)
18 Pitra, p. 601

19 Juster's assertion (*ibid.*, vol. 2, p. 288, note 1) that *Basilica* LX 54.30. repeated the instruction to collect the *aurum coronarium* is incorrect. This
paragraph only repeated the penalties for attempted proselytization of
Christians (ed. Heimbach, vol. 5, p. 895); cf. Starr, *Jews in the Byzantine
Empire*, no. 14 (note), who saw this error but whose references to Juster and
to his own no. 83 are also wrong

20 Ed. Zepos, vol. 4, pp. 1–266; cf. Scheltema, pp. 71–2; Ostrogorsky,
History, p. 28

21 Cf. Andréadès, *Mélanges*, pp. 13–18

22 Theoph. Cont., p. 48 (wrongly by Starr, *ibid.*, no. 28, as p. 61; Doelger,
Regesten 414)

23 Doelger, "Die Frage', p. 11, admitted that the absence of the definite
article before *phoron* (tax) weakened the force of this passage

24 See above, Chapter V, note 2.

25 See Krauss, REJ 87, p. 9 (Esther II.18).

26 Ibn Khurdadhbih, text, p. 111, trans., p. 83

27 See V. Minorsky, 'Marwazi on the Byzantines', *Mélanges Henri Grégoire*, 2
(1950), p. 458

28 Doelger, 'Die Frage', pp. 5–6; pp. 24–5

29 Starr, *ibid.*, no. 44 (note)

30 For other suggestions, see Baron, vol. 3, note 23, note 25 (pp. 321–2)

31 See *Encyclopaedia of Islam*, vol. 3, pp. 97–8, and above, p. 51

32 See Baron, *ibid.*, p. 191, where he rather oddly calls it both at once

33 See above, pp. 114–16

34 Doelger, 'Die Frage', pp. 12–14; Andréadès, *Mélanges*, pp. 22–3; Starr,
Jews in the Byzantine Empire, pp. 14–16

35 See above, Chapter VI, note 33

36 For this theory of lordship over urban workers, see Argenti, p. 45, pp. 49–
50

37 Cf. Ankori, p. 183

38 For the two sources, the twelfth-century *Ioanni Zonarae epitome historiarum*
and the ninth-century Theopanes, see Doelger, *Regesten*, no. 300; for this
explanation, see Starr, *Jews in the Byzantine Empire*, no. 14 and pp. 14–15

39 See above, Chapter VI, note 68

40 See Mann, *Ha-Tekufā*, p. 257, note 3; *idem*, *Jews in Egypt*, vol. 1, p. 73,
vol. 2, p. 74

41 This is Ankori's approach (p. 330, note 79)

42 Neubauer, JQR 9, p. 29; cf. D. Kaufmann, 'A Hitherto Unknown Messianic Movement among the Jews', JQR old series 10 (1898), p. 146

43 For the photocopy, see Mann, *Ha-Tekufā*, p. 255 (? p. 254—there are two
pages numbered '255'); we are greatly indebted to the late Aryeh Rubin-
stein of Manchester for drawing our attention to this point and for eluci-
dating it

44 Baron, vol. 3, p. 190

45 So Doelger in a private communication (letter of September 15 1954) on
Starr, *Romania*, p. 113, who was prepared to accept the existence of a Jewish tax, yet believed it to be not discriminatory but somehow in place of
ordinary taxes

The Vision of Daniel[1]

This source is preserved in a single Hebrew MS., one folio, recto and verso. It belongs to the great collection of the 'Cairo Geniza', that is, to the early medieval Hebrew MSS discovered by Solomon Schechter in the archives room of the Cairo Synagogue (the old synagogue, at Fusṭāṭ, built in 882), at the end of the last century. The MS. was presented by him to the Jewish Theological Seminary of New York, where it is now to be found. As distinct from most of the Geniza material, it has no box mark or other classification.[2] It has been edited twice: by Louis Ginsberg in his volume in honour of Schechter in 1928, and by Yehudā Even-Shmuel in his *Midrashei Geulā* in 1942 (reprinted 1954).[3] So far as we know, it has never been translated.[4] The following translation is of those portions of the text, as printed by Ginsberg, which unmistakably refer to certain emperors, together with parts of the apocalyptic section.

> I, Daniel, stood by the river Ḥebar, and the dread vision was heavy upon me, and I was amazed. And there came to me Gabriel, captain of the heavenly host, and said unto me, 'Know, beloved man and hearken: I have come to tell you that the Mighty Holy One commanded me, "Go, Gabriel, and reveal to Daniel what is to be at the end of days".'[5]
>
> In those days there will arise a king and the sign of his name will be the sum of the letters A R B, and he will be given dominion.[6] He will be the blasphemer before God, and will deal scorn-

fully with God's congregation.[7] He will make mock priests and will anger the Most High by his deeds.[8] And God will destroy him, setting another king in his place who will slay him for the evil of his doings.[9] And this tribe will be exalted from its former state.[10] The sign of his name will be two B's.[11] He will begin by rebuilding the synagogue which the tribe before him had scorned.[12] He will enrich his kingdom with great riches, he will conquer nations and bring peoples under his sway. Then he will become surfeited with his goodness and turn his face against the holy ones of the Most High. He will baptize them by force, against their will, and with much woe, and then he will sell them for slaves and for serving maids.[13] And he will die in his bed in great agony.[14]

And he will pass his sceptre into his son's hand for an inheritance, whose name will be the sign of royalty for beasts—'Leo'. He will make a release and give freedom to the holy nation of the Most High, and the Lord of Lords will increase his kingdom.

.   .   .

And in his days the lowly people will dwell in tranquility.[15] And afterwards there will arise a king who will persecute them by driving out and not by destruction but mercifully. He will set his face against God but he will not succeed. He and four other crowned kings will reign altogether for forty years, all from the same family. He will hurry to make changes in his kingdom, but he too will die.[16]

But from the same house there will reign ⋆ many foes will gather about him to ensnare him but their counsel will be frustrated for he will be worthy of protection. And the land will be filled with good things.[17]

At the beginning of his reign his kingdom will prosper and be exalted to the skies, but in the last days it will be destroyed and Great Tyre will conquer it . . . and in the north there will arise the evil one, the son of wickedness and he will rule over the land of Aftalopon three seasons and half a season.[18] . . . But the Lord God will look upon the face of all the land and burn with fire from heaven the cities of Rome the guilty . . . yet happy are they, yea, happy who on that day are dwelling in Rome and Salonica, in Sicily and in Beroia in Shtriglion and in Ashiniad, in Aram and in Istambolin,[19] while many peoples will war in Aftalopon. . . . And there will be a dearth of crops and cattle, the heavens will storm in thunder, the earth will quake mightily and a great fire from heaven will burn up the dwellers of the earth. The hosts of the unburied dead, the carcasses of birds, beasts and of all creeping things will lie upon the face of the land. And the Lord God will rage, and rain down His fire and pour down His waters, and will cause the seas to quake and their waves to boil. And there will be nothingness, emptiness and chaos. And He will throw them down and drown them in the depths, and the creatures of the deep will swallow them up.

And one who will come from other strongholds will not recognize the land and all that is in it, for mariners will come to mourn the land: 'And is this ⋆ from whence the wealth ⋆ ?'[20] They come and go in their ships, saying one to another, 'Is this the city that men call the perfection of beauty, the joy of the whole earth?'[21] And they mourn her many days. And in those days the kingdom will be given to Rome ⋆ Eshpion,[22] gates and towers ⋆ they will judge ⋆ then the Messiah will reign.

Notes

1   Condensed and revised version of a translation and commentary to appear under the title 'A source for Byzantine Jewry under the Early Macedonians' in BNJ. Stars relate to Lacunae in text, dots to passages omitted

2   See S. Shaked, *A Tentative Bibliography of Geniza Documents* (Paris and The Hague 1964), p. 182; and for the Geniza generally, pp. 12–13

3   See Chapter V note 48

4   Starr, *Jews in the Byzantine Empire*, no. 71, no. 79, no. 93, partially translated the references to Basil, Leo and Romanus; Krauss, REJ 87, translated a few references dispersed throughout his essay

5   A conflation of Daniel VIII.16, where Gabriel revealed prophecies to him on the banks of the river Ulai, and Ezekiel 1:3, where the revelation is on the banks of the Ḥebar, often appearing in this context; cf. e.g. *Sefer Zerubavel*, ed. Even-Shmuel, p. 71 (line 3), p. 73 (line 33) ed. and trans. I. Levi, REJ 68 (1914), pp. 144, 147

6   I.e. Aleph Resh Beth; most probably an allusion to אורב (orēv) = one who lies in ambush, an enemy; see Ginsberg, pp. 313–14; Even-Shmuel, p. 245. Baron, vol. 3, p. 315 (note 6), thought these letters referred to Michael's chief minister Bardas; Starr, *op. cit.*, no. 71, thought they were indecipherable

7   See above, pp. 101–2

8   Theoph. Cont. pp. 244–5

9   This identifies Michael, who was murdered by Basil

10   I.e. the Macedonian dynasty over the Amorian

11   I.e. Basileus Basileus—'Basil, the king'

12   'Synagogue': in the MS. *mikhal*, an unusual derivation from *kahal*. Neither Ginsberg (pp. 314, 319) nor Even-Shmuel (pp. 237, 250) nor Starr, *op. cit.*, no. 71 satisfactorily explained this credit given to Basil. Baron did not discuss it. Krauss, REJ 87, p. 3, suggested that the whole text was by a

converted Jew and dealt with the emperors' treatment of their Christian subjects. But, since it was in Hebrew, it was addressed to Jews. Why, then was there no conversionist propaganda? see *Bar-Ilan Annual 4–5*, pp. 198–9 and our forthcoming BNJ article

13 The penalty of slavery for resisting conversion, or for apostasy, is not to be found in the legislative sources. However, the text need not mean this. Against Ginsberg, p. 315, Baron, vol. 3, p. 179 and Krauss, REJ 87, p. 8, cf. Even-Shmuel's suggestion (p. 250, p. 237, note 34) of a metaphorical meaning: Basil 'sold', i.e. 'gave up' the Jews to slavery, that is to Christianity

14 Basil died a lingering death after going half-mad from grief at the sudden death of his favourite son, and after suffering an accident, or a murderous attempt, while hunting; see R. H. Jenkins, *Byzantium: The Imperial Centuries* (London 1966) pp. 195–7

15 On the problem of Leo and the Jews, see above, pp. 92–4

16 The forty years are 919–959, i.e. including the reign of Constantine VII. But the reference is to Romanus, who, in addition to recognizing Constantine as 'co-emperor', gave his three sons the same title; see Ostrogorsky, *History*, p. 239. On the 'merciful' Romanus, see above, p. 99

17 See Even-Shmuel, p. 251 where this sentence ends the passage on Constantine VII transferred from the apocalyptic sections

18 'Aftalopon' = *heptalophos* (seven hilled) i.e. Rome, identifying it with 'Great Tyre'; Ginsberg, p. 321 (his note to his line 7). 'Three seasons and half a season' is the traditional period for the wicked precursor of the Messiah to rule; cf. e.g. *The Prayer of Rabbi Shimon ben Yohai*, ed. Even-Shmuel, p. 277 (line 149)

19 On the last five places, see Even-Shmuel, pp. 246–7. The Rome where 'happy are they' is explicitly opposed to Aftalopon

20 For an attempt to fill these lacunae, see *ibid.* p. 252 (line 47)

21 Lamentations, II.15

22 'Eshpion' = *sophianon* (cf. Krauss, p. 27, note 3) or *sophion*, a palace built by Justinian II for his wife Sophia, see A. N. Stratos, *Byzantium in the Seventh Century* vol. 2 (Athens 1966), p. 951 (in Greek); identifying the 'second' Rome, i.e. the Rome as opposed to 'Great Tyre', the Rome of the Messiah, to be Constantinople

A Note on Byzantine-Jewish Historiography

The peculiarities of the Byzantine Jewish situation have an historiographical parallel. While the Jews of early medieval western Europe and the Jews under Islām for centuries attracted the attention of historians, Byzantine Jewish studies developed much later, and in their own way. Joseph Perles began his essay on Greek usages in Hebrew, from which we quoted in Chapter VIII and which he published in 1893, by a confession of ignorance. Little was known, he regretted, of the fate of the Jews under the Byzantine régime. They themselves were too oppressed to write their story. Only in the plaintive songs of the synagogue was it possible to get a hint of the relations of Byzantium with the Jews. And no Jewish sources existed for the persecutions of Leo III, Basil I and Leo VI. Perles said nothing of Heraclius or of Romanus.[1] Perhaps this confession was natural enough before the first edition of Aḥīmaʿatz in 1895, and before Adler's edition of Benjamin of Tudela which first appeared in the *Jewish Quarterly Review* for 1904, though it is strange that Asher's edition seems to have made so little impression on Perles.

The founder of Byzantine-Jewish historiography was Samuel Krauss. However, it is remarkable that, when in 1904 he was working on the material which he had used two years earlier for the *Jewish Encyclopaedia*, and which found its final form in his *Studien* of 1914, he too was pessimistic. He had taken up this subject, he said, as one took up a poor, forlorn orphan. The history of Byzantine Jewry was unknown and unremembered. Between 1902 and 1904, what he had already done had not inspired a single contribution worthy of the name. It was his hope that the growing political impact of events in Greece and in the Balkans (i.e. the struggle of the new independent states and the decay of Ottoman power in Europe) would encourage Jewish historians to turn to this neglected field.[2] There were two reasons for this neglect. The first was, as we have mentioned more than once, that Byzantine Jews were completely overshadowed by their neighbours, the Jews of the Gaonate, the great Talmudists of medieval France and Germany. The second was that general Byzantine studies were scarcely out of their infancy. Perles' essay appeared only in the second number of the *Byzantinische Zeitschrift*. Krauss' *Studien* invaluable in its day, has become of little more than academic interest because of the tremendous advances since its publication, particularly in critical editions of general Byzantine sources.

Byzantine-Jewish historiography really only began to develop in the third and fourth decade of this century. This development had two origins. The first was the work of Jacob Mann. In the Geniza material which he edited and discussed in his *Jews in Egypt*, he also came across MSS. with a Byzantine bearing which aroused his interest. In a number of articles, for example in his 'Changes in the Service of the Synagogue', and in the first volume of his *Texts and Studies*, he laid the foundations for all subsequent research. The second origin was the growing interest in the economics and the social structure of Byzantium. The work of Doelger and of Andréadès (not necessarily in its directly Jewish context) and, later the work of R. Lopez, led to a knowledge of specifically Byzantine conditions, of a social and economic framework, which, with all its controversial and problematic aspects, could make it possible to re-assess the Byzantine-Jewish relation, to modify Perles' idea of a dumb, continuously browbeaten sect. The work on the Byzantine circus parties by Grégoire led to the possibility of a further re-assessment: to the idea of Byzantine Jewry as an active and important social element in its own right.

These possibilities were largely brought to fruition by the work of Joshua Starr, who gave Byzantine Jewish historiography an entirely new dimension. His untimely death, shortly after the Second World War, was a serious blow to all historical scholarship.[3] Starr's contribution was twofold. On the one hand a long series of articles, beginning with 'An Iconodulic Legend and its Historical Basis', which appeared in *Speculum* for 1933, has provided, and will continue to provide for many years, the inevitable departure point for the discussion of a great variety of specific topics. On the other hand, his great collection of source references in his *Jews in the Byzantine Empire* will, for all its occasional errors, long remain the irreplaceable key without which no intelligent approach to Byzantine-Jewish study can be made at all. Joshua Starr inspired many: during the last thirty years, a great deal of valuable work has been done, directly or indirectly related to Byzantine Jews, for example by S. D. Goitein and by S. Assaf on social and economic topics, by Z. Ankori on the Karaites and on other heterodox movements. So far as we know, no connected account of Byzantine Jews, since Krauss, exists and this has been the attempt here. Our great debt to our predecessors and contemporaries need hardly be stressed, particularly to Starr.

Of course, it would itself be unhistoric to set down a fundamental change in any process to the accidental brilliance of one man. The period between the two wars saw a gradual change in the climate of opinion about Byzantium itself. The adjective gradually lost its original derogatory meaning. The civilization of the empire, its history, its institutions, its cultural achievements which had indeed been described and emphasized by J. B. Bury in England, or Charles Diehl in France many years before, at last began to attract adequate numbers of historians to make it possible for its special aspects to be adequately investigated. Thus, the Jewish aspect, too, began to receive greater attention. The gradual recognition of the uniqueness of the Byzantine contribution made possible the gradual recognition of the special interest of Byzantine Jews. However, even so, an historical peculiarity does remain. It will be remarked that the Bibliography which follows both seems inflated for a book of this size and contains relatively few items of obviously Jewish reference. For this there are two reasons. The first is that real Byzantine Jewish sources are very limited; there is no escape from a process of inference which must use other sources. The second is that modern writing on the subject is limited too, and so it has to be approached from a wide variety of disparate material, for Byzantine-Jewish historiography, if not the forlorn orphan of Krauss, remains still to be wholeheartedly adopted.

Notes

1 Perles, p. 569
2 Krauss, *Studien,* Introduction
3 See A. G. Duker, 'Joshua Starr', *The Joshua Starr Memorial Volume* (New York 1953), pp. 1–7

Bibliography

Abel, M., *Histoire de la Palestine depuis la conquête d'Alexandre jusqu'à l'invasion arabe*, vol. 2 (Paris Librairie Lecoffre 1952)

Abel, M., 'L'Ile de Jotabé', *Revue Biblique* 47 (1938), pp. 510-38

Abraham ibn Daud, *Sefer ha-Kabala*, ed. and trans. Gerson D. Cohen, *The Book of Tradition* (London: Routledge and Kegan Paul 1969)

Abū Muʻin Nāṣir, *Sefer Nameh*, trans. G. Le Strange, *Nāṣir-i-Khosrau's Diary of a Journey through Syria and Palestine in 1047 A.D.*, Palestine Pilgrim Texts Society No. 4 (London 1893)

Abū ʻOthman, ʻAmr ibn Baḥr al Jāḥiẓ, *Risāla fīradd 'alā al-Naṣara*, ed. J. Finkel (Cairo: Salafyah Press 1926), trans. O. Rescher, *Excerpte und Uebersetzungen aus den Schriften des Philologen und Dogmatiken Gāḥiẓ au Baçra (150–250 H)*, vol. 1 (Stuttgart: Selbstverlag 1931)

Acta 42 martyrum Amoriensium, ed. V. Vasilievsky and P. Nikitin, *The Tale of the 42 Amorian Martyrs*, Mémoires de l'Académie impériale des Sciences de St Pétersbourg, viii série, classe historico-philologique, vol. 7, no. 2 (in Russian) (St. Petersburg 1905)

Adler, E. N., 'Un document sur l'histoire des Juifs en Italie', REJ 67 (1914), pp. 40-3

Adontz, N., 'La lettre de Tzimiscès au roi Ashot (Ašot)' BYZ 9 (1934), pp. 371-7

Agapius of Menbidj, *Kitāb al-'Unwān*, ed. and trans. A. Vasiliev, Part II, section 2, PO 8, pp. 399-500

Aḥimaʻatz of Oria, *Sefer Yuḥasin*, ed. A. Neubauer, *Medieval Jewish Chronicles* (Anecdota Oxoniensa, Semitic Series II) (Oxford 1895), pp. 111-32

Amari, M. *Storia dei Musulmani de Sicilia*, vol. 1 (reprinted) (Catania: R. Prampolini 1933)

Ananias of Shirak, 'The tract on Easter', trans. F. C. Conybeare, BZ 6 (1897), pp. 572-84

Anastasii adversus Judaeos disputatio, MPG 89, cols. 1233-5

Anastos, M. V., 'The Argument for Iconoclasm as presented by the Iconoclastic Council of 754', *Late Classical Studies in Honour of A. M. Friend Junr.* (Princeton University Press 1954), pp. 177–88

Anastos, M. V., 'The Ethical Theory of Images formulated by the Iconoclasts in 754 and 815', DOP 8 (1954), pp. 151–60

Andréadès, A., 'The Jews in the Byzantine Empire', *Economic History* 3 (1934–1937), pp. 1–23

Andréadès, A., 'Les Juifs et le Fisc dans l'empire byzantin', *Mélanges Diehl*, vol. 1 (Paris 1930), pp. 7–29

Andréadès, A., 'La population de l'empire byzantin', *Bulletin de l'institut archéologique bulgare* 9 (1935), pp. 117–26

Andréadès, A., 'Public Finances', *Byzantium* (Oxford: Clarendon Press 1948), pp. 71–85

Andréadès, A., 'Sur Benjamin de Tudèle', BZ 30 (1930), pp. 457–62

Ankori, Z., *Karaites in Byzantium* (Jerusalem and New York: Columbia University Press; Weitzmann Science Press of Israel 1959)

Ankori, Z., 'Some Aspects of Karaite-Rabbanite Relations in Byzantium on the Eve of the First Crusade', PAAJR 24 (1955), pp. 19–25; 24 (1956), pp. 166–73

Annae Comnenae Alexiadis, ed. and trans. B. Leib, 3 vols. (Paris: Association Guillaume Budé; Société d'Édition 'Les Belles Lettres' 1937–43)

Anonymi auctoris chronicum ad annum Christi 1234 pertinens, trans. J. B. Chabot, Scriptores Syrii, series 3, vol. 14, fasc. 1 (Paris: Corpus Scriptorum Christianorum Orientalium; Catholic University of America; Catholic University of Louvain 1920)

Antiochi monachi homilia LXXXIV, MPG 89 cols. 1688–92

Antonini Placentini itinerarium, ed. P. Geyer, *Itinera hierosolymitina saeculi IV–VIII* (Vienna 1898), pp. 195–218 (*Corpus scriptorum ecclesiasticorum latinorum*, vol. 39); and in MPL 72, cols 897–918

Antony of Novgorod, *Book of the Pilgrims*, ed. K. M. Loparev, *Pravoslavnii Palestinskii Sbornik* no. 51, vol. 17, part 3 (in Russian) (St Petersburg 1899)

S. Arethae martyrium MPG 115, cols. 1249–89

Argenti, P., 'The Jewish Community in Chios during the Eleventh Century', *Polychronion: Festschrift Franz Doelger* (Heidelberg: C. Winter 1966), pp. 39–68

Ashburner, W., 'A Byzantine Treaty of Taxation' *Journal of Hellenic Studies* 35 (1915), pp. 76–84

Assaf, S., 'An Early Elegy on the Destruction of Jewish Communities in Palestine' *Bulletin of the Hebrew Palestine Exploration Society* 7 (1940), pp. 60–7 (in Hebrew)

Assaf, S., 'Egyptian Jews in the time of Maimonides', Moznaim 3 (1935), pp. 414–32 (in Hebrew)

Assaf, S., 'Jewish Executioners', *Tarbitz* 5 (1934–35), pp. 224–6 (in Hebrew)

Assaf, S., 'On the Beginning of the Jewish Settlement in Jerusalem after the Arab Conquest', *Texts and Studies in Jewish History* (Jerusalem: The Rabbi Kook Institute 1946), pp. 17–23 (in Hebrew)

Assaf, S., 'On the Family Life of Byzantine Jews' *Sefer ha-Yovel la-prof. S. Krois*, pp. 169–77 (in Hebrew) (Jerusalem: Reuben Mass 1936–37)

Assaf, S., 'R. Yehudă of Barcelona on the Epistle of Joseph, King of the Khazars', *Jeschurun* 11 (1924), Hebrew Section, pp. 113–17

Assaf, S., 'New Documents on Proselytes and on a Messianic Movement', *Tzion* 5 (1940), pp. 113–24 (in Hebrew)

Avi-Yonah, M., 'The Economics of Byzantine Palestine', *Israel Exploration Journal* 8 (1958), pp. 39–51

Avi-Yonah, M., *Geschichte des Juden im Zeitalter der Talmud in den Tagen von Rom und Byzanz* (Berlin: W. de Gruyter 1962)

Baer Y., *A History of the Jews in Christian Spain*, 2 vols. (Philadelphia: Jewish Publication Society of America 1961, 1966)

Bardenhewer, O., *Geschichte der altkirchlichen Literatur*, 4 Vols. (Freiburg: Herder 1913–32)

Bardy, G., 'Montanisme', DTC 10, cols. 2355–70

Bardy, G., *Les Trophées de Damas*, PO 15, pp. 173–291

Bareille, G., 'Baptême des Hérétiques', DTC 2 cols. 228–9

Baron, S. W., *A Social and Religious History of the Jews*, 2nd edition, vols. 3, 4 and 5 (New York: Columbia University Press 1957)

Basilicorum Libri LX, (in 7 vols.) vol. 1, ed. H. J. Scheltema and N. Van der Wal (Groningen-Gravenhage 1955); vols. 2–6, ed. G. E. Heimbach (Leipzig 1833–70); vol. 7, ed. J. Mercati and F. C. Ferrini (Leipzig 1897)

Basset, R., 'Recherches sur la religion des Berbers' *Revue de l'histoire des religions* 61 (1910), pp. 291–342; Eng. trans. *Encyclopaedia of Religion and Ethics*, vol. 2, pp. 506–19

Baynes, N., 'The Icons before Iconoclasm', *Harvard Theological Review* 44 (1951), pp. 93–106

Baynes, N., 'Idolatry and the Early Church', *Byzantine Studies and Other Essays* (London: Athlone Press 1960), pp. 116–43

Bell, H. I., *Egypt from Alexander the Great to the Arab Conquest* (Oxford: Clarendon Press 1948)

Beneshevitch, V. N., 'On the History of the Jews in Byzantium from the 6th to the 9th centuries', *Yevreiskaya Misl'* 2 (1926), pp. 197–224; 305–18 (in Russian)

Benjamin of Tudela, *Sefer Mas'aot*, ed. and trans. A. Asher, 2 vols (Berlin 1840); M. N. Adler (London 1907)

Bialoblocki, S., *Die Beziehungen des Judentums zu Proselyten und Proselytentum* (Berlin 1930); Hebrew version, *Bar-Ilan Annual* 2 (1964), pp. 44–60

Bleik, P., 'On the Relations of the Jews to the Government of the Eastern Roman Empire 602–634', *Khristianskii Vostok* 3 (1914), pp. 175–94 (in Russian)

Blumenkranz, B., 'La conversion au Judaïsme d'André, Archevêque de Bari', JJS 14 (1963), pp. 33–6

Blumenkranz, B., *Juifs et Chrétiens dans le monde occidental 430–1096* (Paris and the Hague: Mouton & Co. 1960)

Bon, A., *Le Péloponnèse byzantin* (Paris: Presses Universitaires de France 1951)

Brătianu, G., 'La fin du regime des partis à Byzance et la crise antisémitique du vii-ième siècle', *Revue historique du sud-est européen* 18 (1941), pp. 49–67

Bréhier, L., *Histoire anonyme de la première croisade* (Paris: Les classiques de l'histoire de France de Moyen Age fasc. 4 1924)

15

Bright, W. 'Cyrillus', *Dictionary of Christian Biography*, vol. 1, pp. 763–73

Browe, P., 'Die Judengesetzgebung Justinians' *Analecta Gregoriana* 8 (1935), pp. 101–46

Browning, R., 'The Patriarchal School at Constantinople in the XIIth Century' BYZ 32 (1962), pp. 167–202

Brutzkus, J., *The Letter of a Khazar Jew of the Xth Century* (Berlin 1924)—in Russian

Budge, E. A. Wallis, *The Chronography of Abū 'l Faraj (Bar Hebraeus)* (London: Oxford University Press 1932)

Bury, J. B., *A History of the Eastern Roman Empire* (London: Macmillan 1912)

Bury, J. B., *A History of the Later Roman Empire*, 2 vols. (London: Macmillan 1923)

Butler, A. J., *The Arab Conquest of Egypt and the Last Thirty Years of the Roman Dominion* (Oxford: Clarendon Press 1902)

Calder, W. M., 'Epigraphy of Anatolian Heresies', *Studies Presented to Sir William Mitchell Ramsay* (Manchester University Press 1923), pp. 59–91

Caro, G., 'Ein juedischen Proselyt (?) auf dem Thron vom Byzanz' MGWJ 53 (1909), pp. 576–80

Cassidori senatoris variae, MGH: auctorum antiquissimorum XI; chronica minora 2, ed. Th. Mommsen (Berlin 1894)

Chabot, J. B., *Le Chronique de Denys de Tell-Mahré*, Bibliothèque de l'école des hautes études, fasc. 112 (Paris 1895)

Chabot, J. B., *Le chronique de Michel le Syrien*, 4 vols. (Paris 1899–1910)

Chalandon, F., *La Domination normande en Italie et en Sicile*, 2 vols. (Paris 1907)

Chalandon, F., *Essai sur le règne d'Alexis I-er Comnène (Les Comnènes*, vol. 1) (Paris 1900)

Charanis, P., 'The Jews in the Byzantine Empire under the First Paleologue' *Speculum* 22 (1947), pp. 75–7

Charanis, P., 'A Note on the Population and Cities of the Byzantine Empire in the 13th Century', *Joshua Starr Memorial Volume* (New York: Conference on Jewish Relations 1953), pp. 135–48

Choricii Gazei Laudatio Aratii ducis et Stephani, ed. R. Foerster and E. Richsteig (Leipzig: Teubner 1929)

Codex Iustinianus, ed. P. Krueger, *Corpus iuris civilis*, vol. 2 (Berlin 1954) (reprint)

Codex Theodosianus, trans. and commentary C. Pharr, M. B. Pharr, and T. S. Davidson (Princeton University Press 1952)

Cohen, Gerson D., 'The story of the Four Captives', PAAJR 29 (1960–61), pp. 55–131

Constantini Porphyrogeniti de ceremoniis aulae byzantinae ed. and trans. A. Vogt, *Le Livre des Cérémonies*, 2 vols. (Paris: Association Guillaume Budé: Société d'Édition 'Les Belles Lettres' 1935, 1939)

Couret, A., *La prise de Jérusalem par les Perses* (Paris 1897)

Couret, A., *La Palestine sous les empereurs grecs* (Grenoble 1869)

Cowley, A., 'Bodleian Geniza Fragments' JQR old series 19 (1906–7), pp. 250–6

Chronicum anonynum, ed. and trans. I. Guidi, Scriptores Syrii, series 3, vol. 4 part 1 (Paris 1903)

Chronicum miscellaneum ad annum Domini 724 pertinens ed. E. W. Brooks, trans. J. B. Chabot, Scriptores Syrii, series 3, vol. 4, part 2 (Paris 1904)

Chronicum pascale, MPG 92, cols. 69–1130

Crum, W. E., *Catalogue of the Coptic Mss in the British Museum* (London: British Museum 1905)

Cumont, F., 'La conversion de Juifs byzantins au IX-ième siècle' *Revue de l'instruction publique en Belgique* 46 (1903), pp. 8–15

Cumont, F., 'Une formule grecque de renonciation au judaisme' *Wiener Studien* 24 (1902), pp. 230–40

Cyrilli scythopolitani vita Sabae (1) ed. E. Schwartz, *Texte und Untersuchungen zur Geschichte der altchristlichen Literatur*, vol. 49, part 2 (1939); (2) ed. with a Slavonic version, I. Pomyalovsky, *Life of the Holy St Saba* (St Petersburg 1890) (in Russian)

Davidson, I., *Thesaurus of Medieval Hebrew Poetry* 4 vols. (New York: Jewish Theological Seminary of America 1924–33)– in Hebrew

Delehaye, H., *Les Saints stylites*, Analecta Bollandiana: Subsidia Hagiographica 4 (Brussels: Societé des Bollandistes 1923)

Delehaye, H., *Les origines du culte des martyrs* Analecta Bollandiana: Subsidia Hagiographica 20 (Brussels: Societé des Bollandistes 1933)

S. Demetrii martyris miracula, MPG 116, cols. 1203–426

Dendias, M. A., 'Leukas or Arta: Elucidation of one place in the Itinerary of Benjamin of Tudela', *Ipeirotica Chronica* 6 (1931), pp. 23–8 (in Greek)

Devréesse, R., 'La fin inédite d'une lettre de S. Maxime: un baptême forcé des Juifs et des Samaritains à Carthage en 632', *Revue des sciences religieuses* 17 (1937), pp. 25–35

Devréesse, R., *La patriarçat d'Antioche depuis la paix de l'église jusqu' à la conquête arabe* (Paris: J. Gabalda 1945)

Doctrina Jacobi nuper baptizati, (1) ed. I. Bonwetsch, *Abhandlungen der koeninglichen Gesellschaft der Wissenschaften zu Goettingen*, XII. 3 (Berlin 1910); (2) ed. and trans. F. Nau, PO 8, pp. 711–80; (3) a later Ethiopic version ed. and trans. M. S. Grébaut, 'Sargis d'Aberga', PO 3, pp. 556–643

Doelger, F., *Beitraege zur byzantinischen Finanzverwaltung besonders des 10 und 11 Jahrhunderts*, *Byzantine Archiv* (9) (Berlin: *Byzantinische Zeitschrift* 1927)

Doelger, F., 'Die Frage der Judensteuer in Byzanz', *Vierteljahrschrift fuer Sozial- und Wirtschaftsgeschichte*, 26 (1933), pp. 1–24

Downey, G., *Constantinople in the Age of Justinian* (Norman: University of Oklahoma Press 1960)

Downey, G., *A History of Antioch in Syria from Seleucus to the Arab Conquest* (Princeton University Press 1961)

Duchesne, L., 'Note sur le massacre des chrétiens himyarites', REJ 20 (1890), pp. 220–4

Duker, A. G., 'Joshua Starr', *Joshua Starr Memorial Volume* (New York: Conference on Jewish Relations 1953), pp. 1–7

Duemmler, E., *Gesta Berengari imperatoris* (Halle 1871)

Duemmler, E., *Auxilius und Vulgarius* (Leipzig 1866)

Dunlop, D. M., *History of the Jewish Khazars* (Princeton University Press 1954)

Dvornik, F., *Les légendes de Cyril et Méthode vues de Byzance* (Prague: *Byzantinoslavica*: Supplementa 1 1933)

Ecloga Leonis et Constantini cum appendice, ed. A. G. Monferratus (Athens 1889)

Elisha bar Shināyā, *al-burhān 'alā sahīh al-'imān*, trans. L. Horst, *Des Metro-*

politen Elias von Nisibis Buch Beweis der Warheit des Glaubens (Colmar 1886)

Emin, N. O., *Researches and Essays on Armenian mythology, archaeology, history, and literary history*, Lazarevskii Institut: Etnografitcheskii fond Emina, vols. 1, 2 (Moscow 1893–6) (in Russian)

Emmanuel, I. S. *Histoire des Israëlites de Salonique* (Paris: Thonon 1936)

Ensslin, W., 'The Government and Administration of the Byzantine Empire', CMH IV, part 2, pp. 1–54

S. Epiphanii adversus haereses, MPG 41 cols. 173–1199

Ermoni, V., 'Les evêches de l'Égypte chrétienne', ROC 5 (1900), pp. 637–41

Ermoni, V., 'Abjuration', *Dictionnaire d'archéologie chrétienne et de liturgie*, vol. 1 (Paris: ed. F. Labrol and M. Leclerq Librairie Letouezy 1924), cols. 98–103

Eusebii historia ecclesiastica, MPG 20 cols. 9–909

Eustathii Thessalonicensis Metropolitae de Thessalonica urbe a Latinis capta, MPG 136, cols. 9–140

Eustathii Thessalonicensis Metropolitae opuscula, ed. T. L. Tafel (Frankfurt 1832)

Eustratus of Saba ('Antiochus Strategus'), *Khabar kharābi-l-baiti-l-mukaddasi* ('Account of the Destruction of the Holy Dwelling'), (1) Arabic text ed. P. Peeters, 'La Prise de Jérusalem par les Perses', *Mélanges de l'université S. Joseph* 9 (193–4), pp. 3–42; (2) Georgian text ed. and trans. N. Marr, *Texts and Studies in Armeno-Georgian Philology*, vol. 9 (St Petersburg 1909) (in Russian); (3) Georgian text trans. F. Conybeare, 'The Capture of Jerusalem by the Persians', *English Historical Review* 25 (1910), pp. 502–17

Euthymii Zigabeni adversus Hebraios, MPG 130, cols. 257–305

Evagrii historia ecclesiastica, ed. J. Bidez and L. Parmentier (London 1898)

Fedden, H. R., 'A Study of the Monastery of St Anthony in the Eastern Desert', Université égyptienne: Bulletin of the Faculty of Arts 5 (1937), pp. 1–60

Ferrari della Spade, G., 'Privilegi degli Ebrei nell'Impero Romano Cristiano', *Muenchener Beitraege zur Papyrusforschung und antiken Rechtsgeschichte* 35 (1945), pp. 102–47

Fischel, W., *Jews in the Economic and Political Life of Medieval Islam* (London: The Royal Asiatic Society 1937)

Fournel, H., *Les Berbers: Étude sur la conquête de l'Afrique par les Arabes, d'après les textes arabes imprimés*, 2 vols. (Paris 1875, 1881)

Frančes, E., 'La ville byzantine et la monnaie aux VIIe et VIIIe siècles', *Byzantinobulgarica* 2 (1966), pp. 3–14

Frančes, E., 'L'État et les métiers à Byzance' *Byzantinoslavica* 23 (1962), pp. 231–249

Freshfield, E. H., *A Manual of Eastern Roman Law* (Cambridge University Press 1928) (trans. of *Procheiros Nomos*)

Freshfield, E. H., *A Manual of Later Roman Law* (Cambridge University Press 1927) (trans. of *Ecloga ad Procheiron Mutata*)

Freshfield, E. H., *A Manual of Roman Law* (Cambridge University Press 1926) (trans. of *Ecloga*)

Freshfield, E. H., *A Provincial Manual of Roman Law* (Cambridge University Press 1931) (trans. of the 'Calabrian Code')

Freshfield, E. H., *A Revised Manual of Roman Law* (Cambridge University Press 1927) (trans. of *Ecloga privata aucta*)

Freshfield, E. H., *Roman Law in the Later Roman Empire* (Cambridge University Press 1938) (trans. of *Eparchion Biblion* 'The Book of the Prefect')

Frey, J. B., 'Inscriptions juives inédites' *Rivista di archeologia cristiana*, 8 (1931), pp. 83–125

Frey, J. B., 'La question des images chez les Juifs à la lumière des récentes découvertes' *Biblica* 15 (1934), pp. 265–300

Fuller, J. M., 'Caelicolae', *Dictionary of Christian Biography*, vol. 1, p. 589

Galanté, A., *Les Juifs de Constantinople sous Byzance* (Istanbul, Imprimerie Babok 1940)

Gay, J., *L'Italie méridionale et l'empire byzantin* (Paris 1904)

Georgii Cedreni compendium historiarum, MPG 121 cols. 24–1165; 122 cols. 9–368

S. Georgii Chozebitae vita, ed. H. Leclerq, *Analecta Bollandiana* 7 (1888), pp. 95–144; 336–59

Georgii monachi hamartoli chronicum, ed. C. De Boor, 2 vols (Leipzig 1904)

S. Germani patriarchae Constantinopolitani epistolae dogmaticae, MPG 98 cols. 148–221

S. Gregentii archiepiscopi Tephrensis disputatio cum Herbano Judaeo, MPG 86 cols. 621–784

S. Gregorii epistolae, ed. P. Ewald and L. M. Hartmann, MGH: Epistolae I, II (Berlin 1891, 1901)

Ginsberg, L., *Ginzei Schechter: Geniza Studies in honour of Dr Solomon Schechter*, 2 vols. (New York: Jewish Theological Seminary of America 1928–9)

Goitein, S. D., 'A Letter from Seleucia (Cilicia)' *Speculum* 39 (1964), pp. 298–303

Goitein, S. D., 'Historical Evidence from the Pen of A Doctor and Liturgical Poet in Byzantium' *Tarbitz* 27 (1948), pp. 528–35 (in Hebrew)

Goitein, S. D., 'The Documents of the Cairo Geniza as a Source for Mediterranean Social History JAOS 80 (1960), pp. 91–100

Goitein, S. D., 'The Main Industries of the Mediterranean Area as Reflected in the Cairo Geniza', *Journal of the Economic and Social History of the Orient* 4 (1961), pp. 168–97

Goitein, S. D., 'Obadya, a Norman Proselyte' JJS 4 (1953), pp. 74–84

Golb, N., 'Notes on the Conversion of European Christians to Judaism in the 11th Century', JJS 16 (1965), pp. 69–74

Golb, N., 'A Proselyte who fled to Egypt at the beginning of the 11th century', *Sefunot* 8 (1964), pp. 85–104 (in Hebrew)

Grabar, A., *L'empereur dans l'art byzantin* (Paris: Publications de la Faculté des Lettres de l'Université de Strasbourg Fasc. 75, 1936)

Grabar, O., 'Islamic Art and Byzantium', DOP 18 (1964), pp. 69–88

Grégoire, H., 'Epigraphie chrétienne', BYZ 1 (1924), pp. 695–710

Grégoire, H., Études sur l'épopée byzantine' *Revue des études grecques*, 46 (1933), pp. 69–129

Grégoire, H., 'Le peuple de Constantinople ou les bleus et les verts', *Comptes rendus de l'académie des inscriptions et belles lettres* (1946), pp. 568–78

Grégoire, H., 'Les sources d'histoire des Pauliciens', *Bulletin de l'académie royale de Belgique*, 22 (1936), pp. 95–114

Grierson, P., 'The Debasement of the Bezant in the 11th Century', BZ 47 (1954), pp. 379–94

Griveau, R., 'Histoire de la conversion des Juifs habitants la ville de Tomei en Égypte', ROC 13 (1908), pp. 298–313

Grunebaum, G. V., 'Byzantine Iconoclasm and the influence of the Islamic Environment' *History of Religions* 2 (1962), pp. 1–11

Guilland, R., 'Étude sur l'hippodrome de Byzance', *Byzantinoslavica* 25 (1964), pp. 234–53; 23 (1962), pp. 203–26

Halévy, J., 'Examen critique des sources relatives à la persécution des chrétiens de Nedjran par le roi juif des Himyarites', REJ 18 (1889), pp. 16–42; 161–178; 21 (1890), pp. 73–7

Halévy, M., 'On the History of Rumanian Jewry in the Middle Ages', *Mizraḥ u-Maʿarav* 3 (1929), pp. 279–81 (in Hebrew)

Ḥazon Daniel (The Vision of Daniel), (1) ed. L. Ginsberg, *Ginzei Schechter* (q.v.), vol. 1, pp. 313–23 (in Hebrew); (2) ed. Y. Even-Shmuel, *Midrashei Geulā* (Tel-Aviv: Massadah Publishing Company 1942 and 1954), pp. 232–52 (in Hebrew)

Hesserling, D. C., 'Le livre de Jonas' BZ 10 (1901), pp. 208–17

S. Hieronymi epistolae, MPL 22, cols. 235–1224

Hilkowitz, K., 'On the problem of the participation of the Jews in the capture of Jerusalem by the Persians in 614', *Tzion* 4 (1939), pp. 307–16 (in Hebrew)

Hirschberg, H. Z., *The History of the Jews in North Africa* (Jerusalem: Mosad Bialik, vol. 1, 1965) (in Hebrew)

Historia conversionis Abramii Judaei, ed. H. Matagne, *Acta Sanctorum Oct. XII* pp. 762–9

Hitti, P. K., *History of the Arabs* (London: Macmillan 1956)

Ibn Khurdādhbih, *Kitāb al-masālik wa'l-mamālik* ('The Book of Roads and Provinces') ed. and trans. M. de Goeje (Leyden 1889)

Iustiniani digestorum seu pandectorum libri L ed. Th. Mommsen and P. Krueger, *Corpus iuris civilis*, vol. 1 (Berlin 1954) (reprint)

Iustiniani novellae, ed. R. Schoell and W. Kroll, *Corpus iuris civilis*, vol. 3 (Berlin 1954) (reprint)

Janin, R., *Constantinople byzantine: développement urbain et répertoire topographique* (Paris: Institut français d'études byzantines 1950)

Janin, R., 'Les Juifs dans l'empire byzantin', *Echos d'Orient* 15 (1912), pp. 126–33

Jeffery, A., 'Ghevond's text of the correspondence between 'Omar II and Leo III' *Harvard Theological Review* 37 (1944), pp. 269–332

Jeffery, A., 'Three Documents on the History of Christianity in South Arabia', *Anglican Theological Review* 27 (1945), pp. 185–205

Jenkins, R. H., *Byzantium: The Imperial Centuries*, A.D. 610–1071 (London: Weidenfeld and Nicolson 1966)

Jenkins, R. H., 'Social Life in the Byzantine Empire', CMH vol. 4, part 2, pp. 79–104

Joannes Psaltes, *Hymn on the Homerite Martyrs*, ed. and trans. E. W. Brooks, PO 7, pp. 613–14

Joannis Asiatici historia ecclesiastica, Book 2, ed. and trans. F. Nau, ROC 2 (1897), pp. 455–93

S. Joannis Chrysostomi orationes VIII contra Judaeos, MPG 48 cols. 842–944

Joannis Malalas chronographia, ed. L. Dindorf, CSHB 1831; Slavonic version trans. M. Spinka and G. Downey, *Chronicle of John Malalas, Books VIII–XVIII* (Chicago 1940)

Joannis Mosci pratum spirituale, MPG 87 cols. 2852–3116

Joannis Zonarae annales, MPG 134 cols. 52–1413; 135, cols. 9–387

Joannis Zonarae epitome historiarum, vol. 3 ed. L. Dindorf (Leipzig 1870)

John of Ephesus, *Ecclesiastical History*, third part trans. R. P. Smith (Oxford 1860)

John of Ephesus, *The Lives of Simeon and Sergius*, ed. and trans. E. W. Brooks, 'The Lives of the Eastern Saints', PO 17, pp. 84–111

John of Nikiu, *Chronicle*, trans. R. H. Charles (London: Texts and Translations Society 1916)

Jones, A. H. M., *The Later Roman Empire, 284–602*, 3 vols (Oxford 1964)

Josephi Genesii historia de rebus Constantinopolitanis, MPG 109 cols 985–1156

Juster, J., 'La condition légale des Juifs sous les rois visigoths', *Études d'histoire juridiques offertes à Paul Frédéric Girard*, vol. 2, pp. 275–338 (Paris Librairie, Paul Geuthner 1913)

Juster, J., *Les droits politiques des Juifs dans l'empire romain* (Paris: Librairie Paul Geuthner 1912)

Juster, J., *Les Juifs dans l'empire romain* (Paris: Librairie Paul Geuthner 1914)

Kahana, A., *Sources of Jewish history*, 2 vols. (Warsaw: Di welt 1922–3) (in Hebrew)

Katz, S., 'Pope Gregory the Great and the Jews', JQR new series 24 (1933), pp. 113–36

Kaufmann, D., 'A Hitherto Unknown Messianic Movement Among the Jews particularly those of Germany and the Byzantine Empire', JQR old series 10 (1898), pp. 139–51

Kazan, S., 'Isaac of Antioch's Homily against the Jews', *Oriens Christianus* 45 (1961), pp. 30–53; 46 (1962), pp. 87–98; 47 (1963), pp. 89–97; 49 (1965), pp. 57–78

Kazhdan, A. P., 'Eustathius of Thessalonica: A Byzantine Pamphleteer of the 12th Century', *Vizantiiksii Vremenik*, new series, 27 (1967), pp. 87–106

Kisse ve-ippodromin shel Shlomo ha-melekh (1) ed. A. Jellinek, *Beth Ha-Midrasch*, vol. 2 (Leipzig 1853), pp. 83–6; (2) ed. and trans. J. Perles, MGJW, pp. 122–39; (3) extract in *Jewish Encycopaedia*, vol. 11, p. 442

Kitzinger, E., 'The Cult of Images in the Age before Iconoclasm', DOP 8 (1954), pp. 83–150

Kraeling, C. H., 'The Jewish Community of Antioch', *Journal of Biblical Literature* 51 (1932), pp. 130–60

Krauss, S., 'Un nouveau texte pour l'histoire judéo-byzantine', REJ 87 (1929), pp. 1–27

Krauss, S., *Studien zur byzantinisch-juedischen Geschichte* (Leipzig 1914)

Kukules, F., 'A Hebrew-Greek Glossary' BZ 19 (1910), pp. 422–9 (in Greek)

Kulakovsky, Y. A., 'A Criticism of the Information of Theophanes on the last Years of the Government of Phocas', *Vizantiiskii Vremenik*, old series, 21 (1914), pp 1–14 (in Russian)

Labriolle, P., *La crise montaniste* (Paris: Bibliothèque de Fondation Thiers Fasc. 31 1913)

Labriolle, P., *Les sources de l'histoire de Montanisme* (Collectanea friburgensis fasc. 15) (Paris: University of Fribourg 1913)

Ladner, G. B., 'Origin and significance of the Byzantine Iconoclastic Controversy' *Medieval Studies* 2 (1940), pp. 127–49

Lagrange, M. J., 'La secte juive de la Nouvelle Alliance au pays de Damas' *Revue Biblique* 9 (1912), pp. 213–40; 321–60

Laurent, V., 'L'oeuvre canonique du concile in Trulo (691–692)', *Revue des études byzantines* 23 (1965), pp. 7–41

Leges visigothorum, ed. K. Zeumer, MGH: Legum Sectio 1—Leges nationum germanicum, vol. 1 (Hanover-Leipzig 1902), pp. 426–56

Leonti Neapolitani episcopi sermo contra Judaeos, MPG 93 cols. 1597–1609; MPG 94 cols. 1272–6; 1381–8

Levi, I., 'Eléments chrétiens dans le Pirkê Rabbi Eliézer', REJ 18 (1889), pp. 83–90

Lewin, M., 'Ein notiz zur Geschichte der Juden im byzantinischen Reiche', MGWJ 19 (1870), pp. 117–22

Loos, M., 'Le mouvement paulicien à Byzance' *Byzantinoslavica* 24 (1963), pp. 258–86; 25 (1964), pp. 52–68

Lopez, R. S., 'The Dollar of the Middle Ages', *Journal of Economic History* 11 (1951), pp. 209–34

Lopez, R. S., 'The Role of Trade in the Economic Readjustment of Byzantium in the Seventh Century', DOP 13 (1959), pp. 69–85

Lopez, R. S., 'The Silk Industry in the Byzantine Empire', *Speculum* 20 (1945), pp. 1–42

Maas, P., 'Die Chronologie des Hymnes des Romanos', BZ 15 (1906), pp. 1–44

McGiffert, A. C., *Dialogue between a Christian and a Jew* (Marburg 1869)

Macler, F., *L'histoire d'Héraclius par l'évêque Sébéos* (Paris 1904)

Mann, J., 'Changes in the Divine Service of the Synagogue due to Religious Persecution', *Hebrew Union College Annual* 4 (1927), pp. 242–310

Mann, J. (untitled communication to conference) JAOS 47 (1927), p. 364

Mann, J., *The Jews in Egypt and in Palestine under the Fāṭimid Caliphs*, 2 vols. (London: Oxford University Press 1920–2)

Mann, J., 'Messianic Movements in the Days of the First Crusade', *Ha-Tekufā* 23 (1925), pp. 243–61 (in Hebrew)

Mann, J., *Texts and Studies in Jewish History and Literature*, 2 vols. (Cincinnati: Hebrew Union College Press 1931) (Philadelphia: Jewish Publication Society of America 1935)

Mann, J., 'Une source d'histoire juive au xiii siècle', REJ 82 (1926), pp. 362–77

Marcus, J., 'Eliezer ben Kalir', *Horeb* 1 (1934), pp. 21–31 (in Hebrew)

Marcus, J., 'Studies in the Chronicle of Aḥīmaʻatz', PAAJR 4 (1933–34), pp. 85–91

Marmorstein, L., 'Les signes du Messie' REJ 52 (1906), pp. 181–6

Marshall, F. H. and Mavrocordato, J., 'Byzantine Literature', *Byzantium* (Oxford: The Clarendon Press 1948), pp. 221–51

Martin, E., *A History of the Iconoclastic Movement* (London: SPCK: Church Historical Society Publications, new series, no. 2 1932)

ʻAli al-Masʻūdi, *Murūj al-dhahab wa maʻādin al-juhaz*, ed. and trans. B. de Meynard and P. de Courtelles, *Le livre des prairies d'or et des mines de pierres précieuses* (Paris 1861–78)

Mayerson, P., 'The First Muslim Attacks on Southern Palestine A.D. 633–A.D.

634' *Transactions and Proceedings of the American Philological Association*, 95 (1964), pp. 155–99

Meyendorff, J., 'Byzantine Views of Islam', DOP 18 (1964), pp. 115–32

Michaelis Atteliates historia, CSHB 1853 (ed. I. Bekker)

Michaelis akominati quae supersunt, ed. S. P. Lampros, 2 vols. (Athens 1879–80) (in Greek)

Miller, W., *Essays on the Latin Orient* (Cambridge University Press 1921)

Moberg, A., *The Book of the Himyarites* (Skrifter utgivna av Kungl. Humanistika vetenskapssamfundet, 7) (Lund 1924)—CWK Gleerup; London: Humphrey Milford, Oxford University Press; Paris: Édouard Champion; Leipzig: O. Harrassowitz

Molho, M., *Histoire des Israélites de Castoria* (Salonica 1938) S. Behar

Monceaux, P., 'Les colonies juives dans l'Afrique romaine' REJ 44 (1902), pp. 1–28

Monnier, H., *Les nouvelles de Léon le Sage* (Bibliothèque de l'Université du Midi, fasc. 17) (Bordeaux 1923)

Montgomery, J. A., *The Samaritans* (Philadelphia 1907)

Moravscsik, G., 'Barbarische Sprachreste in der Theogonie des Johannes Tzetzes', BNJ 7 (1930), pp. 353–7

Munier, H., 'La géographie de l'Égypte d'après les listes coptes-arabes' *Bulletin de la sociéte d'archéologie copte* 5 (1939), pp. 201–43

Nau, F., 'Deux episodes de l'histoire juive sous Théodose II', REJ 83 (1927), pp. 184–206

Nelson, B. N. and Starr, J., 'The Legend of the Divine Surety and the Jewish Moneylender', *Annuaire de l'institut de philologie et d'histoire orientales et slaves*, 7 (1939–44), pp. 289–338

Nemoy, L., 'Al-Qirqisānī's Account of the Jewish Sects and of Christianity', *Hebrew Union College Annual* 7 (1930), pp. 318–97

Nemoy, L., *Karaite Anthology* (Yale Judaica Series, 7) (New Haven: Yale University Press 1952)

Neubauer, A., 'Abou Ahron, le babylonien', REJ 23 (1891), pp. 230–7

Neubauer, A., 'The Early Settlement of the Jews in Italy', JQR old series 4 (1892), pp. 606–25

Neubauer, A., 'Egyptian Fragments II (B)', JQR old series 9 (1896–97), pp. 26–9

Neuman, A. A., *The Jews in Spain*, 2 vols. (Philadelphia: Jewish Publication Society of America 1942)

S Nicephori patriarchi, antirrhetici tres adversus Constantinum copronymum MPG 100 cols. 206–533

S Nicephori patriarchi epitome historiarum, ed. C. De Boor (Leipzig 1880)

Nicole, J., *Le livre du préfet* (Bordeaux 1893)

S Niconis armeni monaci vita, MPG 113 cols. 975–88

Noailles, P., *Les collections de nouvelles de l'empereur Justinien*, 2 vols. (Bordeaux 1912, 1914)

Noailles, P. and Dain, A., *Les nouvelles de Léon VI le Sage* (Paris 1944)

Ostrogorsky, G., 'Das steuersystem im byzantinischen Altertum und Mittelalter', BYZ 6 (1931), pp. 229–40

Ostrogorsky, G., 'Les débuts de la querelle des images', *Mélanges Diehl* 1 (1930), pp. 235–55

Ostrogorsky, G., *History of the Byzantine State* (trans. J. M. Hussey) (Oxford: Blackwell and Rutgers University Press 1956)

Ostrogorsky, G., *Pour l'histoire de la féodalité byzantine*, (Brussels: Corpus Bruxellense Historiae Byzantinae, Subsidia I: Éditions de l'Institut de Philologie et d'Histoire Orientales

Papadopulos-Kerameos, A., 'A Hebrew-Greek Glossary', *Festschrift zu Ehren des Dr A Harkavy* (St Petersburg 1908), pp. 68–90; p. 177 (in Greek)

Pargoire, J., *L'église byzantine de 527 à 847* (Paris: Bibliothèque de l'enseignement de l'Historie Ecclésiastique 1923)

Parkes, J., *The Conflict of the Church and the Synagogue: A Study in the Origins of Anti-Semitism* (Philadelphia: Jewish Publication Society of America 1961) (reprint)

Patlagean, E., 'Contribution juridique à l'histoire des Juifs dans la Méditerranée médiévale: les formules grecques de serment', *REJ* 124 (1965), pp. 137–56

Peeters, P., *Le Trefonds oriental de l'hagiographie byzantine* (Analecta Bollandiana: Subsidia hagiographica 26) (Brussels: Societé des Bollandistes 1950)

Pereḳ Eliahū, ed. Y. Even-Shmuel, *Midrashei Geulā*, pp. 49–54

Perles, J., 'Juedisch-byzantinische Beziehungen' *BZ* 2 (1893), pp. 569–84

Petaḥiā of Ratisbon, *Sivuv ha-rav rabi Petaḥiā*, (1) ed. and trans. A. Benisch, *The Travels of Rabbi Petahiah of Ratisbon* (London 1856); (2) ed. and trans. L. Gruenhut, 2 vols., *Die Rundreise des R. Petachjah aus Regensburg*, Jerusalem Frankfurt (1904–5); (3) trans. E. N. Adler, *Jewish Travellers*, London: George Routledge (1930) pp. 64–91; (4) Palestine section ed. A. Ya'ari, *Palestine Journeys by Jewish Pilgrims* (Tel-Aviv Zionist Federation, Youth Section (1946), pp. 48–55 (in Hebrew)

Philostorgii historia ecclesiastica, ed. J. Bidez, *Die griechischen christlichen Schriftsteller der ersten drei Jahrhunderte*, vol. 21; MPG 65 cols. 460–624

Pitra J. B., *Juris ecclesiastici Graecorum historia et monumenta* 2 vols. (Rome 1864, 1868)

Popov, N. A., *The Emperor Leo VI the Wise and his Reign* (Moscow 1892) (in Russian)

Poznanski, S., 'Meswi al-Okbari, chef d'une secte juive au dixième siècle' *REJ* 34 (1897), pp. 161–91

Procopii caesariensis: De Aedificiis; Anecdota sive historia arcana; de bello Gallico; de bello Persico; ed. J. Haury (Leipzig 1963–4) (reprint)

Quaestiones ad Antiochium ducem, MPG 28 cols. 589–709

Rampolla y Tindaro, M., 'Martyre et sépulture des Machabées', *Revue de l'art chrétien* 10 (1899), pp. 290–305; 377–92; 457–65

Ramsay, W. M., *Cities and Bishoprics of Phrygia*, 2 vols. (Oxford 1895, 1897)

Ramsay, W. M., *Historical Geography of Asia Minor* (London 1882)

Ramsay, W. M., 'The Jews in Graeco-Asiatic Cities', *Expositor* 5 (1902), pp. 19–33; 92–109

Reinach, A., 'Noe Sangariou: étude sur le déluge phrygien et le syncrétisme judéo-phrygien', *REJ* 65 (1912), pp. 161–80; 67 (1913), pp. 1–43; 213–45

Reinach, T., 'Un contrat de mariage du temps de Basile le Bulgaroctone', *Mélanges Schlumberger*, vol. 1 (Paris 1924), pp. 118–32

Romanos, J. A., 'Histoire de la communauté israélite de Corfu' REJ 23 (1891), pp. 63–74

Rosanes, S. A., *History of the Jews in Turkey* (vol. 1) (Tel-Aviv 1930) (in Hebrew)

Rosenthal, J., 'On the History of Heresies in the Time of Sa'adia', Ḥoreb 9 (1945), pp. 21–37

Roth, C., 'On the History of the Jews in Cyprus', *Sefer Zikaron le Yitzḥak ben Tzvi*(Jerusalem: The Ben Tzvi Institute 1954) pp. 285–99 (in Hebrew)

Roth, C., *History of the Jews in Venice* (Philadelphia: Jewish Publication Society of America 1930)

Roth, C., 'The Lombard Lordships', *World History of the Jewish People*, pp. 109–111 (Tel-Aviv: Massadah Publishing Company 1966)

Runciman, S., *Byzantine Civilization* (London: Edward Arnold 1933)

Runciman, S., *The Emperor Lecapenus and his Reign* (Cambridge University Press 1929)

Runciman, S., *A History of the Crusades* (vols. 1 and 2) (Cambridge University Press 1951–2)

Sacramentarium Gelasianum, MPL 74 cols. 1049–1244

Schechter, S., 'An unknown Khazar Document' JQR new series 3 (1912–13), pp. 181–219

Schechter, S., 'Notes on Hebrew MSS in the University Library at Cambridge', JQR old series 4 (1891–2), pp. 90–100

Scheiber, A., 'Fragment from the Chronicle of 'Obadyah, the Norman Proselyte: From the Kaufman Geniza', *Acta Orientalia* 4 (1954), pp. 271–96

Scheltema, H. J., 'Byzantine Law', CMH vol. 4, part 2, pp. 55–77

Schirmann, J., *An Anthology of Hebrew Verse in Italy* (Berlin: Schocken 1934) (in Hebrew)

Schirmann, J., 'The Beginnings of Hebrew Poetry in Italy', *World History of the Jewish People*, pp. 249–66

Schlumberger, G., *L'Épopée byzantine à la fin du dixième siècle* (vol. 1) (Paris 1896)

Scholem, G., *Major Trends in Jewish Mysticism*, Third revised edition (New York: Schocken Books 1961)

Schroetter, R., 'Trostschreiben Jacob's von Sarug an die himjaritischen Christen', *Zeitschrift der Deutschen Morgenlaendischen Gesellschaft*, 31 (1877), pp. 360–405

Sefer Eliyahū, ed. Even-Shmuel, *Midrashei Geulā*, pp. 29–48 (Tel-Aviv: Massadah Publishing Company 1942 and 1954) (in Hebrew)

Sefer Zerubavel, (1) ed. A. Jellinek, *Beth-Hamidrasch* (Leipzig 1854), vol. 2, pp. 54–57; (2) ed. Y. Even-Shmuel, *Midrashei Geulā*, pp. 55–88, in Hebrew; (3) ed. and trans. I. Levi, 'L'Apocalypse de Zerubabel', REJ 68 (1914), pp. 131–50; 69 (1920), pp. 57–63; 71; 108–121

Severus, Patriarch of Antioch, *History of the Patriarchs of the Coptic Church of Alexandria* ed. and trans. B. Evetts, PO 1, pp. 99–214, 381–518; PO 5, pp. 1–215

Shabbetai Donnolo, *Sefer Ḥakhmoni*, ed. D. Castelli, *Il commento di Sabbeta Donnolo sul libro della creazione*(Florence 1880)

Shabbetai Donnolo, *Sefer ha-Yakar*, ed. M. Steinschneider, Donnolo, *Fragment des aeltesten medizinischen Werkes in hebraeischer Sprache* (Berlin 1867)

Shaked, S., *A Tentative Bibliography of Geniza Documents* (Paris and The Hague: Mouton and Co. 1964)

Sharf, A., 'An Unknown Messiah of 1096 and the Emperor Alexius' JJS 7 (1956), pp. 59-70

Sharf, A., 'Byzantine Jewry in the Seventh Century', BZ 48 (1955), pp. 103-15

Sharf, A., 'Jews in Byzantium', *The World History of the Jewish People* (Tel-Aviv: Massadah Publishing Company 1966), pp. 49-68; 393-8; 455-6

Sharf, A., 'The Jews, the Montanists and the Emperor Leo III', BZ 59 (1966), pp. 37-46

Sharf, A., '*The Vision of Daniel* as a Source for the History of Byzantine Jews', Bar-Ilan Annual 4-5 (1967), pp. 197-208 (in Hebrew)

Simon, M., 'La polémique anti-juive de S Jean Chrysostome et le mouvement judaïsant d'Antioche', *Annuaire de l'institut de philologie et d'histoire orientales et slaves* (Mélanges Franz Cumont, vol. 1), 4 (1936), pp. 403-21

Simon, M., *Recherches d'histoire judéo-chrétienne* (Sciences économiques et sociales: études juives, 6) (Paris: Mouton & Co.: Sorbonne, École Pratique des Hautes Études 1962)

Simon, M., *Verus Israel: Étude sur les relations entre Chrétiens et Juifs dans l'empire romain (135-425)* (Paris: Éditions de Boccard: Bibliothèque des Écoles Françaises d'Athènes et de Rome, Fasc. 166 1965)

Singer, C. and D., 'The School of Salerno', *History* 10 (1925), pp. 242-6

Slouchz, N., *Hébraeo-Pheniciens et Judéo-Berbers—introduction à l'histoire des Juifs et du judaïsme en Afrique* (Archives Marocaines 14) (Paris 1908)

Socratis historia ecclesiastica, MPG 67 cols. 29-1724

Sonne, I., 'Note sur une Keroba d'Amittaï publiée par Davidson', REJ 98 (1934), pp. 81-4

Starr, J., 'A Fragment of a Greek Mishnaic Glossary', PAAJR 6 (1935), pp. 353-367

Starr, J., 'Byzantine Jewry on the Eve of the Arab Conquest', JPOS 15 (1935), pp. 280-93

Starr, J., 'An Eastern Christian Sect: the Athinganoi', *Harvard Theological Review* 29 (1936), pp. 93-106

Starr, J., 'The Epitaph of a Dyer in Corinth', BNJ 12 (1936), pp. 42-9

Starr, J., 'On the History of Naḥrai ben Nissīm of Fusṭāṭ', *Tzion* 1 (1935-36), pp. 435-53; 2 (1936-37), p. 92 (in Hebrew)

Starr, J., 'An Iconodulic Legend and its Historical Basis', *Speculum* 8 (1933), pp. 500-3

Starr, J., *Jews in the Byzantine Empire 641-1204* (Athens: Verlag der Byzantinisch-Neugriechischen Jahrbüchen 1939)

Starr, J., 'Le mouvement messianique au début du viii-ième siècle', REJ 102 (1937), pp. 81-92

Starr, J., 'Notes on the Byzantine Incursion into Syria and Palestine', *Archiv Orientálnī* 8 (1936), 91-5

Starr, J., *Romania* (Paris: Éditions du Centre 1949)

Starr, J., 'St Maximus and the Forced Baptism at Carthage in 632', BNJ 16 (1940), pp. 192-6

Stein, E., *Histoire du Bas Empire* (reprinted) (Paris-Brussels-Amsterdam: vol. 1 1959; vol. 2 1949), Desclée de Brouwer

Stephanides, B. K., 'The Adrianople Codices', BZ 14 (1905), pp. 593-4 (in Greek)

Stratos, A. N., *Byzantium in the 7th Century* 2 vols. (Athens: Bibliopoleion 'Estias' 1965-6) (in Greek)

Sukenik, E. L., *The Ancient Synagogue of Beit-Alpha* (Jerusalem 1932)

Sukenik, E. L., 'The Ancient Synagogue of el-Ḥammeh', JPOS 15 (1935), pp. 152-7

Symeonis Junioris epistola ad Justinum Juniorem, MPG 86 cols. 3216-20

Symeonis Metaphrastis S. Symeonis Stylitae vita, MPG 114 cols. 337-92

Tafel, T. L., *De Thessalonica ejusque agro* (Berlin 1839)

Teall, J. L., 'The Grain Supply of the Byzantine Empire', DOP 13 (1959), pp. 87-139

Teicher, J. L., 'The Origins of Obadyah, the Norman Proselyte', JJS 5 (1954), pp. 36-7

Teshuvot ha-Geonim, Sha'arei-Tsedek (Salonica 1792) (in Hebrew)

Teshuvot ha-Geonim, ed. A. Harkavy, *Zikron la-rishonim ve-gam la-aharonim*, vol. 4, part 1 (Berlin 1887) (in Hebrew)

Theodori Balsamonis diaconi ecclesiasticarum canonum collectio, ed. W. Voellus and H. Justel, *Bibliothecae iuris canonici veteris*, vol. 2, pp. 1223-1359 (Paris 1661)

Theophanis chronographia, ed. C. De Boor, 2 vols. (Leipzig 1883, 1885)

Theophanis continuator, ed. I. Bekker CSHB (1838)

Tobiah ben Eliezer, *Leḳaḥ Tov*, ed. S. Buber (Vilna 1880)

Tobiah ben Moses, '*Otzar Neḥmad*, extract ed. P. F. Frankel, 'Ueber Ben Koreisch', MGWJ 30 (1881), p. 471

Trinchera F., *Syllabus Graecarum membranarum* (Naples 1865)

Tritton, A. S., *The Caliphs and their Non-Muslim Subjects: A Critical Study of the Covenant of Umar* (London: Oxford University Press 1930)

Tscherikover, V. A., Fuks, A. and Stern, M., *Corpus papyrorum judaicorum*, vol. 3 (Harvard University Press for the Magnes Press, Jerusalem 1964)

Tucci, R. di, 'Benjamino di Tudela e il suo viaggio' *Bolletino della R. Soc. Geogr. Italia* 7 (1941), pp. 496-517

Uspensky, F., 'Benjamin of Tudela's Notes on his Journey', *Annaly* 3 (1923), pp. 5-20 (in Russian)

Vailhé, S., 'Les Juifs et le prise de Jérusalem en 614', *Echos d'Orient* 12 (1909), pp. 15-17

Vasiliev, A. A., *Byzantium and the arabs* 2 vols. (St Petersburg 1900, 1902) (in Russian)

Vasiliev, A. A., 'The Emperor Michael III in Apocryphal Literature', *Byzantina-Metabyzantina* 1 (1946), pp. 237-48

Vasiliev, A. A., 'The Iconoclastic Edict of the Caliph Yazid II, A.D. 721', DOP 9-10 (1956), pp. 23-47

Vryonis, S., 'Byzantine Δημοκράτια and the Guilds in the Eleventh Century', DDOP 17 (1963), pp. 287-314

Williams, A. L., *Adversos Judaeos: A Bird's Eye View of Christian Apologiae until the Renaissance* (Cambridge University Press 1935)

Wuestenfeld, H. F., *Geschichte des Fatimid Chalifen nach arabischen Quelle*, Abhandlungen der koeniglichen Gesellschaft der Wissenschaften zu Goettingen, 27 (1881)

Yaḥya ib Saʿīd al-Antakyā, *Al-kitāb alladhi sannaʿahu*, ed. and trans. J. Kratᵣ chkovsky and A. A. Vasiliev, 'Histoire de Yahya ibn Saʿid d'Antioche', PO 18, pp. 705–833; PO 23, 349–520

Zachariah of Mityline, *The Syrian Chronicle*, trans. F. J. Hamilton and E. W. Brooks (London 1899)

Zepos, J. and P., *Ius Graecoromanum*, 8 vols., Athens (1931) and Darmstadt (1962: Scientia Aalen)—*Ecloga ad Procheiron mutata*, vol. 6; *Epanagoge aucta*, vol. 6; *Epitome legum*, vol. 4; *Liber juridicus alphabeticus* vol. 6 (the 'Minor Synopsis'); *Michaelis Atteliatis ponema*, vol. 7; *Peira*, vol. 4; *Synopsis Basilicorum*, vol. 5 (the 'Major Synopsis)'

Zimmels, H. J., 'Scholars and Scholarship in Byzantium and Italy', *World History of the Jewish People* (Tel-Aviv: Massadah Publishing Company 1966), pp. 175–88

Zunz, L., *Literaturgeschichte der synagogalen Poesie* (Berlin 1899)

Zunz, L., *Die Ritus des synagogalen Gottesdienstes* (Berlin 1919)

Byzantine Emperors from Constantine I to the Fourth Crusade

324–337	Constantine I	641	Constantine III[2]
337–361	Constantius		and Heraclonas
361–363	Julian	641	Heraclonas
363–364	Jovian	641–668	Constans II[3]
364–378	Valens	668–685	Constantine IV
379–395	Theodosius I	685–695	Justinian II
395–408	Arcadius	695–698	Leontius
408–450	Theodosius II	698–705	Tiberius III
450–457	Marcian	705–711	Justinian II
457–474	Leo I		(regained throne)
474	Leo II	711–713	Philippicus
474–475	Zeno	713–715	Anastasius II
475–476	Basiliscus	715–717	Theodosius III
476–491	Zeno	717–741	Leo III
	(regained throne)	741–775	Constantine V
491–518	Anastasius I	775–780	Leo IV
518–527	Justin I	780–797	Constantine VI
527–565	Justinian I	797–802	Irene
565–578	Justin II	802–811	Nicephorus I
578–582	Tiberius II	811	Stauracius
	Constantine[1]	811–813	Michael III
582–602	Maurice	813–820	Leo V
602–610	Phocas	820–829	Michael II
610–641	Heraclius	829–842	Theophilus

842–867	Michael III	1056–1057	Michael VI
867–886	Basil I	1057–1059	Isaac I Comnenus
886–912	Leo VI	1059–1067	Constantine X
912–913	Alexander	1067–1071	Romanus IV[5]
913–959	Constantine VII	1071–1078	Michael VII
920–944	Romanus I[4]	1078–1081	Nicephorus III
959–963	Romanus II	1081–1118	Alexius I Comnenus
963–969	Nicephorus II		
969–976	John I Tzimisces	1118–1143	John II Comnenus
976–1025	Basil II		
1025–1028	Constantine VIII	1143–1180	Manuel I
1028–1034	Romanus III	1180–1183	Alexius II
1034–1041	Michael IV	1183–1185	Andronicus I
1041–1042	Michael V	1185–1195	Isaac II Angelus
1042	Zoe and Theodora	1195–1203	Alexius III
1042–1055	Constantine IX	1203–1204	Isaac II (again, together with Alexius IV)
1055–1056	Theodora (regained throne)	1204	Alexius V

Notes

1 Tiberius I was the Roman emperor (14–37)
2 Because Tiberius II was also called Constantine
3 Constantius was also known as Constans
4 See above, Ch.I, note 7a
5 1067–8 was a period of confusion with no recognized emperor

Index

Index

233

Lithuania, 173
Liutprand (Bishop of Cremona), 142
'Living Testimony', doctrine of, 20, 21, 25, 61
Lombard, Lombardy, 135, 171, 178
Lopez, R., 206
Louis II (German Emperor, 855–875), 91
Lucca, 172

Maccabeans, 34
Macedonian Emperors, 82, 86, 90, 96, 98, 99, 100, 102, 105 (note 50), 107, 108, 111, 113, 117, 203 (note 10)
Magians, 50, 194
Maḥzor Romania, 179–80
Maimonides, 141, 153
'Major Synopsis', 112, 113
Makkā, 33
Maliḥā, 174
Mamora, Sea of, 138, 158 (notes 2 and 5)
Mann, Jacob, 206
Manuel I (Emperor, 1143–1180), 133, 135, 139, 140, 142, 146, 155, 156, 157, 183
Manzikert, 184
Martina (widow of Heraclius), 55
Masada, 170
Mastaura, 119, 129 (note 48), 178, 179
Mas'ūd ibn Kilij Arslan, 136, 142
Maurice (Emperor, 582–602), 45, 46, 47, 71
Meander, 119
Medea, *see* Persia
Mediterranean, 2, 43, 64, 73, 107, 108, 115, 124, 138, 144, 145, 151, 158 (note 2), 167, 172
Megali himera, 180
Melitene, 45, 83
Menaḥem of Otranto, 99
Merchant of Venice, 184
Merkabah, Ma'aseh Merkabah, 169
Mesopotamia, 62
Messianism, Christian, 25, 64, 65, 67, 81 (note 81), 124–5, 147, 155

Messianism, Jewish, 62–6, 74, 102, 110, 124–6, 141, 147, 196, 203, 204 (notes 12 and 22)
Messianism, Muslim, 63–4
Meyuḥas b. Eliahū, 174
Mezzuzot, 33
Michael I (Emperor, 811–813), 75
Michael II (Emperor, 820–829), 76–7, 81 (note 81), 125, 182, 193
Michael III (Emperor, 842–867), 15, 85–6, 101–2, 203 (note 9)
Michael VII (Emperor, 1071–1078), 184
Michael III (Patriarch of Constantinople, 1169–1180), 147
Michael Sicidites, 140
Midrashim, 28–9, 122, 169, 178
Milesarion, 190
'Minor Synopsis', 155, 182
Mishawayh (Meswi) of 'Ukbara, 150–151
Mishnā, 24, 25, 175
Mishnaic glossary, 180–1
Mohar, 119, 178, 186 (note 59a)
Monks, 11, 13, 74, 100, 115, 126
Monophysites, 12, 27, 42, 53, 109
Montanists, 65–7, 72, 176
More judaico oath formulae, 156–7
Moses, 63
Moses of Bari, 167, 168
Moses of Cyprus, 151
Moses of Thebes, 134
Muḥammad, 52, 68
al-Mukaddasi, 104 (note 33)
Muslim, Muslims, 1, 2, 15, 16, 43, 49, 52, 63, 64, 75, 83, 86, 90, 95, 96, 97, 98, 99, 100, 101, 102, 107, 108, 110, 111, 112, 116, 123, 126, 132–3, 141, 150, 154, 163–4, 165, 174, 183, 184, 194, 196
  and iconoclasm, 68, 69, 72, 73
al-Mu'taḍid (Caliph, 892–902), 183
al-M'utāsim (Caliph, 833–842), 75
Mytilene, 138, 139, 145

Na'ara, 70
Na'arān, 44, 57 (note 4)
Nahum, 196